10-

The Sasanian Era

This Volume is dedicated to the memory of

Mary Boyce (1920 - 2006)
and
Boris Marshak (1933 - 2006)

The Sasanian Era

The Idea of Iran

Volume III

Edited By

Vesta Sarkhosh Curtis

and

Sarah Stewart

in association with The London Middle East Institute at SOAS
and
The British Museum

Supported by the Soudavar Memorial Foundation

Published in 2008 by I.B.Tauris & Co Ltd
6 Salem Road, London W2 4BU
175 Fifth Avenue, New York NY 10010
www.ibtauris.com

In the United States of America and Canada distributed by
Palgrave Macmillan a division of St. Martin's Press
175 Fifth Avenue, New York NY 10010

ISBN 978 1 84511 690 3

The Idea of Iran Vol. 3

Library of Congress Catalogue Card Number: available

Typeset by P. Fozooni

Printed and bound in Great Britain by TJ International Ltd, Padstow,
Cornwall from camera-ready copy edited and supplied by the editors

Contents

List of Figures

Scyphate gold dinar of Peroz with legend πιρωζο þα—υανοþαυο   95
= pirōzo šauanošauo "Pirōz Shahan-shah". Collection of Aman ur
Rahman, Islamabad/Dubai.

Seal with the Pahlavi legends KTK "Kadag" and ktkst'n 'wst'nd'l   97
"provincial administrator of Kadagistān" (after Gyselen 2002: 222, fig. 43).

Acknowledgements

The editors are grateful to the Trustees of the Soudavar Memorial Foundation for sponsoring the symposia and making the publication of the proceedings possible. In particular, we are indebted to Mrs Fatema Soudavar-Farmanfarmaian for her help, advice and involvement in the planning of each symposium.

This double volume would not have been possible without the input and expertise of Dr. Parvis Fozooni, who once again has formatted and typeset this volume with his usual dedication and eye for detail. We are also grateful to Helen Knox for copyediting the papers, and to Dr Elizabeth Pendleton for her help.

We would like to thank Iradj Bagherzade, Alex Wright and staff at I.B.Tauris for their help in producing the publication.

Finally, our thanks go to the authors who submitted their papers within the given deadline, thereby making it possible to publish this series in record time.

Introduction

Vesta Sarkhosh Curtis (The British Museum)
and
Sarah Stewart (The London Middle East Institute at SOAS)

This is the third volume of the *Idea of Iran* and deals with the Sasanian period. The previous two volumes covered the early period – the formation of the Achaemenid empire – and the Parthian era. The success of the symposia, which began as a lecture series in the summer of 2004, would not have been possible without the generous support of Mrs Fatema Soudavar Farmanfarmaian and fellow trustees of the Soudavar Memorial Foudation. Their enthusiasm and commitment to the projects have created such confidence amongst supporters of Iranian studies that this programme has become a major event in the academic calendar in London. From the beginning it has been our aim to publish the proceedings on a regular basis; but the turnaround has exceeded expectation thanks to the dedication of our contributors and, in particular, Dr Parvis Fozooni.

The second volume in the series, *The Age of the Parthians,* covered 400 years of Iranian history ending with the collapse of the Parthian empire in 224 CE. The current volume is the proceedings of two symposia and begins with the advent of the Sasanian dynasty and the reign of Ardashir I. This is an extraordinarily fertile period in Iranian history for it is during the reign of the early Sasanians kings that we see the beginnings of an Iranian state and the formation of a centralised religion. This phenomenon is covered by contributors from different disciplines. What we see here is a comprehensive coverage of various aspects of kingship, religion and society through the eyes of experts in numismatics, philology, history, art history and archaeology.

The paucity of primary sources for this period has meant that there has been substantial scholarly debate over much of the extant material. As in previous volumes we have attempted to challenge traditional views and present a re-appraisal of current thinking with regard to existing evidence. Contributors to the early Sasanian period discuss the characteristic features of the Sasanian state during its formative years including how the centralisation of power and religion manifested itself through coinage, art and architecture. Contributors dealing with the late Sasanian period cover aspects of language, economics, religion and military expansion as well as evidence from an archive found in Bactria.

An important phenomenon that has largely been neglected by scholars of pre-Islamic Iran is the transition from an oral to a written tradition during the Sasanian period This development had far-reaching consequences for the way in which Iranian history was transmitted, the nature and purpose of recorded history and the ability of rulers and priests to centralise and transmit knowledge.

Philip Kreyenbroek argues that the state propaganda of the early Sasanian kings drew on written accounts that were based on oral traditions. He gives examples of traditions that began in oral transmission for example the account of Ardashir's lineage, and compares them with later versions once they were written down. In this way he is able to show how these stories and legends were used to serve the purposes of Sasanian state propaganda, through the preservation of certain histories or versions of history and the exclusion of others: 'propaganda, in other words, played a key role in early Sasanian state-building, and the court was evidently capable of making the population accept as national history a version of events that was not based on fact, but had been drawn up for this very purpose'. Linked to this idea of 'state-building' was the notion of the piety of the early Sasanian monarchs, nowhere better expressed than in the *Letter of Tansar* where the high priest asserts that state and religion are twins. The accepted view of Shapur I's piety is questioned by Kreyenbroek in view of this king's welcoming attitude towards the prophet Mani. At court he was granted extended privileges. Kreyenbroek therefore challenges traditional views about Shapur's religious commitment to Zoroastrianism. He suggests and it was in fact the prelate Kirder who, over the course of an exceptionally long career, succeeded in presenting a uniform version of Zoroastrianism throughout the realm. This would not have been possible before the written composition and transmission of religious texts.

The consolidation of church and state is also the subject of Michael Alram's contribution. He discusses the importance of the power and identity of the early Sasanian kings as witnessed through coinage. He charts the progression of the royal title from 'king' to 'king of kings' to 'the divine Mazdayasnian king of the Iranians whose seed is from the gods'. In this way the monarch creates 'a new identity for his dynasty as well as for the Sasanian state'. Both obverse and reverse of these coins emphasise the importance of kingship and the divine right of the king to rule. This is manifested variously through the religious symbolism of kingly glory, or *kwarenah* and those divine beings or *yazatas* associated in with the investiture of the king. The reverse of Ardashir's coins emphasise the link between religion and kingship with the depiction of a fire altar placed on a royal throne. Under Shapur I, a fire altar is flanked by a figure, a symbol that becomes the hallmark of Sasanian coins until the seventh century CE. Alram presents a new double dinar of Shapur I which shows the triumph of the mounted king over the captive Roman emperor Philip the Arab on the reverse. The coin inscription describes Shapur as king of kings of the Iranians and non-Iranians which, until the discovery of this coin, was only known from Shapur's inscription at Ka'ba-i Zardusht and coins of his son and successor Ormazd I. The royal title is now fully extended and indicates the diversity of the Sasanian realm.

State planning and monumental buildings are further testament to the centralisation of Sasanian Iran under Ardashir I. Dietrich Huff examines the architecture of Firuzabad/Ardashir Khurreh as an example of the power and authority of the first Sasanian monarch. Ardashir's meticulously detailed plan of his new city reflects his understanding of the strategic importance of location: "...to create a kind of miniature model realm with residents, city and countryside, set into an order which symbolises his conception of an ideal state". By choosing a location surrounded by mountains, the king ensured that Ardashir Khurreh (Gur) would be protected from attack by the heavy Parthian cavalry. The fortress of Qaleh Dukhtar overlooking the plain provided further protection.

Touraj Daryayee continues with an analysis of kingship in early Sasanian Iran, as seen through monumental inscriptions and coin legends. He gives a detailed breakdown of the composition of the royal titles both from religious as well as political points of view. He moves away from a traditional concept of Iranian civilisation as a "static unchanging phenomenon" and draws attention to the various distinct traditions surrounding the notion of kingship that existed on the Iranian plateau in the third century. These are: the Avestan tradition, the Old Persian Achaemenid royal ideology, the Hellenistic notion of kingship introduced by Alexander and the Seleucids, the Arsacid tradition and finally the Persian tradition of the Sasanians from their homeland. All these traditions were unified by the Sasanian dynasty in Persis. Daryayee looks for continuities in the notion of kingship with reference to the imperial ideology of previous dynasties. The image of a deified king, which was unknown in the Zoroastrian tradition, appears both in the iconography and inscriptions on Seleucid and Parthian coins, and was adopted by the early Sasanian rulers.

The consolidation of the Sasanian empire is also reflected in the art and architecture of the early Sasanian period. Prudence Harper examines the consolidation of Sasanian dynastic power through an examination of the visual expressions of power and authority during this period. The art of the imperial court under Ardashir and Shapur depicts large rock reliefs commemorating the investiture and victories of the king of kings. This tradition drew on earlier prototypes known from Achaemenid, Hellenistic and Parthian art, but introduced a unified dynastic imagery which became a hallmark of a central Sasanian imagery. With the expansion of the Sasanian empire "a related but distinct imagery arose" in the borderlands. This is evidenced by Sasanian silver plates as well as the newly discovered rock reliefs at Shamarq in northern Afghanistan.

Nicholas Sims-Williams takes us from the heartlands of the Sasanian empire to ancient Bactria, or modern Afghanistan. He discusses the recent

discovery of more than 150 documents in Bactrian, an Iranian branch of the
Indo-European language family and also the language of the administration.
These documents shed light on governance and society in the east, the
relationship of this region with Sasanian Iran and in particular between the
Sasanians and nomadic peoples such as the Hepthalites from the north-east
who, until the arrival of the western Turks in the middle of the sixth century,
were ruling over Bactria. Sims-Williams examines documents that give
fascinating insights into the lives of members of the aristocracy for example
through marriage contracts and correspondence. Through family names and
names of the calendar months, we discover the nature of the relationship
between Bactria and Sasanian Iran. The change from local month names to
Middle Persian month names and vice versa suggests a certain dependence or
"cultural independence from Iran".

Shaul Shaked examines the two main sources of information for religion
during the Sasanian period and highlights the differences between them. On the
one hand is the Pahlavi religious literature, compiled in the Islamic period and
transmitted through the Zoroastrian priesthood, and on the other hand there are
the royal chroniclers, also dating from the Islamic period, but writing in Arabic.
Shaked questions the religious commitment of the early Sasanian kings in the
same way that Kreyenbroek questions the piety of Shapur I. But whereas
Kreyenbroek develops his argument around the presence of the prophet Mani at
the Sasanian court of the time, the focus of Shaked's study is the term *Eran* and
Aneran, commonly used in Sasanian inscriptions, and its relationship to the
term *hu-dēn and duš- dēn,* used to designate followers of the good religion as
opposed to upholders of the evil religion. Through a detailed discussion of
certain texts Shaked concludes that the epithet *Aneran* was very common and
had different implications according to whether it was used by kings or priests.
For the Sasanian king and his court, the term referred to someone who was
ethnically not Iranian. For the priesthood, the term described someone who
belonged to a "religion other than Zoroastrianism".

James Howard-Johnston looks at the grand picture of late Sasanian Iran and
compares the military achievements of the first Sasanian rulers, Ardashir I and
Shapur I, with those of Kavad I and Khusrau I and II. He asks how the view,
commonly held by scholars, of a predominantly feudal empire that was inferior
when compared to that of Rome, can be upheld in the light of what we know to
be the highly developed State administration and military prowess of the late
Sasanians. Regional cohesion and resilience, in the author's view, were key to
the Sasanian response to the military incursions into Iran. These, coupled with
huge investment in military and civil infrastructure are what Howard-Johnston
suggests explain the scale of achievement of the late Sasanian rulers.

Philippe Gignoux tackles the question of economic data in the Sasanian
period despite the dearth of source material. He looks at Pahlavi literature and
Bactrian documents as well as references in early Arabic and Persian literature
and provides interesting and vital information about certain transactions. These

give us an idea of the cost of all sorts of things ranging from animals, medicine and meat, to ritual ceremonies performed by priests.

Philip Huyse's paper returns us to the issue of orality and literacy that Philip Kreyenbroek discusses in the first paper of this volume. He also mentions the lack written sources which makes the oral tradition, and the way in which it is understood and dealt with by modern scholars, all the more significant. Huyse draws our attention to the vocabulary linked to 'memory' for example the different ways of reciting prayers, and the fact that texts were spoken and listened to rather than read. He demonstrates, through various texts, such as the *Denkard*, and passages from the *Yashts* and the *Vendidad*, that Zoroastrians continued to maintain characteristics of the oral tradition well into the Islamic period. He suggests that it is not until the story of Khusrau and his page that we have clear evidence that priests were trained in the art of writing as well as the memorisation of texts. He also outlines the debate amongst scholars regarding the date of the introduction of the Avestan script as well as the writing down of the *Avesta*.

The present volume provides a fascinating view of Sasanian Iran by ten eminent scholars. They combine new discoveries with new interpretations of hitherto accepted views of extant material.

1

How Pious Was Shapur I?

Religion, Church and Propaganda under the early Sasanians

Philip G. Kreyenbroek
(Georg-August University, Göttingen)

The early Sasanian kings are widely assumed to have been motivated by strong religious sentiments, and to have initiated reforms that eventually led to profound changes in the character of the Zoroastrian religion. This view of early Sasanian ideals and policies was engendered above all by sources originating in that period, whose essential veracity has long been taken for granted. The aim of this paper is to re-examine some of the assumptions underlying this acceptance of contemporary sources, and to review the available evidence for the history of Zoroastrianism under the early Sasanians, in the light of a different understanding of the function of these sources.

That the current understanding of Sasanian piety is not unproblematic is suggested, for instance, by the fact that Shapur I (240–272 CE), who is widely held to have been a staunch Zoroastrian, welcomed the non-Zoroastrian Mani to his court, and apparently accorded him impressive privileges. Either Shapur I was not aware that Mani was a *jud-din* (non-Zoroastrian) from whom the faithful should keep their distance, which would imply that his definition of Zoroastrian identity was very different from ours; or, alternatively, he did not care, in which case he does not fit our idea of a staunch Zoroastrian. In other words, something is obviously wrong with our understanding of early Sasanian realities. It will be suggested here that some commonly held views need, not so much revision, but a certain refinement.

Our modern, western concept of history is generally based on written sources, and seeks to offer as factual and objective an account of the past as possible. For us, anything else is not history. However, most of the information we have about the early Sasanians ultimately goes back to contemporary Iranian sources, many of them oral, which did not seek to give a objective account of history, but were created in order to make the population accept a version of events that was likely to further the ends of those who sponsored their creation. The role and importance of state-sponsored propaganda in pre-Islamic Iran — both under the Achaemenids and the Sasanians — appears to have been underrated by many Iranists.

Furthermore, the most important new development in early Sasanian Zoroastrianism, which was to exert a profound influence on both Zoroastrian theology and practice, was the view of that religion as a more or less unified system of belief and observance that was supported by a hierarchical religious organization comparable to that of the Christian Church. These developments mainly affected the way in which statesmen and the higher echelons of the priesthood thought about and presented their religion. While other changes and reforms certainly took place that affected people's religious lives more directly, it seems unlikely that the religious lives of ordinary Zoroastrians changed to an extent that would justify speaking of a "religious revolution".

The limited range of our sources compounds the difficulty of arriving at a factual account of early Sasanian religious history. There is some relevant material in the contemporary inscriptions, notably those of Shapur I and Kirder. Furthermore, we have a number of texts in Middle Persian, Persian and Arabic, which were written down in their present form some considerable time after the early Sasanian period. The most important of these for our purpose are the *Letter of Tansar*, *Kārnāmag-i Ardashir-i Pābagān*, and Abū 'l-Qāsem Ferdowsi's *Shahnama*.

To begin with the *Kārnāmag*, the first thing we are likely to notice is that the *Kārnāmag-i Ardashir-i Pābagān*, "The Life and Times of Ardashir son of Pabag", in fact informs us that Pabag was not Ardashir's father at all! He is said to have been Ardashir's maternal grandfather, who gave his daughter in marriage to Sasan, a descendant from the last Achaemenid, Dara. Admittedly, the grandfather eventually adopted the grandson, and Sasan obligingly vanished from the scene. A consideration that is not addressed here (but would definitely have been addressed in real life) is that it seems unlikely that, in Zoroastrian law, an adopted son of Pabag could still claim the rights of a descendant of Sasan. Such a difficulty might of course have been resolved, but all things considered it seems more plausible to understand the account of the *Kārnāmag* as a fabrication, aiming to combine the legitimacy implied by Achaemenid descent with the problematic fact of a prominent father named Pabag, whose non-Achaemenid origins were presumably well known to the general public.

If we accept that the tradition found in the *Kārnāmag* was not based on fact, the next question is, what are the implications of this for the processes of the construction of history — and thus of public opinion — in Sasanian times generally? It is interesting to note in this connection that Ferdowsi's account in the *Shahnama* — written some 700 years after the question had ceased to be relevant — is still obviously based on the same tradition. Ferdowsi tells us that when Dara died, his son Sasan went into hiding, doing menial jobs. Sasan had a son who was also called Sasan, and in fact there was an unbroken line of four Sasans until the advent of a historical person named Ardashir. Thus Ferdowsi, writing in the second half of the tenth century CE, repeated a tradition that was inspired by the preoccupations of the early Sasanian court in the third century CE, which he still regarded as authoritative 700 years later. The most likely explanation for this is that this forged tradition had become so dominant in Iran since early Sasanian times that it eclipsed any alternative accounts that were based on historical truth.

That Ferdowsi made use of source material that had originally been approved by the Sasanians is confirmed by his handling of the history of the Parthian dynasty. The Parthian kings ruled Iran for almost four centuries, and their history would surely have been worth including in a history of pre-Islamic Iran such as Ferdowsi aimed to write. However, between elaborate accounts of Alexander and stories about the Seleucids on the one hand, and the tale of Ardashir we discussed just now on the other, we only find the following words about the Parthians:

> *Chu kutāh šod šāx wa ham bixešān   naguyad jahāndār tārīxešān*
> *K'azišān joz az nām našenide'am   na dar nāme-ye Xosrawān dīde'am.*[1]

> As their dynasty was uprooted, the Commander does not tell their history
> So I have not heard, or read in the Book of Kings, anything but their name.

Had Ferdowsi had access to non-Sasanian-controlled sources about the Parthians, he would surely not have been so succinct. While it is clear why the Sasanians sought to play down the importance of the Parthians as much as possible, Ferdowsi would hardly have had any reason for doing so if he had had the information at his disposal. Similarly, in his treatment of the history of Mazdak, Ferdowsi begins with a very positive account of that figure, an account that can hardly be based upon an official Sasanian source. Then, obviously following a different tradition that was inspired by the court of Khusrau I, he suddenly turns around and calls Mazdak a heretic.

This suggests that, while Ferdowsi was prepared to use any sources available to him, the official version of early Sasanian history had become so dominant that it had led to the disappearance of any more factual accounts that may once have existed. Propaganda, in other words, played a key role in early Sasanian state-building, and the court was evidently capable of making the population accept as national history a version of events that was not based on fact, but had been drawn up for this very purpose.

One is reminded here of another case of a presumably non-factual account of events that was reproduced with remarkable accuracy in a range of sources, namely the story that the ruler of Achaemenid Iran, who was defeated by Darius I, was not Bardiya (Smerdis), son of Cyrus and brother of Cambyses, but a Magian named Gaumata. The point of the story, it seems, was to stress the legitimacy of Darius by claiming that, when he appeared, the factual ruler of Iran was illegitimate and, worst of all, a liar — a concept the Persians had just learned to equate with wickedness. In fact, whether the story of Gaumata was based on fact or thought up as propaganda, it implies that Achaemenid court circles took it for granted that the people could be made to accept inaccurate information. Given the improbability of the claim that an Iranian king could rule for any length of time while remaining in hiding, and the brilliant use the tale makes of the accepted notions of the day (*viz.* that lying is the essence of wickedness), it can confidently be assumed that this account originated in the propaganda section of Darius' court. From there, however, it spread far and wide: Herodotus[2] reproduces it with only a few minor alterations.

Reasons have been given elsewhere[3] for the assumption that bards or storytellers, the precursors of modern *naqqāl*s, played a key role in transmitting such versions of events, and may have been hired by the court to do so. The result of such a scenario would be that the version in question was repeated again and again among the people, who would listen to the narrative uncritically as to a fairy tale, and thus became hallowed by familiarity. Whatever the precise truth of this hypothesis, it seems fair to assume that the Iranian State could and did invent versions of history when it was to its advantage to do so.

The list of unreliable claims made in early Sasanian sources for political expediency can perhaps be increased by the following instance. The inscription of the high priest Kirder (on whom see further below) that was found at Sar Mashhad,[4] ends with a passage which is badly preserved but clearly contains references to a spiritual journey, during which Kirder saw heaven and hell and met a female figure who presumably represented his *dēn* or "heavenly counterpart". However, the journey was actually made, not by Kirder himself, but by a male figure who was Kirder's "likeness" or "counterpart",[5] a concept that otherwise appears to be unknown to Zoroastrianism. P. Gignoux[6] suggests that the expression "Kirder's counterpart" was used because Kirder physically remained on earth. However, in the only other account of a spiritual journey in Pahlavi, the *Ardāy Wīrāz Nāmag*,[7] no need is felt for such a division: the protagonist's spirit visits the realms of heaven and hell while his body remains on earth, and no further explanation appears to have been necessary. One of the questions raised by this mysterious inscription, therefore, is why it insists that Kirder had an alter ego. The text has given rise to a great deal of scholarly debate, and is widely regarded as a testimony to Kirder's profound religiosity. It has indeed been suggested, largely on the strength of this passage, that Kirder was a shaman, which would be remarkable in a statesman of such finesse.[8] In light of the considerations given above, another interpretation seems more likely. It seems possible that the story of Kirder's spiritual journey was conceived before Mani, Kirder's great rival, had been executed, or before his spiritual authority had dwindled in Iran. Mani's spiritual authority was based on his direct experience of the supernatural through the communications of his alter ego or "twin" (*nrjmyg*). It could be surmised, therefore, that Kirder felt that, for his authority to equal his rival's, he needed to claim a similar, direct experience of the supernatural. Kirder's alter ego might then also have been inspired by Mani's.

Non-factual accounts of history and a preoccupation with religion seem to have been hallmarks of the political culture of early Sasanian Iran. This leads one to consider the question of the connection between the two, and to ask in what way the early Sasanians benefited from reinventing their own history and being represented as especially pious. The known facts are as follows: with no better cause, apparently, than the will to power, a family of local Persian leaders challenged the ruling Parthian dynasty, and eventually overthrew it. The available evidence suggests that Iranian culture disapproved of such changes of power, unless the new monarch was shown to be somehow legitimate; witness the stories of Cyrus the Great being the grandson of the last Median king,[9] and of Darius fighting an impostor rather than the legitimate heir (see above). The available evidence suggests that the Sasanians claimed legitimacy on at least two grounds: (1) that they descended from the ancient Achaemenid kings, and (2) that they were superior,[10] a concept that evidently subsumed being more pious. The *Letter of Tansar*, part of which has been shown to go back to a contemporary document, states that the faith needed to be restored by a man of upright judgement, and that Ardashir was such a man.[11] Tansar's main argument was that, given the loss of values in Iranian society, the country needed both a strong leader and a religious revival; since state and religion are twins, one cannot function without the other.[12]

Ardashir I, in short, presumably realized that he needed the support of the Zoroastrian clergy, and cultivated good relations with it. But what of his successor, Shapur I who, as we saw earlier, invited the non-Zoroastrian Mani to his court and gave him great freedoms? It has been suggested that the King thought of Manichaeism as "reformed Zoroastrianism".[13] However, all available evidence suggest that, in early Sasanian times as later, Zoroastrian religious life focused strongly on orthopraxy — observing traditions and having rituals with Avestan liturgies performed by a hereditary priesthood. None of these elements were shared by the Manichaean tradition, so that such an explanation would imply that the King was remarkably ignorant about his own religion. As an alternative, one might surmise that the King was well aware of the importance of religion for Sasanian rule, but that he was not wedded to one particular religious tradition. The fact that a new religion, Christianity, was making considerable headway in neighbouring Byzantium, may have suggested the wisdom of sitting on the fence, until it was clear whether Manichaeism would have similar success.

It could be argued moreover, that under a king who was deeply committed to Zoroastrianism, the prelate Kirder would not have had to fight so hard in the early stages of his career to put his religion on a safe footing in the Empire. Moreover, Kirder was still alive at the time of Narseh I (293–302), i.e. some sixty years after the accession of Shapur I, which means that he must have been extremely young when he served that King. One may legitimately wonder, then, whether a particularly pious king would appoint as his court *Hērbed*,[14] who was presumably responsible for religious affairs throughout the land, a man who can hardly have been much older than twenty.

Turning to the evidence of the inscriptions, we find that Shapur I — or at least his public persona — focuses on the size of his kingdom and his many victories. He adds that these successes are due to the help of *Yazdān* (God, the gods), who made him their "personal protégé" (*dstkrt*).[15] To show his gratitude, Shapur established many fire temples in all the lands, treated Zoroastrian priests with benevolence, and furthered institutions for the gods. He also demonstrated his generosity by announcing the foundation and upkeep of a great many sacred fires for himself and his family, as well as regular sacrifices for the souls of some of his courtiers. The same inscription describes the King's efforts to establish and further Zoroastrian institutions by granting them special privileges in the realm.[16] In other words religion, and thus Zoroastrianism, played a key role in the public image of the King: it illustrated his position as the gods' protégé, and thus as a rightful sovereign. At the same time, as we saw earlier, the King offered warm hospitality to the non-Zoroastrian Mani. We learn from the inscriptions of Kirder that Shapur I in fact left the administration of Zoroastrian religious affairs entirely to the former, and also made him responsible for administering his private pious foundations.[17] In other words, as far as Zoroastrianism was concerned, what the King owed to the State was carried out by Kirder; in so far as he wished to further Manichaeism he no doubt delegated his authority to Kirder's great rival, Mani.

Perhaps spurred on by this rivalry, and possibly also by personal ambition and piety, Kirder displayed enormous energy in promoting Zoroastrianism. By his own statement, the results of his activities included the following: (1) the number of religious rituals was multiplied throughout the land; (2) many Bahram fires[18] were founded; (3) the priesthood was made prosperous; (4) charters were sealed for many fires and their priestly servants (*mgwn'*); (5) testaments, documents, and various other documents henceforth needed Kirder's seal. Moreover, when Shapur I conquered the lands around Iran, Kirder made sure that the Zoroastrian priests and fires found there did not suffer harm. He put in order the affairs of these priesthoods, and caused the Zoroastrian religion and the righteous priests to be much respected there. On the other hand he punished and reprimanded heretics and those who did not follow the proper exegesis (*wc'ly*)[19] in matters of religion and ritual. As a result of these activities, many Bahram fires were established there, many consanguineous marriages contracted, and many non-religious people became religious. The demon worshippers forsook their evil creeds. Many *Gāhāmbār* ceremonies[20] were performed, and the study of various aspects of the religion increased.[21]

Inevitably, Kirder himself must have been the arbiter of the "righteousness" or otherwise of the priests he encountered in foreign lands, which implies that, as far as this could be done, Kirder's own version of Zoroastrianism was imposed on communities whose original beliefs and practices may have been very different.

Kirder eventually brought about the death of Mani, and the defeat of Manichaeism in Iran, under Bahram I (273–276). He reached the height of his power under Bahram II (276–293). When Bahram II became king, no rival religion threatened the supremacy of Zoroastrianism in Iran, and Kirder had been in office for a long time. Bahram II raised him to the status of the high nobility, and apparently allowed him a free hand. According to a triumphant Kirder, the religion and the priesthood became yet more powerful under Bahram's reign, and the gods, water, fire, and cattle were contented, while Ahreman and the devils suffered great harm. The religion of Ahreman and the *dÿws* was driven out of the land and deprived of credence. Jews, Buddhists, Brahmans, Aramaic- and Greek-speaking Christians and Baptisers and Manichaeans[22] were attacked throughout the land. Cult statues were overthrown, dens of demons destroyed, and places and abodes of the *Yazad*s established.[23]

The ambitious high priest Kirder, in other words, directed all his energies towards the establishment of a Zoroastrian "Church", based on the one true version of Zoroastrianism: his own. Kirder's various claims in his inscriptions make it very clear that his understanding of Zoroastrianism was not based on the notion of pluriformity. For him there was only one way of being a righteous Zoroastrian — a view that was probably shared by the leaders of the Manichaean and emerging Christian communities, and was thus "in the air" in Iran at that time. Moreover, he proclaimed these views in his inscriptions, and presumably took care that they should be made known to the public in other ways. Given the importance of such proclamations in influencing public perceptions (witness the evidence discussed above), the implicit understanding of religion found there probably informed the views of many Iranians. However, while such views are often held in emerging religious groups (including, presumably, Zoroastrianism in the early stages of its history) and were later to become commonplace in many religious traditions that were based on writing, they were clearly at odds with the realities of an ancient, established religion whose traditions had always been handed down orally in priestly lineages.

From the fall of the Achaemenids until Sasanian times, Zoroastrianism had survived without the benefit of a central priestly organization. Given that the religious tradition was handed down by many different priestly lineages, there can be no doubt that a variety of beliefs and teachings had become current and acceptable in Zoroastrian communities. Admittedly the notion of one true religion is implied to some extent in earlier Zoroastrian texts, but in practice such a concept had probably long been overshadowed by the manifest multiplicity of the doctrinal and ritual traditions of the various priestly lineages. At least since the time of Alexander, moreover, religion had belonged mainly in the sphere of the community and the family, rather than the nation as a whole. Thus, when the Sasanians came to power Zoroastrianism presumably consisted of a conglomeration of pluriform traditions based on similar fundamental teachings. In many ways it must have been more similar to Hinduism, with which it shares its roots and which accepts the variety of its traditions as part of its essence, than to the theological traditions of Islam or Christianity, which are based upon the theoretical assumption of unity, if not always on its reality.

Kirder, on the other hand, clearly sought to establish an "official" version of Zoroastrianism both in the Iranian heartlands and in outlying regions, where he must have encountered priestly lineages whose traditions diverged considerably from the Persian ones. In seeking to impose — and proclaiming — a "true form of Zoroastrianism", capable among other things of defeating the threat of Manichaeism, Kirder introduced or reinforced the presumably novel concept of Zoroastrianism as a unified "Church", and of a Zoroastrian orthodoxy. When Mani had been executed, Kirder evidently sought to avoid a repetition of the problem by breaking the power of any non-Zoroastrian religion in the Iranian lands, another step in the process of transformation of Zoroastrianism into a State Church. With a political as well as a spiritual side, and a complex but effective priestly hierarchy which had close links to the state, this emerging Church was aware of the potential threat posed by rival organizations, and increasingly capable of dealing with these.

In practice — given the variety of traditions and the largely oral character of the religious tradition — the Iranian culture of early Sasanian times was hardly capable of imposing a unified version of religion or indeed a Zoroastrian "orthodoxy", but the new concept of religion was to play a crucial role in the further development of Zoroastrianism as a "Church". Kirder states, for instance, that Zoroastrianism became an object of study;[24] it was clearly a source of power and prestige for the clergy, and an important pillar of the internal administration. Thus the ideal of a Zoroastrian "orthodoxy" (in the sense of a single right way of being a Zoroastrian) developed, which particularly affected the priestly elite: leaders of the ecclesiastical administration and those learned priests who were instrumental in transmitting or composing religious texts. The Pahlavi books, for example, clearly reflect these Sasanian views to a considerable extent, ignoring popular observances, practices and beliefs that did not conform to this ideal of unity.

Ordinary Zoroastrians, on the other hand, although they were made to abandon their statues in favour of fires, and must have felt the weight of the growing power of the priesthood, in most respects seem to have continued their religious lives as before. Evidence is accumulating that Zoroastrian religious life was much richer and more varied than is suggested by most Pahlavi books. Popular observances, such as pilgrimages, and the offerings made to the waters in the cave that was recently discovered at Veshnaveh,[25] seem to have been important aspects of Sasanian Zoroastrianism. A few references to such practices can in fact be found in the Pahlavi books,[26] but on the whole popular religion is not reflected there. Nevertheless, it is precisely at the level of popular observance that ancient practices endured in many corners of the modern Iranophone world, which shows that they were deeply rooted in people's minds and must therefore be regarded as key elements of Sasanian Zoroastrianism.

In order to find popular acceptance, in other words, the early Sasanians needed to be regarded as both legitimate and particularly virtuous, not least in the sphere of religion. Such an image of Ardashir I was promulgated by the high priest Tansar, who represented the King as uniquely capable of restoring Zoroastrianism to its proper form. Whether Tansar was aware of it or not, this discourse implied that the concept of a good and just society directed by a single vision included the notion of a single correct form of practising Zoroastrianism. In the case of Kirder, such a vision seems to have inspired many of his actions, and thus those of the Sasanian state in matters of religion. Many pious institutions were established that were more or less directly linked to state power. This in turn led to the development of a church in our sense of the word, with a powerful priestly hierarchy and a network of fire temples. Leading priests, such as those who were to transmit or compose the Pahlavi books that are our main source of information about post-Achaemenid Zoroastrianism, "studied all aspects of the religion" (KKZ 15) as a result of Kirder's actions, and were presumably influenced by his vision of Zoroastrianism.

What began as discourse of Sasanian propaganda, then, developed into a new dimension of Zoroastrianism: the ancient faith became a state religion based upon an ideal of unity and coherence. In this, Sasanian Zoroastrianism held similar views to the religions that surrounded it, which must have made the concept seem all the more natural and self-evident. Just as Sasanian propaganda tended to disregard objective facts, however, this religious ideology, and the learned books informed by it, tended to ignore the richness and variety of the religious lives of ordinary Zoroastrians. The early Sasanians then, inspired by their own propaganda, laid the foundation of a Zoroastrian "Church", with all this implied. On the other hand, they cannot be said to have revolutionized the religious lives of ordinary believers.

Notes:

1. Ferdowsi 2003: 1179.
2. *History* III: 61–80.
3. Ibid.
4. For the text, translation and commentary see Gignoux 1968: 387–417.
5. *cygwn krtyr hnglpy; cygwn krtyr*, SM 36, 38 *et passim*. See Gignoux 1968: 407–408.
6. Ibid.
7. See Gignoux 1984a and 1984b.
8. Nyberg 1938.
9. Herodotus, *History* I: 107–108.
10. Thus, according to the *Letter of Tansar*, Ardashir I was "more richly endowed with virtues than the ancients and his custom [was] better than the customs of old." (Boyce 1968: 36).
11. Boyce 1968: 36–37.
12. Ibid.
13. Boyce 1979: 113.
14. On the term *hērbed* see Chaumont 1960; Kreyenbroek 1987a; 1987b.
15. The meaning of *dstkrt* seems clear from the context. Old Persian *dastakarta* meant "handmade, handywork", see Kent 1953: 190. The Greek equivalent *ktisma* (Back 1978: 210) means "creature".
16. See e.g. Shapur's inscription at the Ka'be-i Zartošt (ŠKZ); Back 1978: 284–371.
17. *KKZ* 2–3. The inscriptions are discussed in detail by Back (1978: 390–391).
18. The term "Bahram fire" may perhaps refer to fire-temples intended for the community as a whole, rather than private fires. More research is needed, however, to establish the precise meaning of the term in early Sasanian times.
19. Back (1978: 430) translates Phl. *wizār* as "canon", but the widely accepted interpretation of the word as "explanation" (McKenzie 1971: 92) seems to make good sense here.
20. Communal ceremonies that were celebrated at certain points in the religious year, see Modi 1922: 419–428.
21. KKZ 11–14; Back 1978: 418–431.
22. So Boyce 1984: 112.
23. KKZ 8–10; Back 1978: 408–417.
24. "And there was much studying of the religion in many ways" (KKZ 15).
25. See Stöllner and Mir Eskanderi 2003.
26. Thus the offerings of food to the waters are referred to in *Nērangestān* 48–49 (Kotwal and Kreyenbroek 2003: 218–29).

2

Early Sasanian Coinage

Michael Alram
(Kunsthistorisches Museum, Münzkabinett, Vienna)

S ince the invention of coinage in the late seventh century BCE, coins were
not only a medium of exchange, but also the symbol of power and
identity of their respective issuers. Whether we recall the so-called
toxotai, the Achaemenid gold coins showing the "King of Kings" running with
a bow in his hands, or the *glaukes*, the owls of Athens, both coin types were
immediately associated with their issuers in the whole of the ancient world, and
thus they became the symbol of identity of these two world powers.

Ardashir I (224–240)[1]

When Ardashir, son of Pabag, seized power from the Arsacid king Artaban IV
(213–224), he immediately reorganized the monetary system of his new
empire. It was his desire to present himself as the new "King of Kings of the
Iranians" as quickly as possible, not only to his own people but also to his
enemies within and outside Iran.

Ardashir's coinage can be divided into three major phases. His first minting
phase thus begins with his coronation as king of Fars and ends with his victory
over the Arsacid "King of Kings" Artaban IV at the Battle of Hormizdagan,
which is supposed to have taken place in 223/224 — probably Year 1 of the
Sasanian era corresponding with the lighting of the Ardashir Fire as stated in
the Bishapur inscription.

A single type of coin was minted in three different denominations and
presented Ardashir as the new king of Fars (Fig. 1).[2]

This first coin portrait of Ardashir is frontal and conveys an extremely
dynamic image of the king. He wears a high tiara, which is actually of Arsacid
origin (Mithradates II), but which had long been part of the regalia of the king
of Fars. As king of Fars, Ardashir used only the simple title *šāh* ("king"). In
addition he held the honorary title *bay* ("the divine", "His Majesty"), which
was set before the name of the king (*bay Ardašahr šāh*).[3] His father Pabag can
be seen on the reverse. In the legend Ardashir is described as "son of the divine
Pabag, the king" (*pus bay Pābag šāh*).

Fig. 1. Silver drachm of Ardashir as king of Fars, SNS I, type I/1 (mint A). British Museum.

The principal denomination remains the drachm, which corresponds more or less to the Arsacid model in weight and reduced fineness (between 3.49 and 3.77 g and 61 % fineness). In addition half drachms and obols were also minted. At present, the dimension and duration of this issue cannot be deduced from the material itself, but from a numismatic point of view, Ardashir's reign as king of Fars probably did not last very long. This means that he ascended the throne of Fars not very long before 223/224. The mint may be assumed to be Stakhr (Group/Mint A), which served for centuries as the main mint of the kings of Fars.

The second phase of Ardashir's rule, his first as "King of Kings" started immediately after his victory over Artabanus IV and brought with it a radical reordering of Iranian coinage, from both a typological as well as a denominational point of view. In this period the western capital of the Parthian empire, Ctesiphon, was also captured, presumably in 226/227, the year of the founding of the Sasanian Empire, as stated by western sources such as Agathias and Elias of Nisibis.

Ardashir appears now in his new attire as "the divine Mazdayasnian King Ardashir, (king) of (the) Iranians" (*mazdēsn bay Ardaxšahr šāh Ērān*). On the reverse we see a fire altar with the explanatory legend "Ardashir's fire" (*ādur ī Ardaxšahr*). It is the holy fire that was lit at the beginning of each king's reign and it was a symbol of the Zoroastrian faith.

It is remarkable that Sasanian gold coinage began with this type (Fig. 2),[4] which had not been in use in Iran since the time of the Greek Seleucids. The weight of this first Sasanian dinar issue (8.47 g) was based on the old Attic standard, introduced to Iran by Alexander the Great and the Seleucids. The weight is therefore significantly higher than that of a contemporary Roman aureus or a Kushan dinar.

Fig. 2. Gold dinar of Ardashir I, SNS I, type IIa/2 (mint B). British Museum.

Moreover, it is interesting to note that on this first Sasanian gold issue Ardashir only bears the title "King of the Iranians" while on all subsequent issues the longer title "King of Kings of the Iranians" appears.[5]

The new type of coin chosen by Ardashir (Fig. 3) emphasizes the special role that Mazdaism was to play in the Sasanian state from this time on. This does not mean, however, that Ardashir elevated Mazdaism to a kind of "state religion". It is more likely that

Fig. 3. Silver drachm of Ardashir I, SNS I, type IIa/3a (mint B). British Museum.

his main desire was to assert the king's absolute claim to power with regard to the Zoroastrian priests and to see his political course legitimized by religion. Also new is the addition Ērān, expressing the idea propagated by Ardashir of the "realm of the Aryans/Iranians" (Ērān-šāhr), which should provide a clear ideological demarcation from his predecessors, the Arsacids. With its clear political message Ardashir's new coin type should help to create a new identity for his dynasty as well as for the Sasanian state. The type was kept nearly unchanged for centuries and thus became a powerful symbol of the new Iranian empire.

According to my typological analysis published in the new SNS series, type II was struck in two different mints. One mint was probably located in Ecbatana/Hamadan,[6] one of the principal mints of the Arsacid empire, which fell in Ardashir's hands probably shortly after his triumph over Artaban in 223/224. The second mint was in Seleucia/Ctesiphon, which was conquered, as already mentioned, in 226/227.[7] Following the Arsacid tradition in Ctesiphon, in addition to the silver drachm, mainly tetradrachms (Fig. 4) and copper coins were minted in huge quantities.

Fig. 4. Billon tetradrachm of Ardashir I, SNS I, type IIe/3a (mint C). Kunsthistorisches Museum, Vienna.

The third and final phase of Ardashir's reign, which may be roughly dated to c. 229/230 to 240, reflects the apogee of his power. His position as the new "King of Kings" was now undisputed, and all the lands of the former Parthian Empire had been subjugated, with the exception of Armenia. This phase is marked by the introduction of a new coin type on the obverse (Figs 5, 6): it shows Ardashir with a covered, artificial hairstyle.[8] The fabric that covers the top of his head and the korymbos is either with earflaps and neck-guard (Type IIIb) or without (Type IIIa). There is also a new addition to the legend: kē čihr

Fig. 5. Silver drachm of Ardashir I,
SNS I, type IIIa/3a (mint C).
Kunsthistorisches Museum, Vienna.

Fig. 6. Silver drachm of Ardashir I,
SNS I, type IIIb/3b (mint B).
British Museum.

az yazdān ("whose seed [is] from the gods").[9] The full title now runs as follows: "the divine Mazdayasnian King of Kings Aradshir, (king) of (the) Iranians, whose seed is from the gods" (*mazdēsn bay Ardašahr šāhān šāh Ērān kē čihr az yazdān*). If we compare this new title with the title of the Arsacid kings: "The King of Kings, Arsakes, the benefactor, the justice, the excellent, the friend of the Greeks" (*Basileus Basileon Arsakes Euergetes Dikaios Epiphanes Philhellenos*), a complete revival of Iranian kingship becomes obvious.

Typological criteria permit the following conclusion: Types IIIa (Fig. 5) and IIIb (Fig. 6) were again produced at two different mints and the bipartition of minting as noted in Phase 2 also continued in Phase 3. However, the concentration of production has now clearly shifted from Hamadan (mint B) to Ctesiphon (mint C).

With regard to the coin standard and denominations, it should be noted that the final fine-tuning of the new currency system took place in Phase 3. The weight of the gold dinar was reduced by nearly 1 g and was now fixed between 7.20 and 7.40 g. At that weight it was still about 1 g heavier than a Roman aureus (6.40 g). Ardashir also minted double dinars (Fig. 7). The weight of the drachm was raised uniformly to c. 4.20 g, and the average silver content lies at around 90.6 %. A contemporary Roman silver denarius has a weight of only 3 g and a silver content of 45 % — this demonstrates clearly how powerful the new Sasanian currency was.

Fig. 7. Gold double dinar of
Ardashir I, SNS I, type IIIa / 3a
(mint C). British Museum.

Fig. 8. Silver drachm of Ardashir I,
SNS I, type VI/3b (mint B).
Kunsthistorisches Museum, Vienna.

In both mints there are two special issues that each depict Ardashir with special crowns (Fig. 8).[10] These special types appear to have been minted as additions to the principal issues in the two proposed mints and were perhaps related to certain religious celebrations.

In Phase 3 and probably related to Ardashir's great eastern campaign, mints in Sakastan (Sistan) and Marv were also started. As I have shown elsewhere, in Sakastan the so-called "throne-successor coins" — drachms (Fig. 9) and large bronze coins — were minted, while in Marv an issue of small bronze coins was produced.[11]

Fig. 9. Silver drachm of Ardashir I, SNS I, type VIII/3a (Sakastan?). Kunsthistorisches Museum, Vienna.

Shapur I (240–272)[12]

Ardashir's son Shapur took over from his father a completely reorganized monetary system, which he kept nearly unchanged in its principal structures.

The pictorial programme introduced by Ardashir was adopted virtually unchanged (Fig. 10).[13] On the obverse we see the bust of Shapur now with the mural crown of Ahuramazda; it is from this time onwards that each Sasanian king has his individual crown, which symbolized the *khwarrah* or divine aura of the ruler. The reverse of Shapur's coins displays the fire altar in slightly altered form flanked by two attendants also wearing mural crowns — probably dual images of the king in the role of the guardian of the sacred fire.[14]

Shapur's title on the obverse corresponds to that of his father: "The divine Mazdayasnian King of Kings, Shapur, (king) of (the) Iranians, whose seed is from the gods"; the analogous inscription "Shapur's fire" is found on the reverse.[15] It is remarkable that on his coins Shapur merely calls himself "King of Kings of the Iranians", while in his

Fig. 10. Silver drachm of Shapur I, SNS I, type IIc/1b (style indéterminé). Kunsthistorisches Museum, Vienna.

inscriptions he bears the title "King of Kings of the Iranians and Non-Iranians". This longer title does not appear on normal coin issues until the reign of his son and successor, Ohrmazd I (272–273).

On a special issue at the beginning of his reign Shapur wears an eagle-headed *kolah* with the *frawahr* symbol (Fig. 11).[16] The same headgear can also be observed on the jousting relief at Firuzabad.[17]

Fig. 11. Silver drachm of Shapur I, SNS I, type Ib/1a (style A). British Museum.

The average silver content of Shapur's drachms lies above even that of the drachms of Ardashir, namely by 4 %. The drachm now reaches a fineness of around 94 %. This was something the Roman emperor could only dream of; at around the same weight (4.20 g) his antoniniani only had a silver content of just below 45 %. In rare cases tetradrachms of billon continued to be struck. Bronze coins in four different denominations were issued for use as petty cash for daily transactions on the markets. Moreover, lead coins appear for the first time, and they probably also served as petty cash.

Shapur also continued to strike gold coins (Fig. 12). Apart from the dinar, Shapur minted dinar fractions, as did his father, Ardashir. However, it is important to note that Sasanian gold coinage was purely prestigious and had not the economic significance of the Roman aureus.[18]

Fig. 12. Gold dinar of Shapur I, SNS I, type IIc / 1a (style A). Staatliche Museen zu Berlin.

The typology of the coins remains unchanged throughout Shapur's reign; none of the triumphs over the Roman arch-enemy that feature so prominently in the account of his deeds or on the rock reliefs, find even the slightest expression in his coinage so far.

An exception to this is a stylistically related group of drachms, which stands out from all other issues by virtue of its debased silver content (Fig. 13).[19] This phenomenon is all the more remarkable, because, in the more than 400 years of its minting, the Sasanian drachm otherwise displays no serious debasement in the quality of its metal. Metal analyses carried out as part of our SNS project showed that the silver content of these drachms fluctuates between 12 and 62 %.[20] In terms of trace elements, too, they are clearly distinguished from the good-quality silver drachms.

Fig. 13. Billon drachm of Shapur I, SNS I, type IIc/1b (style P). Kunsthistorisches Museum, Vienna.

As we know from Shapur's famous *Res Gestae* at the Kab'a-i Zardusht at Naqsh-i Rustam and also from Roman literary evidence, the Roman emperor Valerian was taken prisoner in the year 260. During the course of this campaign the Roman capital in the east, Antiochia, was taken for the second time, Samosata was plundered, and Shapur's troops advanced as far as Cilicia and Cappadocia. With the capture of Antiochia and Samosata the two eastern Roman mints also fell into the hands of the Sasanians.

Bearing this in mind, further metal analyses were performed on ten antoniniani of Valerianus and Gallienus struck in the mints of Antiochia and Samosata just before the Sasanian conquest (Fig. 14). The analyses revealed that the silver content of the Roman antoniniani displays a similar fluctuation (13.5–31.6 %) to the Shapur drachms minted in base silver. Equally, a qualitative comparison of the trace components showed that both the Roman and the Sasanian coins contain the same elements.[21] This confirms a hypothesis proposed by Robert Göbl many years ago that Shapur reminted antoninianus metal captured as spoils of war in the Roman mints at Antiochia and Samosata.[22] However, where he did this — perhaps in a peripatetic mint that travelled with the army on its campaigns — and what value these inferior drachms were accorded in the Sasanian monetary system, remains unclear.

In this context I must refer to an exceptional new gold coin: the obverse displays a portrait of Shapur I, while the reverse shows not the customary fire altar, but Shapur mounted on a horse with the Roman emperor Philip the Arab (244–249) standing before him (Fig. 15).[23] The obverse inscription bears the

Fig. 14. Billon antoninianus of emperor Valerianus (253–260) from the mint of Antioch. Kunsthistorisches Museum, Vienna.

Fig. 15. Gold double dinar of Shapur I with the Roman emperor Philip the Arab. Private Collection.

familiar title of Shapur, but is extended by the component "King of Kings of the Iranians and Non-Iranians": "the divine Mazdayasnian King of Kings, Shapur, (king) of Iranians and Non-Iranians, whose seed is from the gods". The legend on the reverse which, like the image, is wholly atypical of Sasanian coin typology known hitherto, reads: "This (was at) that (time) when he placed Philippos, Caesar, and the Romans, in tribute and servitude" (ēn ān ka-š firipōs kēzar ud hrōmāy pad bāz ud bandag<īh> estād hēn).[24] The basic concept of the reverse image is adopted from the relief carvings: i.e. the Roman kneeling before the king with arms stretched out (Bishapur I–III, Naqsh-i Rustam) or rushing up to him (Darab), whom Robert Göbl has already — albeit not uncontroversially — identified as Philip the Arab.[25] Shapur strove to record his bravery and glorious deeds for all eternity, as an example to be followed by his descendants. Both the pictorial programme of the five "imperial reliefs" as well as small art objects on which the images are limited to individual events — such as the Paris cameo with the capture of Valerian[26] or the new double dinar commemorating Philippus suing for peace — are part of this endeavour.

Based on a stylistic classification of Shapur's coins, Rika Gyselen suggested that at least four mints (a maximum of eleven) were operating during Shapur's reign. The principal mint remained in Ctesiphon, and the mints in Sakastan and Marv were also operating, at least occasionally. The Marv mint is also the first one which puts its signature on the reverse of a rare issue of gold dinars.[27] Moreover, during the reign of Shapur I the local kings of Marv were permitted to mint bronze coins bearing the inscription *mlwy MLKA* and depicting the image of the king on horseback on the reverse as part of a scene of investiture (Fig. 16).[28]

Fig. 16. Bronze coin of the king of Marv. Kunsthistorisches Museum, Vienna.

Ohrmazd I (272–273)[29]

Under Shapur's son, Ohrmazd I, two important changes took place in the iconography of Sasanian coinage: on the obverse the king's title is extended to "King of Kings of the Iranians and Non-Iranians". On the reverse we now see a scene of investiture: on the left side of the fire altar the king is standing, raising his right hand as a gesture of reference to the god Mithra who is standing on the other side of the altar (Fig. 17). Mithra, identified by his crown which consists of rays, extends the diadem of sovereignty to the king — a coin type which expresses clearly the king's divine right to rule.

A second type shows Ohrmazd holding a "staff" and on the right side of the altar stands a female person, traditionally identified as the goddess Anahita, also with a

Fig. 17. Silver drachm of Ohrmazd I, SNS II, type Ib/2b. Kunsthistorisches Museum, Vienna.

"staff" in her hands (Fig. 18). These "staffs" are probably barsom bundles used in the Zoroastrian rituals.

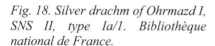

Fig. 18. Silver drachm of Ohrmazd I, SNS II, type Ia/1. Bibliothèque national de France.

Fig. 19. Silver drachm of Bahram I, SNS II, type I/1a. Kunsthistorisches Museum, Vienna.

Bahram I (273–276)

Bahram I returned to the basic reverse type of Shapur I with two standing figures who turn their backs to the fire altar (Fig. 19). Historically important are some rare issues of silver drachms, which bear mint signatures of Marv, Sakastan and Balkh. From Balkh we also know signed bronze coins. If the reading of the mint signature (*BHLY* for Balkh) is correct, this is the first numismatic evidence of an imperial Sasanian mint established in former Kushan territories, and it testifies to direct Sasanian rule in Bactria at the time of Bahram I.[30]

Bahram II (276–293)

No other Sasanian king used as many different obverse and reverse types as Bahram II. In particular, the obverse design with the busts of the king, the queen and a third person is exceptional (Fig. 20). These special designs reflect the king's individual preoccupation with domestic and dynastic issues, which can also be observed in the scenes of his rock reliefs and on silverware.[31]

On the obverse we either see the bust of the king alone[32] or together with an unbearded youth facing the king wearing a high tiara (Median bonnet),[33] as on the so-called throne-successor coins of Ardashir I (Fig. 9). This young man is traditionally interpreted as a crown prince; we should, however, be careful with such interpretations, although I have no better solution to offer at the moment.

Fig. 20. Silver drachm of Bahram II, SNS II, type VI/3. Kunsthistorisches Museum, Vienna.

Another type shows Bahram together with his queen Shapurdukhtag (Fig. 21) and finally the royal couple is faced by a third unbearded bust, often depicted with a diadem in hand (Fig. 22). Queen and tertiary bust wear changing headgears with animal heads attached to them — boar, griffin, horse and eagle are most prominent — but their exact meaning remains uncertain. Jamsheed Choksy has tried to demonstrate that the unbearded busts facing the king or the royal couple represent images of the goddess Anahita and the Iranian god of victory, Verethragna.[34]

Fig. 21. Silver drachm of Bahram II, SNS II, type IV/1. British Museum.

Fig. 22. Silver drachm of Bahram II, SNS II, type VII/5. Kunsthistorisches Museum, Vienna.

For the reverses of his coins Bahram has chosen the type of his predecessor, but he sometimes also shows the scene of investiture with the king on the left side of the fire altar making the gesture of reference and on the right side a female figure, most probably the goddess Anahita (as on the obverse), who extends the diadem to the king (Fig. 22).

From the eastern mints only Marv sometimes appears as a mint signature on dinars and drachms. A new signature is that of Ray (Fig. 23) and another mint with the signature *hwpy*; the meaning of this word, however, remains uncertain (it could be the signature of an unknown mint or, as Lukonin has suggested, the word *xūb* = good).[35]

According to the stylistic analyses of Rika Gyselen[36] some of the principal mints, which have already been in operation under Shapur I were still working for Bahram II and even for Narseh. In some cases we are able to reconstruct a stylistic continuum of coin issues that stretches from the time of Shapur I until Narseh, and it therefore gives us good reason to assume that this group of coins

Fig. 23. Silver drachm of Bahram II from the mint of Ray, SNS II type VI/3. British Museum.

showing the same handwriting was produced in one and the same mint.

Narseh (293–303)–Ohrmazd I (303–309)

In the reign of Narseh one important phenomenon occurs for the first time in Sasanian coinage: Narseh is depicted with two different crowns on his coins. However, these two types were not issued contemporaneously but clearly mark two successive stages in the king's coinage (Figs 24–26).

From Narseh's famous Paikuli inscription we know that after the death of Bahram II Narseh had to fight for his throne. His rival was Bahram III, king of Sakastan, who was forced by a certain Bahram to take the diadem. But the Sasanian nobles had chosen Narseh, king of Armenia, to become "King of Kings". The reign of Bahram III lasted for only a very short time (four months according to Tabari) and whether he struck coins or not has always been disputed.

In an article published in 1959, Robert Göbl tried to show that all the coins that were attributed by Paruck and others to Bahram III (Fig. 26) actually belong to Narseh, as Herzfled and Vasmer had already stated before him.[37] This hypothesis was based mainly on a careful study of the coin legends and on Göbl's assumption that, according to the Sasanian convention of individual crowns, each ruler was forced to adopt a new crown if his reign was interrupted by usurpation or captivity. This is because the crown symbolized the *khwarrah* or divine aura of the ruler. The new crown was based on the old one, but represented an enhanced form.

Fig. 24. Silver drachm of Narseh, SNS II, type Ia/1a. Private Collection.

Fig. 25. Silver drachm of Narseh, SNS II, type Ib/4a. Private Collection.

There is no question that Göbl was perfectly right in pointing out that the coin legends of his type I (Fig. 26) — showing the crown only with loops — offer not the slightest evidence for reading the name of Bahram. Of course, we are confronted with the problem that most of the coin inscriptions are illegible, but the very few good examples show clearly that on both types the name of Narseh is

Fig. 26. Silver drachm of Narseh, SNS II, type II/5b. British Museum.

intended (*nrshy* or *nshy* but never *wrhr'n*). Therefore Göbl concluded correctly that both types belonged to Narseh. Chronologically, Göbl placed the type showing the crown only with loops (Fig. 26) at the beginning of Narseh's reign and the crown with loops and branches (Figs 24, 25) later. He connected the changing of the crown with the rebellion of Bahram III. The main argument for this chronological sequence was his assumption that the number of emblems on the crown had to be increased, as is the case with the later crowns of Peroz or Khusrau II, whose reigns were also interrupted.

If we compare the size of both issues, it is evident that the issue of Göbl's type I (Fig. 26) was much smaller than the issue of Göbl's type II (Figs 24, 25). This means that type I was struck during a shorter period of time and that the main issue of Narseh was in any case Göbl's type II, which may support Göbl's chronological sequence and historical interpretation.

Altogether this looks quite convincing, but nevertheless it is wrong! Our careful typological and stylistic analysis of Narseh's coin types in the course of the SNS project leads to the conclusion that his coinage starts not with Göbl's type I but with Göbl's type II (Figs 24, 25) and that Göbl's type I (Fig. 26) has to be placed at the end of Narseh's reign. I should mention that the same conclusion was already drawn by DeShazo and published in his *Pahlavi Palaver* 1993.[38] This new chronological sequence is mainly based on the evolution of the busts: from Bahram I to Narseh (type I) the folds of the tunica are always drawn with three triangular strokes on the shoulders; but from Narseh (type II) to Ohrmazd II (Figs 28–30) and Shapur II the folds are drawn in vertical strokes. A further typological argument are the ribbons on the fire altar which become canonical only with our type Ib of Narseh (Fig. 25), which is characterized by a different hairstyle for the king and three dots on the altar column.

At the moment I am not able to give you a convincing historical interpretation. The only known event of historical importance in the second half of Narseh's reign was his defeat against the Roman emperor Galerius in 297 (battle of Erzerum and treaty of Nisibis in 298), but whether this was really the reason why he lost the branches of his first crown, I cannot venture to say. In any case, the new numismatic sequence of Narseh's coin types has one important implication for the dating of his relief at Naqsh-i Rustam: it was not carved at the very beginning of his reign but in the third and final phase.

Altogether not more than ten mints were working for Narseh and Ohrmazd II. Again mint signatures are only known from Sakastan, which sometimes put the letter S on the altar column (Fig. 27), and then from Marv (Fig. 28). For Ohrmazd we also know the mint signature of Ray (Fig. 29).

Ohrmazd introduced a new reverse type with a bust on the altar table. Whether we see this as an image of the

Fig. 27. Silver drachm of Narseh from the mint of Sakastan, SNS II, type Ia/1d. Private Collection.

king or — less likely — a god, the subject is still controversially discussed. On the obverse and reverse of some of Ohrmazd's drachm issues additional letters are engraved (Fig. 30); their meaning, however, remains uncertain. They cannot be signatures for "Versandstempel" (as Göbl thought), but probably functioned as internal control signs of the respective authorities.[39]

Fig. 28. Gold dinar of Ohrmazd II from the mint of Marv, SNS II, type Ia/3h. British Museum.

Fig. 29. Silver drachm of Ohrmazd II from the mint of Ray, SNS II, type Ia/2c. Private Collection.

Fig. 30. Silver drachm of Ohrmazd II, SNS type Ia/3d. Private Collection.

Notes:

1. For a detailed survey of Ardashir's coinage see Alram and Gyselen 2003 (= SNS I).
2. SNS I: type I/1 (mint A).
3. For the meaning of the term *bay* see O. Skjærvø in Alram, Blet-Lemarquand and Skjærvø 2007: Appendix 3.
4. SNS I: type IIa/2 (mint B).
5. SNS I: type II/3.
6. SNS I: types IIa–d/3a (mint B).
7. SNS I: types IIe–d/3a (mint C).
8. SNS I: type III/3.
9. For a detailed discussion of the title see O. Skjærvø in Alram, Blet-Lemarquand and Skjærvø 2007: Appendix 3.
10. SNS I: types IV–VII/3.
11. Alram 2007.
12. For Shapur I see the detailed study of R. Gyselen in Alram and Gyselen 2003 (= SNS I), as well as Alram, Blet-Lemarqand and Skjærvø 2007.
13. SNS I, types II/1–2.
14. On the interpretation of this see SNS I: 36 with references to further literature; cf. also the issues which bear the name of Shapur on both sides of the reverse.
15. On the coin inscriptions of Shapur cf. also Skjærvø's remarks in SNS I: 57–69.
16. SNS I: type I/1a. For the *frawahr* symbol see O. Skjærvø in Alram, Blet-Lemarquand and Skjærvø 2007: Appendix 1.
17. Cf.also Gyselen 2004: nos 77–78, where the *frawahr* symbol can be clearly made out on the *khola*.
18. Cf. also Schindel 2006 and the somewhat divergent view by Gariboldi 2005.
19. SNS I: nos 129–142 (Types IIc/1b; Style P, Groups c/1and c/2).
20. SNS I: 81–87 and 269 with Fig. 58.
21. SNS I: 85–87 with Table 8.
22. Göbl 1971: 25; cf. also Gyselen's remarks in SNS I: 268–271.
23. This coin is published in Alram, Blet-Lemarquand and Skjærvø 2007.
24. For the reading and a detailed philological analysis of the inscriptions see O. Skjaervo in Alram, Blet-Lemarquand and Skjærvø 2007.
25. Göbl 1974. Last confirmed by Meyer 1990; cf. also von Gall 1990: 99–104.
26. Cf. my brief description in Seipel 1996: p. 399, 78.
27. SNS I: pl. 35, A51 and Gyselen 2004: no. AV8.
28. On this see Loginov and Nikitin 1993.
29. The typological classification of the coins from Ohrmazd I to Ohrmazd II is based on Alram and Gyselen (forthcoming); see also Gyselen 2004.
30. See Nikitin 1999.
31. See Herrmann 1998 and Herrmann 2000.
32. Gyselen 2004: no. 146 (SNS II: type I/1).
33. Gyselen 2004: no. 151 (SNS II: type II/2).
34. Choksy 1989. See also Curtis 2007a.
35. See Gyselen 2004: 56 and no. 158.
36. See SNS II = Alram and Gyselen (forthcoming).
37. See Göbl 1959 as well as Göbl 1971 for a typological overview.
38. See DeShazo 1993.
39. For Shapur II cf. Schindel 2004, 227 (= SNS III).

3

Formation and Ideology of the Sasanian State in the Context of Archaeological Evidence

Dietrich Huff
(Deutsches Archäologisches Institut, Berlin)

The formation of the Sasanian state and the achievements of its founder, Ardashir Papakan, are among the most favourite subjects of Oriental historiography, or more precisely, of the historic-legendary literature of late antique and medieval Iran. The difficulties in deciding what among these sources is a trustworthy historical account and what is a mythical narrative, invention or addition by later chroniclers are well known, and not only in the case of Ardashir. There are more reliable but less vivid historical sources such as coins which, besides chronological sequences, may even provide a good deal of iconographic information.[1] The few Sasanian inscriptions on rock and on monuments are of course of the highest value, as are the rock reliefs and other representations, which all give a somewhat broader, but often debatable view, especially of early Sasanian history and culture.

In the case of Ardashir Papakan's political beginnings, we have the rare opportunity to check the literary reports and other documents on his early career through archaeological remains, which his planning and building activities have left on the plain of present Firuzabad in Fars. With state architecture and state planning conceptions generally expressing very authentically the mundane and spiritual ideology of state government, these traces can adjust, correct and supplement literary reports of historical events, and may offer an insight into the tendencies of Ardashir's political aims, and his ideas of kingship and its cosmological background.

Among the literary sources[2] the chapters on the Sasanians in the chronicle of Tabari give the most continuous and comprehensive account of the rise of the Sasanian dynasty. Tabari gives a reliable compilation of older sources, which partly and indirectly go back to Pahlavi books, especially to versions of the official chronicles of the Sasanian court and to the *Khudainama*, a predecessor of the much later *Shahnama*. Although it is evident that these sources tell the history as seen at the time and as the court wished them to be seen, they provide the best information on Sasanian history available.

Ardashir's usurpation of Fars

Tabari, like most of the other sources, reports that Ardashir was a younger son of Papak, chieftain of Khir, a small town east of Istakhr, the provincial capital of Fars, and a grandson of Sasan, principal of the Anahita Fire Temple of Istakhr, who allegedly was related by marriage to the Bazrangi family, the petty kings of Fars under the suzerainty of the Parthian Great King.[3] The early lineage of the Sasan family is obscure and as usual partly embellished in order to connect it with the mythical kings of Iran. Different sources give varying stories,[4] but the family obviously belonged to the nobility of the province of Fars.

By favour of the Bazrangi King Gochihr, Ardashir started his career in his youth first as an apprentice, later as *argbed*, a military governor of the rich city and district of Darabgerd in eastern Fars.[5] From this position he began to enlarge his territories by raiding neighbouring districts, killing their rulers, plundering their treasures and replacing them with his trusted followers. Having annexed large parts of southern Fars, he persuaded his father Papak to assassinate king Gochihr (his patron and alleged kinsman), whose residence was not at Istakhr but in neighbouring Baidha, near the site of ancient Anshan. The assassination took place but Papak tried to bypass Ardashir and demanded the crown of Fars from the Parthian Great King Artaban IV (216–224 CE) for his eldest son Shapur. Artaban refused and, obviously well informed about the background of the assassination, accused Papak and Ardashir of murder and insurgency; but he was unable to bring them to justice.[6]

The political situation with Papak and Shapur as kings of Fars is corroborated by coins, showing King Shapur with a Parthian helmet-crown on the obverse and king Papak with an extravagant headdress on the reverse, both following the Parthian style of looking left.[7] In the inscription of Shapur I (240–272 CE) on the Ka'ba-i Zardusht at Naqsh-i Rustam, "Shapur the king, the son of Papak" is mentioned,[8] and both men are represented in the graffiti on the stone window frames of the so-called Achaemenid Harem at Persepolis — now reconstructed and harbouring the local museum — and in the "Tachara" (Fig. 1). The partly spontaneous but detailed and well-composed sketches give us a realistic impression of courtly dress in late Parthian Fars, showing that the civilizing standards here were by no means inferior to those of the royal Parthian court. Even the artistic quality of most of the earlier Persis coins has proved rather superior to the schematic images of the imperial late Parthian coinage.[9]

The princely figures of the Persepolis graffiti are richly dressed in wide, patterned trousers, a long shirt reaching below the knees, with long sleeves and a necklace or necklace-like collar, an overcoat with decorations on the shoulders, and tied with ribbons across the chest. Papak is standing, his left

Fig. 1. Graffiti from Persepolis. Papak (C) and his son Shapur (A, B, D, E).

hand grasping the hilt of his sword (Fig. 1C), obviously performing some kind of offering with a spoon-like instrument, perhaps putting frankincense on an incense burner.[10] His headdress looks like an early version of the forthcoming Sasanian crown arrangements. Shapur on horseback is recognizable by his Parthian helmet-crown with a crescent as an emblem, as depicted on his coins. His horse is decorated all over with flowers and tassels of different sizes. Most remarkable is the abundant use of ribbons, the lengths of the diadem, which is wound around the head and tied at the neck by a simple knot or later by a bow. The diadem was the most important symbol of royalty since the Hellenistic period.[11] Whereas on the coins, Papak and Shapur still follow the Parthian style with two thin ribbons, depicted as straight lines, hanging down from a knot or bow tied behind the head, the graffiti show rather broad and long bands, sometimes partly pleated, as the open ends of the diadem, hanging or even floating from the bow, which fixes the diadem behind the head, cap or helmet-crown. This detail of the Persepolis graffiti can be seen as a direct predecessor of the long, pleated ribbons, which float horizontally in the air behind the heads of Ardashir, his son Shapur and other royal persons in the large battle relief at

Firuzabad (Fig. 2), where the two Sasanians chase and unhorse their Parthian adversaries.[12] In the Persepolis graffiti, the diadem bands are not only applied to the self-proclaimed kings Papak and Shapur, but also to Shapur's horse, where they decorate the horse's mane, tail, knees and hocks, a custom that becomes ubiquitous for every royal subject in later Sasanian iconography (Fig. 1B). Here we must understand it as an unmistakable demonstration of Shapur's vigorous claim to kingship.

Fig. 2. Detail of Ardashir's jousting relief, Firuzabad.

Following Papak's obviously natural death, which seems to have occurred soon after, Shapur became sole king of Fars.[13] His demand for acknowledgement by Ardashir was of course refused, so he set up an army to march to Darabgerd and subjugate his rebellious brother. Fighting, however, was avoided because he was killed at the very beginning of the campaign by a structure that collapsed at a place called the "Palace of Humai".[14] This is most likely Persepolis, which lies between Istakhr and Darabgerd, and the decaying monuments of which provide an adequate scenario for such a fatality. The Achaemenid buildings there were certainly not inhabitable at the end of the Parthian period, after most had already been burned down by Alexander. But some may have been reused and the graffiti, as well as the fact that Shapur made a stopover there, prove that the place must still have been of importance for the inhabitants of Istakhr, especially for the upper classes. It is quite possible that Shapur set up his camp or headquarters on the terrace in order to organize his army in the plain below. There is no indication in the literary sources that some sympathizer of Ardashir had a hand in the fatal accident.[15]

The path to kingship seemed open for Ardashir. He was crowned and enthroned in Istakhr with the preliminary support of all his brothers.[16] But, notwithstanding future quarrels with the Parthian Great King, internal problems arose. A conspiracy of his brothers and their partisans ended in a massacre among the population of Istakhr, perhaps an unavoidable development at that time, because some of the brothers were older than Ardashir and more entitled as heirs to the throne. No reason is given for the rebellion at Ardashir's long-standing place of — seemingly successful — government in Darabgerd, which was also suppressed with much bloodshed.

Preparing and achieving the overthrow of the Arsacids

Among the mainly mythical and legendary reports, which most chronicles, even Tabari's, give on Ardashir's early years as petty king of Fars, and which praise his further successful territorial annexations and booty-taking, there is little detailed information about the enormous scope of his preparations for his real goal, the overthrow of Parthian rule. In contrast to Papak and Shapur, who might have been satisfied with a status as vassal kings of Fars, Ardashir's general characterization in the sources leaves no doubt that he was determined to end the "illegitimate" Parthian domination and re-establish indigenous Persian rule, which had been interrupted by Alexander's defeat of the Achaemenids.[17] As we have seen, the ruins of Persepolis were still regarded as a memorial of past splendour, although no original historical knowledge of that period had survived in Iran after the conquest by Alexander.

Ardashir's claim of predominance in Iran was paraphrased in Tabari as a divine vocation as ruler of countries, delivered to him by an angel in a dream.[18] It is not necessary to discuss here whether his religiousness was based on genuine devotion or on political calculation, but there is no doubt that he used his proclaimed election by Ahuramazda and his divine mission as an argument for all his activities, and that he speedily established an ecclesiastical organization as an instrument for internal political dominance. The emphasis in Tabari and other sources of his pious activities and provisions, e.g. his early appointment of a high priest immediately after his enthronement as king of Fars,[19] or missions of conversion, as described in the probably late Sasanian Letter of Tansar,[20] may have been later literary additions. But even during his time as a rebel he gave clear proof of his endeavour to promote Zoroastrianism by founding a fire temple, not only as one of his first constructions, but as the only one built of ashlar, instead of the ordinary rubble and mortar used for his palaces.[21] His identification with Zoroastrian faith became all the more evident when he achieved the position of Great King. In his imperial coinage he replaced the Hellenistic motif on the reverse by a fire altar.[22] In his rock reliefs it is Ahuramazda who bestows him with the wreath of kingship (Fig. 3); and in the relief of his investiture at Naqsh-i Rustam his horse tramples on the dead

Artaban IV, characterized by the emblem on his helmet and his double-pointed beard, in the same manner as Ahuramazda's horse tramples on the defeated Ahriman.[23] From this early and also later evidence we may safely conclude that Ardashir, by spreading his divine mission, inspired his followers to agitate and fight for the right cause and convinced them that they would be victorious with the support of God.

Fig. 3. Investiture relief, Firuzabad. Ahuramazda is handing over the ring of kingship to Ardashir. His page, his son Shapur and two knights are standing behind the king.

The question has to be asked, why after being enthroned and crowned in Istakhr, did Ardashir not chose the capital of Fars or a palace nearby for his residence, as probably most of the Persis kings had done before? There may have been a number of reasons. As a far-sighted politician, he no doubt foresaw serious battles to come against the great northern and western provinces and eventually against the army of the Parthian Great King. With such an uncertain future, the easily accessible, exposed situation of Istakhr might have been regarded as precarious, and in the event of a siege Ardashir could probably not rely on the absolute loyalty of the inhabitants after the bloody suppression of his brothers' and their partisans' rebellion. Similar considerations may also have gone against choosing Darabgerd.

We do not know much about Ardashir's fighters and the composition of his army, which must have been a powerful force. For his early raids from Darabgerd he probably started by recruiting pugnacious young people from the town and its surroundings. But as the rebellion after his coronation as king of Fars showed, the majority of Darabgerdis, for whatever reason, were by no means a reliable force to follow him against the Parthian Great King or to guarantee a safe power base. Erratic tales in such sources as that of the noble

Isfahanian citizen Banak with his six sons and probable helpers,[24] who joined Ardashir, may be taken as an example of the many high-ranking sympathizers from other provinces, who like Ardashir, were discontented with Parthian rule and brought with them their dependants. There must have been innumerable other supporters, warlike folk and mercenaries, who were attracted by Ardashir's successful leadership and his doubtless charismatic personality. Among these troops there were certainly landless people, the surplus of a growing population, who hoped for or were promised subsistence or farming land after a successful war.

The availability of a large force of loyal followers must have been another argument for Ardashir's decision not to set up his residence in Istakhr, but to build a new city at a safer place and populate it with his own people, so that it would be a reliable power base for future wars. His basic intention, however, must be looked for at another, not only practical but also ideological level. As we shall see, his aim was to create a kind of miniature model kingdom, with a residence, a city and the countryside around, within an order that symbolized his conception of an ideal state. Archaeological field research has revealed that he carried out this project successfully in the plain of present Firuzabad, 100 km south of Shiraz, which he named Ardashir Khurreh, later abbreviated to Gur.[25] The comparatively small but water-rich plain with an agreeable climate, on the borderline between *sardsir* and *garmsir* — the cold and hot regions — is surrounded by mountain ridges with four accesses, one of them from central Fars.[26] The mountains, however, are not an insurmountable barrier, as the migration routes of Qashqai nomads and an advance thrust of British troops in November 1918 have demonstrated;[27] they might however have been an obstacle for the heavy Parthian cataphracts.

The main reason for Ardashir's choice of Firuzabad, however, must have been the fact that the plain was thinly populated and mostly uncultivated, because large parts of it were under water; the sources call it a lake.[28] In fact, streams of water flow permanently into the plain from three sides and had probably silted up the area around the only outflow, so that in time water had spread and filled every depression at least for large parts of the year.[29] Ardashir must have understood that drainage was possible and would provide him with the necessary virgin land for his colonization programme. In a densely populated and fully cultivated area like Darabgerd or Istakhr he would have faced serious trouble with the long inherited landownership. Here on the contrary, his creation of new arable soil for his adherents would add to his reputation not only as a victorious warlord but also as a wise and prudent ruler, caring for his people.

The gigantic task of draining a plain, founding a city and building an obviously extraordinary palace must have required a tremendous amount of funds, labour and many years of work. It certainly made Ardashir famous beyond his distinction as a successful general all over Iran, and made it clear to the Parthian Great King that his insurrection was not a local affair, but a provocation to which he had to react. Tabari recounts the dramatic story of the highly insulting letter from the Great King, calling Ardashir a Kurd who grew up in the tents of the Kurds, and accusing him of killing, land grabbing and illegitimately posing as a king, and concluding with the charge of building a city and a palace.[30] The letter, together with the announcement that the vassal king of Ahwas had been sent to arrest him and bring him to trial, was a declaration of war. The story in its presented form must be regarded as a literary invention, and the charge of building a city and a palace being treated as serious a crime — if a crime at all — as waging war and killing innocent people, appears today as baseless and excessive. However it is an essentially accurate illustration of the political situation at that time. We have to take into account that in antiquity the foundation of a city was an important royal prerogative. Not without reason did cities in the West as well as in the Hellenized Orient have names like Alexandria, Seleucia, Antiochia, Vologasias or Mithradatkert. In Tabari's fictitious letter the Great King asks Ardashir, "Who has ordered you to build the city?", a realistic and accurate detail, which shows that the Great King insisted on his privilege that, if anybody else was to found a city, he could do so only by order and in the name of the king.

The name Ardashir gave to his new city, Ardashir Khurreh, must have made things worse. Khurreh or *khvarenah*, with the inadequate translation "fortune" or "glory", means a god-given spiritual quality or power, which is the indispensable precondition for kingship.[31] By giving his city a name, thus publicly announcing that he possessed the *khvarenah*, the divine power of kingship, he openly proclaimed himself ruler of Iran, an act of high treason, the most serious of capital crimes, which carried the death penalty. As Ardashir had doubtlessly foreseen the consequences of his activities, these can only be understood as a long-term, well-prepared provocation, which left the Great King with no escape from a final showdown, for which he was probably not at all well prepared. Artaban, who resided in Nehavand, had by no means the support of all Parthian provinces, not even from his brother Vologases V (207–227 CE), who ruled in Iraq, and neither did the great families of the Suren, Karen and Miran side with him, which meant that they kept their important position.[32]

The site of the battle is somewhat obscure. At any rate it did not take place in the plain of Firuzabad as some sources say. Except for one attempt by the vassal king of Ahwas, who was easily repelled,[33] no Parthian army had even tried to reach Ardashir Khurreh. The battlefield for which Tabari and others give the name of Hormizdagan,[34] was very probably between Isfahan and Nehavand and is identified by Widengren from the Nihayat as Gurbadagan, modern Gulpaygan.[35] Tabari and other chronicles, as well as the great battle relief at Firuzabad (Fig. 2), relate that Ardashir himself killed the Parthian king and trod upon his fallen enemy's head or shoulder.[36] Shapur, Ardashir's son and the Crown prince, is said to have knocked down Artaban's scribe, Dadhbundadh,[37] but as the Parthian knight who is unhorsed by Shapur in the

Firuzabad relief wears the royal diadem, as do Ardashir, Shapur and the fallen Artaban, he is clearly a Parthian prince. The relief thus agrees with the report in the Nihayat that Artaban, fleeing with some princes of his family, was caught and killed by the pursuing Sasanians.[38] The chronicles unanimously state that on the day of his victory (September 224 CE), Ardashir proclaimed himself s*hahan shah*, King of Kings.

The relief of his investiture by Ahuramazda in the gorge of Firuzabad (Fig. 3), *c.* 1 km upstream from the battle relief, gives a surprisingly modest view of this imaginary act. Ardashir, followed only by a page, his son Shapur and two more princes or knights, stands opposite Ahuramazda, and receives the ring of kingship with ribbons, which the god holds out to him over a small fire altar. Ardashir raises his left hand in the canonical gesture of greeting or adoration to the god, who holds the barsom bundle.[39] The relief is unfinished. It is not undisputed that it was Ardashir's first representation of his investiture and it was certainly not the major one. The relief at Naqsh-i Rajab, which is stylistically related, presents a richer, partly disputed entourage,[40] and the relief at Naqsh-i Rustam, mentioned above, is certainly the grandest and artistically most refined work of this series.[41] Nevertheless, the two reliefs in the gorge of Firuzabad, the dramatic scene of the cavalry battle, counterbalanced by the unpretentious representation of Ardashir's investiture, form an ensemble, which documents Ardashir's rise to power and establishment of a dynasty for four centuries in a remarkably sensitive way.

Most obvious in these monuments of commemoration is the leading part played by Ahuramazda. However, king and god stand on an equal footing and only by his gesture of respectful salute does the king acknowledge the superiority of the god. The situation is different on the reliefs of the royal Achaemenid rock tombs, where an almost identical scene is given, if we accept the deity above as Ahuramazda on the wings of the *khvarenah*.[42] The king, elevated above the ranks of his subjects, is clearly communicating with the god and saluting respectfully with his raised hand. One may assume that his salute is also directed towards the fire. But it is the god who returns his salute with the same gesture of his hand, holding out the ring of kingship with his other hand towards the king below. The Achaemenid king does not presume to stand on the same level as Ahuramazda.

At the end of the Sasanian dynasty the relation between king and god had gone to the opposite extreme. On the relief on the tympanum of Taq-i Bustan of the investiture of the Sasanian king, probably Khusrau II (591–628 CE), he has unquestionably become the main figure in the scene. Standing on a higher pedestal facing forwards, he does not even turn to face the god, but only reaches out with his arm across his chest and grasps at the ring of royal kingship, which a slightly smaller Ahuramazda holds out to him. A female figure on his other side, generally regarded to be Anahita, and to whom the king pays no attention, pours water from a jug onto the ground and offers him another ring of kingship with the obligatory royal ribbons.[43] The sequence seems symptomatic of the development of self-conception of the king in pre-Islamic Iran.

Darabgerd

Another rock relief, which must be mentioned in connection with Ardashir and his early beginnings, was carved into a cliff above a spring-fed lake *c.* 5 km east of Darabgerd. It shows a Sasanian emperor on horseback, accompanied by his grandees and knights, receiving the submission of two Roman emperors — a third lies dead under the hoofs of the horse — and of the Roman army, including a war chariot. The scene resembles the well-known triumphal reliefs of Shapur I (240–272 CE) in Bishapur and Naqsh-i Rustam and it is strange to find it here. It is even more puzzling that the victorious emperor in Darabgerd does not wear the crenellated mural crown of Shapur, but the early globe-crown of Ardashir. The attribution of the relief has been debated ever since and the different opinions are difficult to judge.[44] Taking into account that both the relief's location and the crown have a connection with Ardashir, one might even speculate that it was conceived as a kind of homage by Shapur to Ardashir. Perhaps it was the intention of the son to share his Roman triumph with the father by presenting the triumph under the first Sasanian crown of Ardashir at the cradle of the empire. At any rate, the relief demonstrates the high esteem in which Darabgerd — in spite of its early rebellion — was held at least during the early period of the Sasanian dynasty.

The relation between this city and Ardashir still existed in the Middle Ages and led to an incorrect version of the facts. Ibn-al Fakih, and others after him, writes that Ardashir built his circular city after the model of Darabgerd.[45] Darabgerd was in fact a much older city than Ardashir Khurreh. The Pahlavi catalogue of Iranian capitals[46] attributes its foundation to a Dara or Darab, i.e. an Achaemenid king, Darius, or a later petty king of Fars of the same name. Regarding Ardashir's early and long-standing position as an *argbed* in Darabgerd, the idea seemed logical and was frequently repeated later on. It seemed all the more justified as the circular city plan, also incorrectly, was regarded as a favourite type under Parthian rule, with the rounded walls of Hatra, the mistakenly Parthian-dated Takht-i Sulaiman/Shiz and other central Asian examples as a confirmation.[47] However, it has always been overlooked that Hamza al-Isfahani, one of the most reliable sources, already had the clearly correct information, that Darabgerd originally had a triangular layout, that its circular wall was only built in the early eighth century by a governor of Fars under Hajjaj ibn Yusuf (661–714 CE)[48] and there was no geometrical, radial-concentric system of streets. Thus Darabgerd became a circular city about half a millennium after Ardashir Khurreh was founded. Doubtless with this neighbouring city as a model, it got its circular wall about half a century before the construction of the circular city of Baghdad, Madinat as- Salam,[49] which the Calif al-Mansur (754–775 CE) pretended to have invented and designed himself, without the existence of a model.[50] Indeed, it is clearly impossible that the spectacular layout of Ardashir Khurreh, together with its history, which was mentioned in nearly every major chronicle, had remained unnoticed at the early Abbasid court.

Even if Ardashir had not been inspired by a circular Darabgerd because he would only have been familiar with the old triangular town, he might have learned something about the shared disposition of city and residence. It is not known whether or how the old triangular town was arranged around or beside the rocky outcrop in the plain, which is now the centre of the circular medieval Darabgerd, and which holds a small multiphase castle, the original date of which is unclear. With steep cliffs and a tiny plateau above three lines of defensive walls it must, in any case, have been much too small for use as a residence of the governor of an important district.[51] The *arg* or fortress where Ardashir was educated and which he took over as *argbed* was most probably not this castle but a ruined place with the significant local name of Qaleh Shah Nishin (Seat of the King), a strong fortification on a high and large rocky massive outcrop on the northern foothills on the edge of the plain, where the road runs from central Fars (Fig. 4).[52] It seems also to have been a custom in Parthian times to place the residence of a ruler not inside a city but outside at some distance.

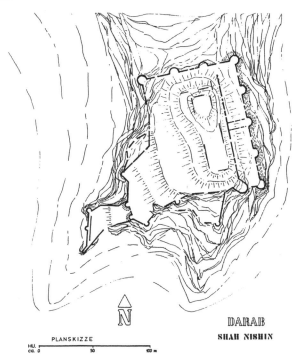

Fig. 4. Sketch plan of the ruined fortress of Shah Nishin, northwest of Darab.

The best-known example is the old Parthian capital of Nisa, where the strongly fortified royal residence, Mithradatkert, present-day Old Nisa, is *c.* 5 km from the much older city, called New Nisa because it survived long into the Islamic period.[53] As we have already seen, Gochihr, vassal king of Fars, also had a residence, not in Istakhr but in Baidha. This was not a naturally protected stronghold but probably a fortified stately manor house within his territorial properties.[54]

Ardashir Khurreh: reality and ideology

When Ardashir started his construction project in Ardashir Khurreh, his palace-fortress was certainly among the very first buildings he constructed. As a far-sighted politician he must have foreseen the danger of attacks by armies of the Parthian Great King and his vassals. Although soldiers could cross the mountain ridges on foot, the main bulk of the army, the cataphracts — heavy Parthian cavalry — were expected to come through central Fars and the northern gorges along the Firuzabad or Mand river, ancient Khunaifighan. Armies from the western Mesopotamian provinces came via Kazerun. Both accesses were blocked by defensive walls across the valleys at Muk in the north, and near Farrashband in the west. The main fortification, today called Qaleh Dukhtar (Fig. 5), was built in the Firuzabad gorge, the Tang-i Ab, opposite the cliffs, where the reliefs were later carved.[55] A defensive wall with bastions was laid across the gorge further upstream. The palace-fortress occupies a triangular plateau *c.* 1 km in length, above the last bend of the river

Fig. 5. View over the mountain ridges with Qaleh Dukhtar and the plain of Firuzabad.

before its exit into the plain. The plateau was fortified by a traverse wall with a large semicircular bastion on the crest of the ridge. The mostly impregnable cliffs along the bend of the gorge had to be walled only in some places. This outer fortification was probably intended to harbour an army or a refugee population of the city for a while in case of emergency (Fig. 6).

Fig. 6. View of Qaleh Dukhtar from the west, the staircase, centre left, the palace, aivan *and domed throne hall (photo courtesy of G. Gerster).*

A second traverse wall with a rather simple gate room cuts off the impregnable tip of the plateau, thus acting as an inner fortification. The traverse wall and the walls lining the edge of the plateau contain long casemate rooms with arrow slots, and there was probably a parapet above the vaulted ceilings, giving shelter for the defenders. There are lower fortification works and towers, making use of every cliff and outcrop, and two outworks reach down to the river, thus completely controlling the road. Two wells, connected with the river by tunnels, provided drinking water.

The palace is situated at the highest point of the plateau, which also houses simple stone-rubble constructions for the garrison. From an entrance courtyard with a cistern, a square tower with a winding staircase gives access to a second higher courtyard, surrounded by large and high halls with wide, bench-like podiums, clearly used for accommodating the higher ranks of Ardashir's followers. A tribune at the end of the courtyard, accessible by an open staircase, seems to have served for the commanders or chieftains addressing an assembly in the courtyard. It is possible that above the tribune, on the edge of the third terrace — which is accessible from the square tower and across the roofs of the halls — the king himself appeared and spoke to his people.

The palace proper on the third terrace contains the *aivan* with side halls, a square, domed throne hall with side rooms and private rooms upstairs. The throne room with its surroundings is built into a huge, round donjon-like tower, standing exactly on the line of the inner traverse wall, one half outside, the other half inside the fortress. To procure this kind of building, Ardashir had to put up with serious statical disadvantages, which, together with obvious technical inexperience and an extremely complex building site, led to early damage and disfiguring emergency constructions. The fact that he nevertheless chose a circular outline for the main part of his palace must probably be explained by ideological perceptions of kingship. Also significant is his positioning of the throne room in the very front line of his fortification, demonstrating that in his view this was the place of the king in battle, comparable to the message that the battle relief in the gorge was meant to transmit.

The dating of Ardashir's palace-fortress to the time before his overthrow of the Parthian Great King does not only result from the logics of historical development. It is corroborated by two pre-Sasanian coins, found during excavation: a copper coin of a king of Characene, and a small silver coin of an unknown south Iranian ruler of the late Parthian period. A silver drachma of Shapur II (309–379 CE) indicates occupation of the place in the fourth century.[56] After the fortress had proved to be a rather futile construction, with no serious attack by an imperial army having taken place[57] and early damage as well as its remote position limiting its value as a residence, it seems to have served its original purpose at least once, at the end of the Sasanian period. Some copper coins of the latest Sasanian type, found with traces of occupation in the casemates,[58] testify to the attempt of the last Sasanian king, Yazdgird III (632–651 CE), to build a last line of defence against the invading Arabs in the heartland of his perishing dynasty.[59]

The location of Ardashir's palace-fortress far from his city, on the main access road to the plain, is quite similar to that of the Shah Nishin, his presumed residence at Darabgerd. Now, however, the choice of the site was clearly determined by strategic considerations. Nevertheless, it is significant that Ardashir obviously did not prepare a residence inside his newly founded city and instead added an extraordinary palace to the fortress in the gorge, unprecedented in Iran at that time. Moreover, after his victory over the Great

King, when the danger of attacks was no longer imminent, he built a second, larger palace in the plain, immediately at the exit of the gorge, thus obviously continuing an early Iranian tradition.

Ardashir built his circular city (Figs. 7 and 8b) in the northern part of the plain near the eastern bank of the river, *c*. 5 km from the exit of the gorge.

Fig. 7. View of the ruined city of Ardashir Khurreh (photo courtesy of G. Gerster).

Medieval chronicles praise its precise configuration "even as though drawn with compasses", and describe very correctly the tower "even as it were the centre point of the circle".[60] The layout is indeed a masterpiece of ancient surveying skills, all the more so as the twenty subdividing radial lines, which formed the street system, not only cover the city, *c*. 1.85 km in diameter[61] — one ancient *mil* — but are spread out all over the plain to distances of up to 10 km, even crossing a mountain ridge (Fig. 8).

The city had a massive wall of clay, possibly with mud-brick facings and bastions; its decayed condition leaves this open. It is surrounded by a moat *c*. 35 m long and an outer wall. The two main axes with four main gates are still clearly visible in the ground, and so are the sixteen sub-radials and at least four concentric circles dividing the outer city area into three rings of — probably — private allotments. In the circular innermost area, *c*. 430 m in diameter, the radial system of division did not continue, but the Sasanian structures were aligned with the main axes, with the tower, the Tirbal or Minar, standing on their point of intersection. This city centre was enclosed by an inner wall and was probably reserved for official buildings only.[62]

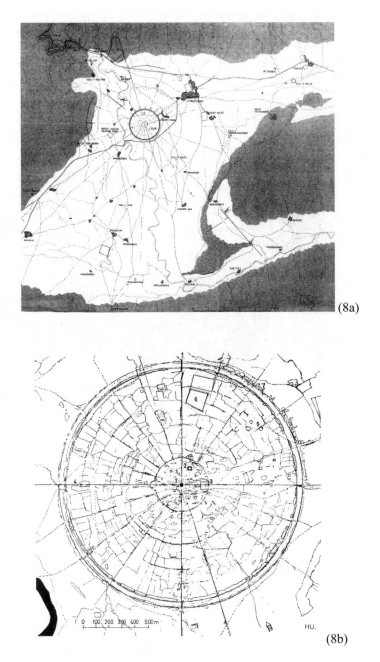

Fig. 8a and b. Map of Firuzabad and plan of the city of Ardashir Khurreh.

The main building, the so-called Takht-i Nishin —Throne-Seat — stands between the northern main axis and one of the two deep depressions, former water basins, still functioning in the Middle Ages and mentioned in chronicles, which also describe the well-cut and polished ashlar of the building and its former brick dome.[63]

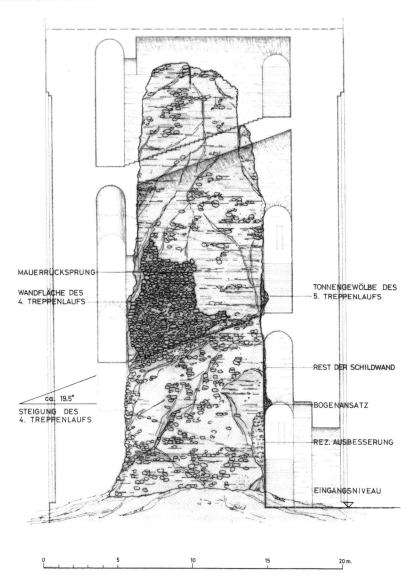

MAUERRÜCKSPRUNG

WANDFLÄCHE DES
4. TREPPENLAUFS

ca. 19.5°

STEIGUNG DES
4. TREPPENLAUFS

TONNENGEWÖLBE DES
5. TREPPENLAUFS

REST DER SCHILDWAND

BOGENANSATZ

REZ. AUSBESSERUNG

EINGANGSNIVEAU

0   5   10   15   20 m.

Fig. 9. The Minar/Tower in the centre of Ardashir Khurreh with the outlines of the destroyed staircase.

Survey established that the ruin was formerly a cubic building with a square domed room *c.* 14 square meters, with wide and deep arched bays at its four sides and connected by wide gates with four lateral annexes, either *aivans* or side rooms.[64] The building was basically a so-called closed *chahartaq*,[65] and may be regarded as a model for future Sasanian fire temples; it continued to be a major element of Iranian architecture throughout the Islamic period.

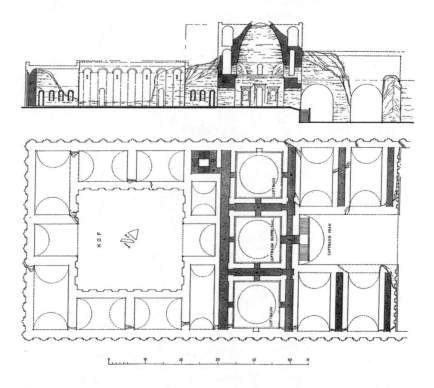

Fig. 10. Ardashir's second palace, the "Atashkadeh", in the plain of Firuzabad. Shaded areas indicate the first floor and a niche above the double stairs in the aivan, *in which would have been the throne seat.*

It seems reasonable to identify it with the fire temple of Ardashir Khurreh, which is mentioned in Tabari's narrative correspondence between Ardashir and Artaban, the place to which Ardashir hoped to send the head of the Parthian Great King.[66] A large ruin on the west side of the Takht-i Nishin seems to have been the Friday mosque of the medieval town, into which the former Sasanian sanctuary may have been incorporated.

In the northern sector of the inner city, opposite the Takht-i Nishin, recent excavations have uncovered parts of an interesting structure containing a small room, with a plaster floor painted with a chequered design, and three bathtub-shaped troughs along the walls, painted red. In an adjoining chamber fragments of wall painting were found, showing persons in a kind of procession, holding an animal resembling a kid. The rare pottery seems to indicate a post-Sasanian date, although the figures, as far as the available documentation allows, seem to stand in the Sasanian traditional pose. The size of the troughs is similar to that of sarcophagi, which one would not expect to find in the centre of a Zoroastrian residential city, opposite a fire temple. Based on current information, an interpretation is not possible at present.[67]

The tower in the city centre, known as Tirbal or Minar,[68] gave rise to mistaken and vague ideas about its original appearance and purpose. Herzfeld was the first to work out its architectural function correctly, which is identical to the staircases in Ardashir's palaces.[69] It was not an open tower with a spiral staircase of the Kairo or Samarra type as formerly thought, but a square compact block of c. 19 m side length, which contained a staircase, winding upwards on mounting vaults between a square central post of c. 9 m side length — the still standing "Minar" — and outside walls, which had already been destroyed in the early Islamic period. Istakhri and other medieval sources point out that the whole plain could be overlooked from the top of the tower,[70] and this must in fact have been the primary reason for locating it there. As the plain was by no means perfectly flat, the surveying work of Ardashir's project of land division, which consisted in laying the radial system all over the plain, could never have been accomplished without the tower as an outlook, to give and correct the directions of the twenty radial lines and to serve as an benchmark for the surveyors, who had to extend each radial, step by step.[71]

During the early times of warfare, the tower might also have served as a signal post; the damaged top of the tower is still visible today from the roof of the round palace building at Qaleh Dukhtat. But these practical aspects were certainly not the only purpose of the most outstanding structure of the city. A staircase, 2 m wide and with an extremely low gradient (13/30 cm), is certainly too extravagant to be a purely technical structure. Moreover, fragments of carved stucco in the debris of the entrance to the tower show that this was a richly decorated high-status building. We will return later to the question of its significance.

As recently as the 1970s the radial and concentric plan of Ardashir Khurreh was still visible in the ground tracing the edges of fields, paths, canals, the remains of walls and qanats, both inside and outside the city walls.[72] About 4 km from the city centre (Fig. 8a), an enclosure wall 1 m thick, with the stone foundations partly preserved, surrounded the city as a twenty-cornered polygon, clearly not a fortification wall, but used to single out a special area of land for particular owners. There was another, narrower polygon or circle of division, halfway between the city and this polygon; Muqaddasi wrote that the estates surround the city in narrow circles.[73] Whereas inside the city Islamic shrines occupy marked locations of the city plan, clearly replacing older sites of importance, some Sasanian ruins stand on the end points of the main axes: a small circular mud-brick fort in the north-east; a walled-in mountain area in the north-west, perhaps a Zoroastrian cemetery; garden terraces, a circular water basin, stairs and a pavilion in the south-west; water installations in the south-east.[74] A number of large gardens lie on or alongside other radials.

The direction of the main axes of Ardashir's layout is not adjusted to the cardinal points, a fact which naturally leads to the assumption that transcendental conceptions or stellar constellations are involved. Although motivations of this kind may have been used as an excuse, the actual reason must have been technical pragmatism. The plain slopes markedly from north-east to south-west, as the centre line of the winding Firuzabad river clearly shows. The north-east–south-west main axis of the layout runs exactly parallel to the river, i.e. straight down the sloping plain, so that there can be no doubt that the plan was an integral part of Ardashir's drainage programme. Although largely levelled in today, the north-east–south-west axis is still recognizable as a former main canal, bringing water into the city moat and leading it from the other side and onto the lower part of the plain. Significantly, the radials coming from higher ground run into the city moat as deep, widening gullies, characterizing these radials as collector canals, which discharged their water into the moat. The north-east-south-west axis with the canal is directed to the western tip of a rocky ridge, which together with the southern mountain range forms a bottleneck through which the Firuzabad river and other streams of water must leave the plain (Fig. 8a).

The intended purpose of Ardashir's drainage programme was probably to dredge the lower riverbed and especially the narrow exit between the rocky spur and the southern mountain chain, in order to increase the speed of the water outflow. This successful operation is not only largely praised in the chronicles, but was also confused with another project: the cutting or tunnelling through a mountain, as already mentioned in the Karnamak-i Ardashir, which simply states: "He [Ardashir] dug through a broad mountain and made a stream of water flow. Many villages and hamlets he made flourish".[75] Ibn al-Balkhi embellished this information and turned it into a dramatic accident, by which Ardashir's great advisor and engineer, Abarsam, who planned and carried out the drainage programme, was drowned with all his workmen when the tunnel was finally broken through and the water gushed forward.[76]

There is in fact a water tunnel, to and through which water from the rich springs in the easternmost part of the plain at Jahdasht is led along the crescent-shaped mountain ridge, which separates the completely arid side valley of Lohrasbeh from the main plain. Further proof that this combination of draining and irrigation was part of Ardashir's programme is an aqueduct wall, which runs straight through the side valley, down to the river, with smaller aqueduct walls branching off on either side, together with the ruins of simple houses and two major settlement sites.[77] The long aqueduct wall did not belong to the twenty radials of Ardashir's layout, however; it ran almost exactly in a north–south direction straight towards the tower in the city centre behind the ridge, which was and is invisible from the side valley. This alone leaves no doubt that the irrigation project of the Lohrasbeh valley was part of Ardashir's master plan and also its surveyor's technical masterpiece.

Tabari mentions a certain Abarsam[78] as Ardashir's special dignitary since his coronation as king of Fars, a General who later repelled the attempted attack against Ardashir Khurreh by the vassal king of Ahvas, sent by Artaban. Abarsam's high position is corroborated by the inscription of Shapur I on the Kå aba-i Zardusht at Naqh-i Rustam, where he is quoted with the honourable name of Abarsam Ardashir-farr.[79] In Ibn al-Balkhi's dramatic but clearly invented story of the tunnel accident, Abarsam appears as the chief engineer, who was drowned with his workmen. Notwithstanding the unreliability of Ibn al-Balkhi's story, it would not be unusual at that time for the most trusted grandee of the king to be involved both with military responsibilities and with the management of Ardashir's colonization work.

In any case we must assume that for his gigantic project of drainage and irrigation, land division and distribution, and for all his building activities, Ardashir had assembled a team of highly qualified experts, specialized in surveying, architectural design, stone-cutting techniques and building crafts, from all over Iran and probably even from abroad. Like the Achaemenids before him and like several of his successors, Ardashir seems to have made use of imported ideas and techniques at least for his fire temple in Ardashir Khurreh. There are Roman examples of the ground plan of the Takht-i Nishin and, as mentioned above, it was not built in the local tradition with rubble and gypsum mortar, using as a measuring unit an Oriental ell or yard (=46.5 cm) as was the case with all his other buildings.[80] Instead the Takht-i Nishin was distinguished by Roman-type ashlar walls of perfectly cut freestones fixed with mortar and additional iron clamps in lead filling and — as further evidence of western influence — was based on a typical western measuring unit of a foot (=29.30 cm).[81] However, the masons' marks show that local workmen were employed here also, and in its final composition the architectural design of the building must have been typically Iranian: the interior square room with four bays may also be seen as a larger version of the palace hall of Qaleh Dukhtar with its four wide gates; and the dome on squinches, which can be reconstructed here in accordance with the palace domes, was in any case an Iranian development.[82]

Ardashir might have achieved his goals of draining, irrigating and distributing land and building a city very much more easily and faster if he had applied the age-old orthogonal Hippodamic system, which was well known all over the antique world, and countless examples of which were present in the Hellenistic-Roman provinces of Iran's western neighbourhood. Significantly, his son and successor Shapur I had already laid out his new city of residence, Bishapur, west of Ardashir Khurreh near Kazerun, on a simple, orthogonal plan, also with two intersecting main streets and a rectangular system of side alleys. Here the northern part of the city was reserved for a large fire temple area, incorrectly interpreted as Shapur's palace, and probably some other official buildings.[83] The fortified palace stood on a mountain next to it, but outside the city walls. Other Sasanian cities founded after Ardashir's reign, followed the same system, e.g. Jundi Shapur and Aivan- i Karkha.[84] It was only Ardashir who evidently preferred circular designs. In addition to his circular city plan of Ardashir Khurreh, he proved this by his round, donjon-like palace in the fortress and by the small mud-brick fort on the eastern access to the plain.

Of the seven cities Ardashir is said to have founded after his first city of residence,[85] only one, Veh Ardashir, has so far yielded archaeological evidence of his activities. On the western bank of the Tigris, opposite the old Parthian capital of Ktesiphon, Ardashir established a city on the site of the already existing settlement of Koche, as a new place for the inhabitants of the former Oriental metropolis of Seleucia further west, which had lost its economic basis, when the Tigris changed its course and the harbour ran dry.[86] Near the site of the famous Taq-i Kisra, the ruin of the late Sasanian main palace and residence, surveys and excavations have discovered a round, massive mud-brick wall, c. 3 km in diameter, with semicircular bastions, probably the fortification which Ardashir built for his forthcoming Mesopotamian capital.[87] There is no geometric layout visible in the excavated areas of the densely occupied interior of the city; it seems that the pre-existing allotments of the settlement of Koche had been preserved.

Historical tradition, as well as his archaeological heritage, characterize Ardashir as a fervently ambitious visionary but at the same time as a realistic and far-sighted politician and general, whose intentions and actions were always based on rational plans and calculation. There can be no doubt that his decision to lay out his colonization project of Ardashir Khurreh on a complicated radial and concentric plan, instead of the normal, easily constructed chessboard pattern, was not perfunctory or of aesthetic insignificance, but a meaningful demonstration. Without understanding his intentions more precisely, one may assume that what he tried to demonstrate was his vision of the Iranian state, with which he was going to replace the feudal system of the Parthian Empire. Although large sections of Parthian rule probably belong to the most prosperous and liberal periods of Iran, Ardashir had also experienced phases of Arsacid weakness against external and internal enemies, a weakness from which he profited without any scruples. His idea of kingship certainly contrasted with the feudal Arsacid system, where the king was dependent on the uncertain loyalty of semi-independent princes and vassals. The proclamation of his divine mission was obviously his main argument, in order to secure the unrestricted loyalty of the nobility as a precondition for an efficient and successful government. And he must have seen that the only appropriate political system for a successful government lay in a centralist or even an absolute monarchy as the worldly representation of cosmic order.

The radial-concentric plan of Ardashir Khurreh symbolizes perfectly the organization of a centralist state, in which all decisions come from one central authority, and in which this authority is surrounded by the social classes of the people, their ranks diminishing the further they are from the centre. In the central area of Ardashir Khurreh, beside the tower only the fire temple occupies a prominent place, as a paradigm for the clergy, which was going to become an institution of foremost influence in the Sasanian Empire.

We do not yet know what other major buildings were erected in the inner circle, apart for the tower and the fire temple. There are significant but small mounds on the north-west–south-east axis, which may contain the remains of Sasanian structures. The majority of irregular rubble stone ruins in and beyond the city centre are clearly of medieval, post-Sasanian date, although they may cover more original Sasanian buildings. However, there is scarcely enough space for a palace, and the tower stands isolated from any major ruin.

Finding a satisfying explanation for the tower, which is unique in such a context, will probably remain a matter for discussion. At the time that the plan was laid out over the plain, the top of the Minar must have been just an open platform, on which the figure of graduation for the twenty radials was drawn; and where measuring and sighting instruments were installed. When surveying work was completed, rooms might have been built on it, otherwise the grand and decorated staircase does not make sense. Of course, the possibility that a sacred fire was installed there cannot be excluded, but there is no evidence or likelihood for this assumption, since the great fire temple was next to it. The alleged pipeline for a fountain on top of the tower, mentioned in some sources[88] is a literary topos, frequently applied to prestigious buildings, and must be ignored. Some sources call the tower a fortress[89] and in fact, with its measurements of 19 m square and *c.* 35 m in height, it might have looked like that to later generations; but it was neither that nor a real palace.

With no comparable precedent available, only the position of the tower on the centre point of the plan of Ardashir Khurreh might provide an argument for a very vague interpretation beyond its practical use. If Ardashir understood kingship as the central element of an ideal state, the tower should have been meant as a symbol of the king or of kingship in general. There might have been a symbolic place for the king, and possibly rooms on the top could have been used for some official or ceremonial purposes in this context. In Bishapur the twin-columns monument with a statue of Shapur I, which was erected next to the intersection of the two main roads of the town by the governor Apasay in honour of the king,[90] is not an actual comparison, but it points to the fact that veneration of the king was a common element in Sasanian society.

The exalted position of king, which Ardashir increasingly claimed for himself over time, is demonstrated by a special architectural arrangement in his second, greater palace, today incorrectly called Ateshkadeh, or Fire Temple (Fig. 10).[91] He had it built in the plain next to the exit of the gorge, without any fortifications and definitely after his victory over the Parthian Great King. Its plan had the same architectural components as his first palace in the fortress, but was three times the size and with a somewhat different arrangement. On the back wall of the great aivan, above the entrance gate to the central domed hall, is located a high, vaulted niche.[92] Halfway up in the niche is a raised dais, accessible from the corridors of the upstairs private area of the palace, on which we have to imagine the king sitting on his throne, giving audience to the people in the aivan and its side halls. We may assume that the position of the king was made even more prominent by paintings, stucco or drapery in and around the niche. The distance between king and people was considerably increased by the fact that the floor level of the aivan was several metres below that of the domed halls, and access to the gate was via a pair of opposing staircases of the Iranian type of open-air staircases, known both from Persepolis and from the late Sasanian palaces of Kangavar and Qasr-i Shirin,[93] and here transferred to the interior of the palace. Leading up from either side to the gate with the throne niche above, they make the prospect even more dramatic for the audience. During assemblies in the central domed hall with its higher floor level, where the upper part of the same niche opens on the other side under a high, decorated arch, the king was probably somewhat less remote towards higher ranks, grandees and nobles.

The refinement of architectural arrangements for royal court ceremonials, which had been achieved under Ardashir, seems to have remained unsurpassed. There are no other palaces preserved to the same extent as those of Firuzabad. However, the Taq-i Kisra, the great aivan of the otherwise destroyed Sasanian palace of Ktesiphon, built during the late Sasanian period probably by Khusrau I (531–579 CE) and known as the Sasanian chief residence, has no comparable installations under its arch, which is nearly twice as large as the aivans of Ardashir.[94] Here the throne must have stood on the floor of the aivan, but no doubt on a high, elevated base. The remoteness between king and people seems to have been achieved here by other means. However, the legendary tales of the king giving audience from behind a curtain, of the heavy golden crown hanging down from the ceiling above his head[95] or of the famous Takht-i Taqdis, subject to far-reaching reconstructions,[96] would not have left any archaeological traces.

Notes:

1. Göbl 1971: Alram 1999: 67–76; Curtis 2007b: 7–20.
2. Tabari 1879: XIV–XVI Introduction by Nöldeke; Gutschmid 1880: 721–749; Christensen 1944: 59–83; Widengren 1971: 711–784.
3. Tabari 1879: 1–4; for the English translation see Widengren 1971: 732–734 and 760–767.
4. Karnamak 1879: 36–38; for the English translation see Widengren 1971: 776–778; Tha´alibi 1900: 473–480.
5. Instead of the apparently rather realistic career of Ardashir in Darabgerd, both the Karnamak and Tha´alibi give the clearly fictitious story of his youth as a page at the court of the Parthian Great King.
6. Tabari 1879: 6–8; Widengren 1971: 734.
7. Alram 1999: 68 and 71, fig. 8; Nasrullahzadeh 2004: 192.
8. Back 1978: 338; Huyse I, 1999: 49 § 36.
9. Alram 1999: 68. cp. figs 1–3 and 5–8.
10. Herzfeld 1941: 309, fig. 402 ; Sami 1958/59 (1338 H): 273–275; Calmeyer 1976: 63–68, figs 3–4; Nasrullahzadeh 2004 (1383 H): 192; Callieri 2003, figs 1–6.
11. Ritter 1965: 3; Huff (in press): 205–209.
12. Hinz 1969: 115–119; Gall 1990: 20–30; Vanden Berghe and Smekens 1984: 62–63, fig. 8.
13. Tabari 1879: 8.
14. Tabari 1879: in the version of Bel ´Ami (Tabari 1869: 69–70) Shapur was betrayed by the other brothers, who deserted and went over to Ardashir; a not very convincing variant, as their rebellion against Ardashir and their massacre shortly afterwards is reported by Bel´ Ami as well. About the importance of the ruins of Persepolis for Parthian Fars see also Wiesehöfer 2007: 47.
15. See, however, Nöldeke's suspicion in Tabari 1879: 10 note 1.
16. Widengren (1971: 736) gives CE 208 as a date. See also Alram (1999: 68) who suggests the years after CE 205.
17. Tabari 1879: 1–3; Karnamak 1879: 36–38.
18. Tabari 1879: 5–6.
19. Even if Tabari's report of Ardashir's appointing a high priest, *mobadan mobad*, immediately after his enthronement (Tabari 1879: 9) is doubted (Widengren 1971: 735), he must have set up or improved the clergy to serve in his newly built fire temple in Ardashir Khurreh, which was definitely not his only foundation.
20. Boyce (1968a).
21. Huff 1972: 517–540.
22. Göbl 1971; Alram 1999: 67–76.
23. Hinz 1969: 126–134; Schmidt 1970: 122–123, pls 80–82.
24. Karnamak: 1879: 46; cf. also Tha´alibi 1900: 478–479.
25. Huff 1974: 155–179. One may consider the possibility — purely speculative — that Ardashir may have tried to realize this project before, e.g. in Darabgerd, and that such an attempt might have caused the rebellion there. The name of Gur, which also means tomb, was changed to Firuzabad, "Place of Victory", by the Buyid ruler Adud-al Daula (948–983 CE), who used the place as a secondary residence to Shiraz.
26. Schwarz 1969: 56–59; Balkhi 1912: 43–46.
27. Bayliss 1987: 414–416.

28. Balkhi 1912: 44; Schwarz 1969: 56. As usual, Alexander is made responsible for the devastation, as he allegedly flooded the plain in order to conquer an Achaemenid city that was believed to have stood there.
29. Temporary inundation or permanent swampy areas could be observed in many plains of Iran, e.g. in the Marvdasht, before modern drainage.
30. Tabari 1879: 11–12. Other insults are "Kurdish shepherd" and "envious highwayman" (Nihayat); see Widengren 1971: 768.
31. Malandra 1983: 88–97.
32. Widengren 1971: 741–745.
33. Tabari 1879: 12–13. But see note 57.
34. Tabari 1879: 14.
35. Widengren 1971: 739–743.
36. Tabari 1879: 15. The sources differ in brutality; cf. the versions of Bel'Ami (Tabari 1868: 73) and the Nihayat (Widengren 1971: 769).
37. Tabari 1879: 14.
38. Widengren 1971: 769; Ghirshman 1962: 125–130, figs 163–166; Vanden Berghe and Smekens 1984: 62–63, fig 8.
39. Ghirshman 1962: 131, fig. 167; Hinz 1969: 119–123.
40. Hinz 1969: 123–126; Schmidt 1970: 123–125, pl. 96–97.
41. Hinz 1969: 126–134; Schmidt 1970: 122–123, pl. 80–82.
42. The interpretations of the personalities and deities on the royal Achaemenid tomb reliefs are highly controversial. The suggestion that the person in the winged symbol was meant to be Ahuramazda, the winged symbol itself the *khvarenah*, was put forward in D. Huff "Probleme um Ahuramazda und Khvarnah", *Avesta-Symposium, Akademie der Wissenschaften Berlin-Brandenburg und Botschaft der Republik Uzbekistan*, Berlin 9. 10. 2001 (in press). The main argument for the identification of the winged symbol without Ahuramazda as the *khvarenah* is its obligatory appearance in all representations of the royal canopy. See also Soudavar 2003: 3–4 and 95.
43. Fukai 1972: pls 1–33; 1984: 51–60; Ghirshman 1962: 192–193, fig. 235.
44. Hinz 1969: 144–171; Herrmann 1969: 63–88.
45. In Schwarz 1969: 56–57; Yaqut 1861: 175.
46. Markwart 1931: 43–94.
47. Ghirshman 1962: 34–35; Matheson 1972: 255; Stein 1936: 117 and 193–194 wavers between a Parthian to a Sasanian date.
48. Hamza 1848: 26; cf. also Creswell 1940: 21 n. 3; Istakhri (in Schwarz 1969: 93) stresses the well-tended new wall, and Stein (1936: 193–194) wonders why the wall is so much better and preserved to a bigger height than the contemporary or later wall of Ardashir's city; see also Encyclopaedia Iranica VII: s.v. Darab II. 5–7.
49. Herzfeld 1921: 106–133; Creswell 1940: 1–38; Lassner 1970; 184–241.
50. Herzfeld 1921: 132 n. 1; Creswell 1940: 21 n. 3.
51. Huff 1995: 429.
52. Huff 1995: 430. The rock with caves in its cliffs is called Ghar-i Siyah, Black Cave. At its foot stand the ruins of a later Sasanian fire temple, Oghlan-Qiz, next to a spring-fed lake (Ouseley II, 1821: 154, pl. 36; Miroschedji 1980: 157–160).

53. Masson 1982: 118–139; Invernizzi 1998: 45–59. That the separation of the ruler's residence from the town was an old rule of Oriental government is confirmed by the remarks of a Byzantine ambassador to al-Mansur, who dared to criticize, among others, the fact that the Calif had built his palace in the middle of his newly founded circular city of Madinat as-Salam, because it was disturbing and inappropriate for the ruler to live among and under the surveillance of the people (Lassner 1970: 57–58).
54. Huff 1991: 46–69: today a tepe with remains of fortifications, partly covered by a village, stands out in a larger area with traces of medieval settlement.
55. For closer descriptions of Qaleh Dukhtar see Huff 1972: 127–171; 1976: 157–173; 1978: 117–147. A small fortress, Naqare Khaneh, above the next river bend upstream is of Islamic date, according to the pottery.
56. Huff 1978: 128, pl. 43; cp. Alram 1999: 70, fig. 4.
57. However, the palace seems to have been raided and pillaged at an early date when it was partly unfinished, by a rival warlord, Mihrak, during an absence of Ardashir and his army. (Karnamak 1879: 52; Ferdowsi 1877: 254). Ferdowsi's information, that Mihrak dispersed part of the booty among his soldiers, seems to coincide with numbers of semi-precious stones and fragments of jewellery found during excavation in obviously unfinished levels of the main courtyard of Qaleh Dukhtar (Huff 1978: 127, note 20).
58. Huff 1978: 140.
59. Gold 1976: 63. "He (Obeyed Allah ibn Ma´mar al Taymi) conquered Ardashir Khorra, and ... Yazdgird escaped and went to Marv".
60. Balkhi 1912: 45.
61. The measurements are based on results of a survey in 1972. A. Stein (1936: 117) gives 1 1/3 mile (c. 2 km).
62. Huff 1972: 518, fig. 1.
63. Balkhi 1912: 45. Large amounts of brick fragments and some complete bricks (32 x 32 x 7.5 cm) were found in and around the ruin.
64. Huff 1972: 519–532.
65. A construction of four arches supporting a dome. If used for fire temples, the constructions had to be closed to the outside by walls in the arches, added rooms or surrounding corridors. See Encyclopaedia Iranica IV, 1990, s.v. Cahartaq I: 634–638.
66. Tabari 1879: 12.
67. An enigmatic Sasanian sanctuary with a room containing large boxes with plaster lids was excavated in Bandian near Dargaz, Khorrasan (Rahbar 1998: 213–250). Another oval structure of Islamic date, excavated in the city centre of Ardashir Khurreh, was hypothetically identified as an observatory for its similarity with the thirteenth-century Rassadkaneh at Maragheh, although an interpretation as a large kiln should not be excluded.
68. Ibn al-Balkhi (1912: 45) gives a muddled description of a composite building, in which features of the Takht-i Nishin — ashlar walls and brick dome — seem to be set on top of the Minar, which is called a platform. Of the names mentioned by al-Balkhi, "Iran" or "Aivan Girdah" obviously refer to the tower, "Gumbad Kirman" or "Girman" to the Takht-i Nishin.
69. Herzfeld 1926: 255.

70. Schwarz 1969: 57; Huff 1969/70: 324–338. The given documentation of the still-standing part of the tower is still valid. The staircase begins exactly under the arch that separates the entrance room and the first flight of steps. The entrance room has a plaster floor, on which fragments of decorative stucco were found. I have revised my theory concerning the upper part of the tower (Fig. 8). As it was certainly built contemporaneously with the palace of Qaleh Dukhtar, the hypothetical niches, would have had a horizontal upper frame, not a vaulted one as in the later great palace. If there was a dome, this would have covered only a room on top of the square (9 x 9 m) central post of the stair tower, as suggested in other reconstructions (Huff 1993: 57). The reconstruction of the upper rooms is purely hypothetical (see below).

71. There is no information on surveying instruments and techniques in Sasanian Iran. But we may assume that standard Roman technology was available.

72. Huff 1974: 165, fig. 1; 1993: 56. Meanwhile most of these traces have disappeared as a result of the introduction of modern mechanized agriculture.

73. In Schwarz 1969: 57.

74. Huff 1974: 165. Significant for the persistence of Ardashir's plan throughout the centuries is the position of the gate building of the late Safavid or Qajar governor's palace garden in modern Firuzabad, which stands exactly on the eastern corner point of the outer polygonal enclosure wall, on its intersection with the eastern radial line. We may assume that an ancient estate or some other ancient installation with a gate leading out onto the eastern road towards the exit of the plain and the circular fort, in the end became the focal point for the development of the modern town of Firuzabad in the Safavid period.

75. Karnamak 1879: 48.

76. Balkhi 1912: 74–75.

77. Huff 1974: 160. Because of a lowering groundwater table the original canal and tunnel, which are still visible and are also indicated by the ruins of medieval water mills, had to be given up and were replaced by a canal and tunnel at a lower level, which nowadays irrigates a reduced area of gardens and fields around the village of Lohrasbeh. The settlements on the riverbank and at the eastern spur of the ridge were also abandoned during the Islamic period. About 1 km east of the latter settlement, several large, round table- or pedestal-like stone objects were unearthed during agricultural levelling work.

78. Karnamak 1879: 9 and 12.

79. Back 1978: 351–352; Gignoux 1986: II/27; Huyse I 1999: 54–55.

80. Huff 1971: 168–171.

81. Huff 1972: 533–536.

82. Huff 1989: 223–236.

83. Ghirshman 1956: Plan de la ville; 1962: 138–149, fig. 176; 1971: 21–36.

84. Ghirshman 1962: 180–181, fig. 221; Adams and Hansen 1968: 53–59; Gyselen and Gasche 1994: 19–35, pls. 1–10.

85. Tabari 1879: 16 note 1 and 19–20.

86. Reuther 1930: 1–9; Fiey 1967: 3–38.

87. Venco Ricciardi 1968/69: 57–68; Invernizzi 1976: 167–175.

88. Balkhi 1912: 45.

89. e.g. Mukaddasi in Schwarz 1969: 59.

90. Ghirshman 1956: Plan de la ville: point F; 1962: 151, fig. 194; 1971: 29–30, pl. 40, 3.

91. e.g. Istakhri and Ibn Hauqal in Schwarz 1969: 58.

92. Huff 1971: 154–158, fig. 13a–a.
93. Reuther 1938: 493–578; Azarnoush 1981: 78, fig. 5.94.
94. Reuther 1930: 15–22; Huff 1971: 150–154.
95. Tabari 1879: 221–222; Tha´alibi 1900: 699–700.
96. Tha´alibi 1900: 698–699; Herzfeld 1920: 1–24 and 103–147.

4

Kingship in Early Sasanian Iran

Touraj Daryaee
(University of California, Irvine)

The idea of kingship and imperial royal ideology in ancient Iran has been the subject of a number of important studies, notably by G. Widengren,[1] R.N. Frye,[2] J. Neusner,[3] C. Herrenschmidt,[4] R. Schmitt,[5] J. Wolski,[6] J.K. Choksy,[7] J. Wiesehöfer,[8] G. Gnoli,[9] P. Briant,[10] A. Soudavar,[11] and most recently by A. Panaino.[12] What each of the studies provides is an elucidation of the notion of kingship and the position of the king vis-à-vis gods and humans in the Achaemenid, Seleucid, Arsacid and Sasanian periods. I believe what needs to be done for ancient Iranian history in general and for the Sasanian period specifically is the highlighting of the points of continuity, rupture and metamorphosis in terms of the idea of kingship. I am, like many, hesitant to see ancient Iranian civilization as a static unchanging phenomenon and I am an opponent of the perpetual infatuation with the concept of "continuity". While there are certainly elements of continuity in many respects, there are more changes and developments that need to be studied in order for us to understand the ancient Iranian world.

This is true for the idea of kingship in Sasanian Iran. I believe one of the biggest problems is that the idea of kingship in the Sasanian period has been discussed rather monolithically and statically, as if the concept in the early Sasanian period (third century) was the same as after Shapur II in the fourth century, or in the time of Khusrau I in the sixth century and Khusrau II in the seventh century. Ardashir I (224–240 CE), Shapur II (309–379 CE), and Khusrau I (531–579 CE) and Khusrau II (590–628 CE) each had a different attitude towards kingship and towards the position of the monarch in *Ērānšāhr*. Not only were these kings the products of their time, but they were also influenced by or reacted to the institution of the Zoroastrian religious hierarchy, which at times aided and at other times confronted the king and his power.[13] Furthermore, the burden of the past traditions on the Iranian Plateau made itself felt on the institution of kingship, where different aspects were emphasized depending on the domestic situation and on interactions with neighbouring powers.[14] I contend that in fact there were different attitudes towards kingship in each of these periods, which were influenced by the Zoroastrian hierarchy and by the power or weakness of the king and the court. In this essay I would like to discuss the notion of kingship and its formation in early Sasanian history of the third century CE, specifically during the reign of Ardashir I, the founder of the dynasty.

In order to understand the notion of kingship in the third century we need to discuss and preview several distinct traditions, which at times interplayed with one another on the Iranian Plateau and which were unified and systematized in the third century under the rule of the house of Sasan in the province of Persis/Pārs. These notions are firstly the Avestan tradition, secondly the Old Persian Achaemenid royal ideology,[15] thirdly the Hellenistic notion of kingship, which was introduced with Alexander the Great and the Seleucids,[16] fourthly the influence of the Arsacids as inheritors of these two former traditions, and fifthly the tradition specifically in Persis, the homeland of the Sasanians.

What kind of kingship did Ardashir I and the early Sasanians wish to emphasize in the third century? In order to understand this mentality and to see the development and formation of royal ideology we can glean details from the coinage[17] and from early Sasanian inscriptions and artistic production. From the very first inscription of Ardashir and his imperial coinage (post-enthronement) we have the following titulature:[18]

mzdysn bgy 'lhštr MLKAn MLKA 'yl'n MNW ctry MN yzd'n
mazdēsn bay ardashir šāhān šāh ērān kē čihr az yazdān

"The divine Mazda-worshipping Ardashir, king of kings of the Iranians, whose image/seed is from the gods/*yazdān*"

As we shall see, each block of this titulature for Ardashir and the succeeding kings points to a specific tradition that was current on the Iranian Plateau. Let us deconstruct the titulature and divide it into proper blocks in order to discuss them individually to gain a better understanding of the notion of kingship. By breaking down the titulature into units so that each reveals its point of origin, we can then obtain a complete view of how Ardashir and the house of Sasan brought these elements together, and provide a specific meaning for kingship in the third century.

I - *Mazdēsn*

The appearance of *mazdēsn* (*mzdysn*) is quite significant for ancient Persian history and for the history of religion on the Iranian Plateau. To my knowledge this is the first time that we find *mazdēsn* used as a legend or inscription in the history of the four pre-Islamic dynasties. Its meaning is quite clear: "Mazda-worshipper" or "adherent to the religion of Mazda".[19] It is only an Aramaean seal which has the legend of *zrtštrš* meaning "Zoroastrian"[20] from the Achaemenid period that can match *mzdysn* in suggesting an adherence to the religion of what we call today Zoroastrianism.[21]

In fact there are all sorts of gestures and symbols providing evidence that the Achaemenids and Parthians were Mazda-worshippers, but it is with Ardashir that we have direct evidence that the upstart king is a Mazda-worshipper. It is also the case that Ardashir and his family were to utilize the Avestan tradition, since it is in the *Avesta* that we find the term *mazdaiiasna-* "Mazda-worshipper".[22] More importantly the appearance of the form *mzdysn* rather than what we should have in Middle Persian (*msdyšn*) (the change from Avestan –zn- > to –sn- is unknown in Western Iranian, it should be -šn-) suggests a learned Western Iranian borrowing from the Avestan tradition.[23]

This is not the place to discuss the written tradition of the *Avesta* and the various dates proposed, most people accepting K. Hoffman's suggestion that the *Avesta* was written down in the fourth century,[24] but the mention of the Nask by Kerdīr in his inscription[25] in the third century should give us some pause regarding the time when the *Avesta* as a written text was at the disposal of the Persians. What one can conclude then, is that in the third century an imperial ideology had formed that was subordinated to the worship of Ohrmazd since it stood at the beginning of Ardashir's titulature. Thus, first and foremost the Sasanians were Mazda-worshippers. This in a way is reminiscent of the Achaemenid period when Darius proclaimed:

> *vašnā auramazdāha adam xšāyaθiya*
> "by the grace/favour of Ahuramazda I am king" (DBI.11–12).

But the Sasanian relation with Mazda here appears closer and more intense. It is not as the Achaemenid kings mention *auramazdā xšaçam manā frābara* "Ahuramazda gave me the realm" or that *ahuramazdāha ragam vartaiyaiy* "I turn myself quickly to Ahuramazda" (DBIV.57). Rather from their first coins and first inscription the Sasanians claim a more intense Mazda-worshiping than previous Iranian dynasties. I believe this attitude towards Ohrmazd and other *yazata*s (Middle Persian *yazdān*) was such because they believed they had a special privilege vis-à-vis *yazata*s and humans. That is, their proximity to Ohrmazd and other *yazata*s made them a special kind of being which, although not necessarily a Zoroastrian tradition, was a grafted-on aspect of the Persian encounter with Hellenism in the proceeding centuries.

II - *Bay*

The use of *bgy*/*bay* for the ruler is significant because at no time in the Achaemenid period did the Persian kings use *bay* "god, lord" to refer to a human.[26] The basic meaning of the word as an agent noun clearly means "distributor", which in the Old Persian inscriptions came to mean "god".[27] In Sasanian times *bay* was used to designate the king and people of high importance, usually translated as "Majesty", but also as "god" or "divine". In fact there is no reason not to assume that *bay* designated the king as divine. One finds a similar non-Iranian tradition in the post-Achaemenid period, under the influence of Hellenism in Iran. Parthian *bagpuhr* reflects the Hellenistic influence of the title θεοπάτωρ "son of God",[28] which appears on Seleucid and then on Parthian coinage.[29] There is no lack of divine association at this period for rulers, a good example being Parthian *bagpuhr*, Sogdian *βγpwr* from (Sanskrit *devaputra*), which was the title associated with the Chinese emperor *fagfur*[30] known as *huángdì* "god-king".[31]

The Sasanian king being designated as *bay* ("divine") meant that he was someone who stood closer to the gods and not to humans. P.O. Skjærvø in his exposition on the palaeography of the third-century Middle Persian, has suggested that the title *bgy* means "divine", where according to him the title still stood for the divine status of the king, rendering the Greek θέος.[32] I believe that indeed the early Sasanian rulers may have wanted to be known as divine entities, and hence *bay* stood for exactly what resonated in the minds of the Persians, i.e. "divine" at the time. This was not a tradition that would continue in the Sasanian period. As the Zoroastrian hierarchy grew its power stripped away such a claim, and by the fourth century CE "Majesty" was understood to be the designation of *bay*, although by then it was little used. By then *Xwadāy* — meaning a suzerain — was used and associated with Sasanian rulers, but by the early Islamic period it became specifically used for designating "god" in Persian.[33] Only Mohammad Reza Shah Pahlavi, who was to revive this title as part of the imperial propaganda as mandated by the court in the late 1970s, was called *Xwdāyegān* (certainly *pluralis maiestatis* by then!).

In the Seleucid period we find local governors and rulers in Persis who minted coins with the legend *prtrk' zy 'lhy'* / *fratarakā ī bayān*. As later Persis coinage has rulers who call themselves MLKA / *šāh*, we may assume that the Fratarakā were not independent rulers and were probably subordinate to the Seleucids.[34] The meaning of this legend has been subject to several important studies by Wiesehöfer,[35] Skjærvø,[36] and Panaino.[37] Panaino takes the legend to mean "the governor (for the sake/for the account = in the name) of the gods", referring to the gods, namely Ahuramazdā, Mithra and Anāhitā, that were upheld by the Achaemenids.[38] Skjærvø, with whom Panaino agrees in principle, takes the legend to mean "the one (set) ahead (of others) of = by the god".[39] I simply take the legend to mean "Fratarakā of the gods". These Fratarakās then were protectors of the *bayān* "gods", but these *bayān* I believe were not Ahuramazdā, Mithra and Anāhitā as Panaino maintains, but the Achaemenid kings themselves. In an article on the iconography of the coinage of the Fratarakās, Callieri made the important observation that the paraphernalia, namely the banner, the funerary monuments[40] and the gesture of the person standing before it all, emphasize a tie with the Achaemenid kings. I believe, as Callieri has rightly pointed out, that the *bayān* are none other than the Achaemenid kings, who after their death became deified through the Hellenic tradition.[41] This may be exactly the reason for which we may read the title *bay* on the coinage of Ardashir and the early Sasanians as "divine", in its Hellenistic sense.

I think the reasoning that this usage was not part of the Persian tradition does not justify ignoring innovation as a factor in the history of Iranian religion and traps us in the idea of the "unchanging" nature of Persian kingship in antiquity. Just because the Achaemenids did not claim divine descent does not mean that the Sasanians could not. Then the Sasanian kings could very well be "Mazda-worshipping", kings who were "divine" themselves.

III - MLKAn MLKA / *Šāhān Šāh*

This part of the titulature is well known. The Achaemenid title of *xšayāθiya xšayaθiyānām* borrowed from the kingdom of Urartu (*šar šarrani*) signified Persian ascendancy in the Near East in the sixth century BCE.[42] It must be emphasized, however, that with the pre-Imperial coins of Ardashir, he and his family members followed very closely the Persis tradition of being MLKA, or simply "Kings", as the title stood with his brother Shapur and his father Pabak.[43] But something happened once he was able to defeat Ardavān and become the "King of Kings". This may certainly have been due to the change in the power relation between the kings of Persis and their Parthian overlords, where Ardashir before his defeat or conquest of the surrounding regions could at best have been *šāh ī pārs* in defeating the various local rulers. There is no doubt that the title King of Kings makes its appearance from the Parthian period in the middle of the first century BCE and that the new claim to descend from the Achaemenids was caused by successive victories over the Romans.[44] Thus, this is part of the Achaemenid tradition of kingship, which passed through the Parthians to the Sasanians.

What is new and significant here is that Ardashir was the first ruler to claim to be "King of Kings" of *Ērān*. Here one sees the use of Avestan terminology, reinforcing the existence of a strong Avestan — written or oral — tradition so that it could be utilized by Ardashir. In effect the "King of Kings of Ērān" brings together the Old Persian tradition via the Parthians and that of the Younger Avestan tradition of the Kavi's rule over the *airiianam dahyunam*, although even that was probably altered by the Sasanians, creating an **airiianam xšaθram*, i.e. *Ērānšahr*,[45] at it was never used in the previous empires.[46]

The problem here is whether the Sasanians themselves were instrumental in the transposition of the mythical homeland of the Aryans onto the Iranian Plateau, or whether the idea was already current on the plateau. A safe supposition would be that, at least in the province of Persis, the idea of *Ērān/Ērānšahr* would have been known to some, such as the Mages or Pabak who, according to later tradition, was the custodian of the Adur-Anahīd temple. We should remember that the Ābān Yašt is important in that various heroes and potentates make sacrifices to Lady Anahitā to overcome their enemies, by the banks of the River Vaŋhvai Daiti in *airiianam dahyunam*. So it could very well be that through the cult of Anahitā we have the establishment of *Ērānšahr* by the Sasanians. We should remember the statement by Plutarch about the Achaemenid king Artaxerxes II receiving royal initiation at the sanctuary of a θέα πολεμιχή "warlike goddess", comparable to Athena in Greece and Ištar (having the same epithet *bēlit* "lady") in Mesopotamia.[47] For Ardashir I we also find the statement by Agathias that the king went through an initiation ceremony. Was this ceremony related to the cult of Anahīta, which Artaxerxes II had dedicated himself to? More interesting is that according to Persian tradition, his grandfather Sasan was in charge of the fire temple called Anāhīd,[48] and when Ardashir defeated the rebels he sent their heads to the Anāhīd temple.[49]

IV - MNW *ctry* MN *yzd'n* / *kē čihr az yazdān*

Lastly we come across the very interesting and recently much discussed "*kē čihr az yazdān*", whose meaning seems to be clear, i.e. "whose image/seed is from the deities/gods". This statement, of course, is contrary to the traditional Persian notions of kingship in the Achaemenid period, but I see nothing particularly traditional about the early Sasanians. In fact they had come to the scene to change the history of Iran in the name of bringing back order as it once existed. We should not forget the accusation levelled against Ardashir I in the *Tansar-nāmeh* that the upstart king had brought innovation.[50] Not only during the reign of Ardashir I, but also during the reign of Khusrau I, many changes and innovations were made in the name of restoring lost knowledge or resurrecting the Persian tradition from oblivion.[51]

Let us examine the phrase *kē čihr az yazdān*. In the *Avesta, čiθra* stands for both *semen* and for "form, appearance". Middle Persian *čihr* "form, shape, appearance", Manichaean Middle Persian *cyhr* "face", Parthian *cyhr* "form, appearance", and supported by Pashto *cēr* "similar", Gāndhārī *cirorma* "face-covering", where it has survived in Persian as *čihre* "face, appearance", and here is best defined as "image". The second sense of *čiθra-* is better attested as "seed" or "origin".[52] It can be seen in Old Persian *ariya čica-* of "Aryan lineage", Middle Persian *čihr* "seed, origin, essence", Manichaean Middle Persian *cyhr* "essence, origin, offspring", Manichaean Parthian *cyhrg* "essence, nature", and Pazand *čihara* "essence, origin, source".[53] While the first *čiθra-* has been explained as being cognate with Vedic *citrā* "brilliant, shining, excellent, outstanding", the second *čiθra-* has remained problematic. Pisani believed that the secondary *čiθra-* was an interrogative pronoun *ci-* with the locative *tra*, much like Sanskrit *ku-tra*, meaning "who are you?" or "where do you come from?" thus seeking origin.[54] Sanskrit *citrah* "bright", is related to Avestan *čiθra-* "visible form",[55] or "manifest", and with its other meaning "family, race, seed",[56] when one accepts Duchesne-Guillemin's suggestion that both *čiθra*s in fact have a common meaning. This can be seen by pointing to the idea that seed or semen is conserved in the stars and connected with light.[57] According to the *Bundahišn*, when Ahreman brought death to the primordial bull and Gayōmard, their seed or semen was purified in the following manner:

> *šusr ī gāw abar ō māh pāyag burd ānōh bē pālūd hēnd ...*
> *ka gayōmard andar widerišnīh tōhm be dād ān tōhm*
> *pad rōšnīh ī xwaršēd be pālūd hēnd*

> "The semen of the bull was brought to the moon station,
> there it was purified... when Gayōmard, emitted seed,
> while passing away, that seed was purified in the light of the sun".[58]

Thus we can posit a single *čiϑra-*, referring to the seed of life.[59] In the royal Achaemenid inscriptions the following passages refer to the idea of seed/origin[60] (DNa.8–15):

> *adam Dārayavahuš xšāyaθiy vazraka xšāyaθiya*
> *xšāyaθiyānām xšāyaθiya dahyūnām vispazanānām xšāyaθiya*
> *ahyāyā būmiyā vazrakāyā dūraiapiy Vištāspahyā puça*
> *Haxāmanišiya Pārsa Pārsahyā puça Ariya Ariya ciça*

> "I am Darius the great king, king of kings, king of countries
> containing all kinds of men, king in this land far and wide,
> son of Hystaspes, an Achaemenian, a Persian, son of a Persian,
> an Aryan, having Aryan lineage [lit. seed]."[61]

Which brings us to Ardashir's *mzdysn bgy 'rthštr MLK'n MLK' 'yr'n MNW ctry MN yzt'n / mazdēsn bay ardashir šāhān šāh ērān kē čihr az yazdān.*[62] If we accept that *čihr* stands for both image/face and seed,[63] the meaning of this Middle Persian phrase could be "the divine Mazda-worshipping Ardashir, king of kings of the Iranians, whose image/seed is from the gods/*yazdān*".[64]

To which *yazdān* or gods is Ardashir connecting his seed/image? Before answering this question, I would like to return to the issue of *bay*. As mentioned at the beginning of this essay it was stated that the Fratarakā simply honoured and probably deified the Achaemenid kings, and so the *bayān* referred to those Achaemenid kings. By doing this the Fratarakās were attempting to gain some legitimacy in Persis. As we know from later Middle Persian and Persian texts, the Sasanians claimed they were related to Dārāy-e Dārāyān, the Achaemenid kings worthy of worship by the Fratarakās. The model, however, that was used to deify the Achaemenid kings was the Hellenic tradition, which began with Alexander and was carried to its logical conclusion by the Seleucids, influencing the Persis overlords.[65]

But what about *yazdān*? Being from the race or seed/image of gods is not unique to this case in antiquity. Being the mirror image of the gods such as Ohrmazd, Anahīta or Mithra is also documented by the early Sasanians themselves. All we have to do is to look at early Sasanian rock reliefs. A. Gariboldi has made the very pertinent observation that the early Sasanian reliefs show the king and the gods as having similar physical features, size, clothes, horse and harnesses.[66] In terms of proportion, the Sasanian king is an exact image of the *yazatas/yazdān*. One has to wonder about the power and belief of the early Sasanian kings about themselves and where they stood and what was their function and relation to gods and men. I believe the legend on the coins and the inscriptions of Ardashir I and Shapur I meant exactly what is showed pictorially on the rock reliefs, that they were divine and that they were made in the image of the gods and were related to them.

In a detailed study, Antonio Panaino has attempted to demonstrate that the Sasanian kings, much like their Achaemenid predecessors, were not divine or in any sense sacred rulers. According to Panaino it is really our misunderstanding or a simplified reading of the Sasanian inscription when the king of kings states that he is ἐκ γένος θεῶν, a defied king.[67] In other words, according to him, the Sasanian king's function was as *cosmocrator* without any special relation to the gods. This was because the Zoroastrian religion prevented human beings from making such a claim, as was the case with Christianity and the Byzantine king.[68]

It should be emphasized that in the Sasanian period we do not have a monolithic or static institution of kingship, and in fact the idea of kinship went through several distinctive changes. Most importantly, as Panaino himself states, the institution of Zoroastrianism had an impact on the way in which Sasanian royal ideology was made manifest. However, in the early Sasanian period Ardashir I, who was an upstart, brought together the existing traditions of kingship, a combination of Persian ideology along with that of the Hellenistic tradition of deified kingship, to justify his family's rule over *Ērānšahr*. He not only became a divine king,[69] he also created a genealogy which connected himself to the mythical Kayanid dynasty,[70] Furthermore, he transposed the mythical homeland of the Aryans, as mentioned in the *Avesta*, onto where he came to rule, thereby creating the realm of *Ērānšahr*. Thus, the various traditions were drawn upon by Ardashir to create a new phase in ancient imperial ideology, and also in the history of Iran. As an upstart you could not bring any more legitimacy to your rule than to claim to be from the seed of the gods.

Furthermore it be should remembered that the institution of Zoroastrianism could not have impacted on the idea of early Sasanian kingship very much because it was an institution in its infancy. The Zoroastrian church in the third century could not have put any demands on the king of kings to claim very much of anything. This changed in the fourth century, when church and king faced Christianity as a real threat to the empire and Zoroastrian fervour was needed to mount an attack against the new foe across the border. The newly formed and invigorated Zoroastrian religious hierarchy caused the idea of kingship to be redefined.

It is only with Shapur II in the fourth century CE that the Sasanian imperial royal ideology went through a change, mainly due to the power of the Zoroastrian religious hierarchy and its important architect, Adurbād ī Mahrsapandān. From this time the king became a *cosmocrator* as a man who mediated between gods and men, but in the third century Ardashir I was not simply a king who had earthly duties, he was divine, just as his Roman counterparts from the time of Augustus to the fourth century CE were. Ardashir claimed exactly what he was, a *bay* whose image was made like/from the seed of *yazdān* "gods" and the rock reliefs support this idea along with the Greek attestation ἐκ γένος θεῶν.[71] We should remind ourselves that the Near Eastern idea of deification was very much alive across the Euphrates in the third century CE. One of the magistrates of Palmyra, who was the stratēgos, recalled his position in the following manner during the time of Severus Alexander:

'STRTG LQLNY' BMYTWYT' DY 'LH' 'LKSNDRWS QSR
"Stratēgos of the *colonia* during the presence of the deified Alexander Ceaser"[72]

In conclusion we can state that the early Sasanian imperial ideology was mainly a reworking of the Avestan, Old Persian and Hellenic notions of kingship: by using the Avestan tradition the Sasanians established that they were indeed *Mazdēsn* or Mazda-worshippers (something new in terms of the epigraphical evidence). But now through the tradition of Persis, where the Fratarakās emulated the Hellenic cult of a deified king, Ardashir claimed a connection with the *bayān*: i.e. the early Sasanians remembered the Achaemenids[73] and saw them as *bayān* just as the Fratarakās had. The Parthian royal ideology contributed to the Sasanians in that the Old Persian tradition was kept alive by them with the title of "King of Kings". The last element, Ardashir being an exact image of the gods, suggested a very non-Iranian tradition, but it was adopted by both the Seleucids and the Parthians and, in an interesting way, by the early Sasanians. Of course Ardashir I may not have known that it was not Iranian in origin, but for him and his family it was part of an established tradition in Persis and the Iranian world. Thus, early Sasanian kingship was a hybrid idea drawing strength from Zoroastrian, Persis, Parthian and Hellenic traditions to justify its rule over *Ērānšahr* as a deified king of the Iranians.

Notes:

1. Widengren, 1959: 242–257.
2. Frye, 1964: 36–54.
3. Neusner, 1963: 40–59.
4. Herrenschmidt, 1976: 33–65.
5. Schmitt, 1977: 384–395.
6. Wolski, 1990: 11–18.
7. Choksy, 1988: 35–52.
8. Wiesehöfer, 1996: 55–66.
9. Gnoli, 1998: 115–139.
10. Briant, 2002, especially Chapter 6.
11. Soudavar, 2003.
12. Panaino, 2004: 555–594.
13. Gignoux, 1984a: 72–80.
14. Wiesehöfer has also rightly emphasized similar sentiments about the danger of seeing Arsacid kingship as a "fixed, unchangeable phenomenon", 1996: 58.
15. See Ahn, 1992.
16. See Daryaee, 2007: 1–12.
17. For the chronology of Ardashir's coinage see the important article by M. Alram, 1999: 67–76.
18. For a complete list of Ardashir's titulature see P. Huyse, 2006: 182–183.
19. Avestan *mazdaiiasna* "he who sacrifices to (Ahura) Mazdā", but by the Sasanian period this was not the meaning that was understood for the word, but simply one who was a worshiper of Ohrmazd and what we call today a Zoroastrian, see Skjærvø, 2003: 50, ff. 8.
20. Schmitt, 1997: pp. 922–923.
21. For the context of the seal found see Briant, 2001: 113.
22. Bartholomae, 1961: 1160.
23. Nyberg, 1974: 130.
24. Hoffmann, 1975: 316–325.
25. Gignoux, 1991, KSM 29: 29.
26. *Bay* is used in the epic tradition as the designation for king Wištāsp, Gheiby, 1999, passage 40.
27. Bailey, 1989: 403.
28. Humbach, 1988: 104–105.
29. Gariboldi, 2004a: 367.
30. Borhan-e Qate', 1982: 1494.
31. Bailey, 1989: 404.
32. Skjærvø, 2003: 49, ff. 6.
33. Shayegan, 1998: 50.
34. For the Frataraka see Wiesehöfer, 1994; and more recently Wiesehöfer 2007: 37–49.
35. Wiesehöfer, 1994: 105–110.
36. Skjærvø, 1997: 93–104.
37. Panaino, 2003: XX.
38. Panaino, 2003: 283.
39. Skjærvø, 1994: 102.
40. Potts believes that although the Fratarakās may have been ignorant of the original function of the funerary monuments of Ka'ba and Zendan, they still had ideological significance, 2007: 270–271.

41. Callieri, 1998: 35–36.
42. Piras, 2002: 207.
43. Alram, 1999: 72, fig. 8.
44. Neusner, 1963: 50–51.
45. MacKenzie, 1998: 535.
46. Gnoli, 1989: 2.
47. Piras, 2004: 251.
48. Ṭabari, 1999: 4.
49. Ṭabari, 1999: 15.
50. Boyce, 1968a: 47.
51. Daryaee, 2003: 44–45.
52. Nyberg, 1974: 55.
53. Gershevitch, 1959: 214.
54. Pisani, 1933: 214; Lincoln, 1992: 119.
55. Panaino considers the meaning "visible form" as a further semantic development of the second meaning due to its connection with Apam Napāt 1992: 94.
56. Mayrhofer, 1976: 705.
57. Duchesne-Guillemin, 1955: 98.
58. Bahār, 1369: 69.
59. Lincoln, 1992: 119.
60. Skjærvø, 2003:53, ft. 10.
61. Kent, 1953: 137–138.
62. Back, 1978: 281.
63. Daryaee, 2002: 113–116.
64. Similar to Skjærvø's reading, 2003: 53; Soudavar disagrees with this divine notion of the early Sasanian kings. He takes the opposite view of what čihr means in the context of imperial ideology, 2006: 1.
65. Daryaee, 2007: 11–12.
66. Gariboldi, 2004b: 32.
67. Panaino, 2003: 282–283.
68. Panaino, 2004: 584–585.
69. Widengren, 1959: 245.
70. Daryaee, 1998:121–149; Daryaee, 2001–2002:1–14.
71. Huyse, 1999, 1.2.4: 22.
72. Millar, 1993: 149.
73. Shahbazi, 2001: 69.

5

Image and Identity: Art of the Early Sasanian Dynasty

Prudence O. Harper
(Curator Emerita, Metropolitan Museum of Art, New York)

In the early third century CE a new Sasanian dynasty assumed control in Iran and Mesopotamia, a region that had been exposed for centuries to the cultural traditions of the Greco-Roman world. Throughout an area extending from the eastern Mediterranean coast to western central Asia and from the Caucasus Mountain region to the Persian Gulf, a rich and varied array of Greco-Roman images were in use by artisans employed both by official and private patrons. In the lands held by the Romans to the west of Iran, in Asia Minor, the Levant and the Syro-Mesopotamian region, as well as in territories ruled by the Kushans in Bactria to the east of Iran, the surviving monuments and artefacts illustrate a broad reliance on western, Hellenized models.

When the two earliest Sasanian monarchs, Ardashir I (224–240 CE) and Shapur I (240–272 CE), established political control in Iran and parts of Mesopotamia, a primary and immediate concern was the creation of a distinctive set of dynastic images. Initially in the coinage and glyptic and then in immense rock-carved reliefs and on silver vessels, a dynastic programme gave visible definition to Sasanian authority. Almost a millennium earlier, the new Achaemenid rulers of Iran, in the late sixth century BCE, had similarly acted to create a unified visual imagery of empire on seals, coins and sculptures, and in the second century BCE the Arsacid king, Mithradates I, the first to rule over an extensive Parthian empire, made a comparable political statement with the development of distinctive dynastic images.[1]

Continuity with the art and imagery of the Arsacid era is evident in the designs and motifs appearing on the earliest Sasanian monuments. Still there is a significant difference in conception and scale between the earliest Sasanian dynastic art, the third-century rock reliefs in Persis, and such late Parthian works as the reliefs at Tang-i Sarvak in southern Elymais, created to celebrate regional and political authority under the Arsacids. Prominent location, monumental size and, by the end of Ardashir's reign, clarity of focus and design are three of the most important features of the early Sasanian works.[2]

The trend towards a simplified composition can be traced in the reliefs of Ardashir from the battle scenes at Firuzabad, incorporating three, vigorous, single combats and a complex and obscure court scene at Naqsh-i Radjab to a simple, balanced composition at Naqsh-i Rustam in which two immobile, equestrian figures confront each other and demonstrate in concrete visual terms the interdependent relationship between god and king. Even when Roman patterns and models contributed to the Sasanian designs, as they surely did in the victory scenes of Shapur I, what the Iranians rejected in the foreign models is as notable as what they kept.[3] There are no miscellaneous battle paraphernalia, no scenery elements to define the place or setting in real or natural terms, no supporting figures to suggest historical accuracy or distract the viewer from the primary, dynastic message. Some details were, of course, essential to a proper understanding of the image. As on the coins, the forked beard of the last Parthian king, Ardavan, is carefully depicted in the investiture relief of Ardashir I at Naqsh-i Rustam in spite of the fact that it is hardly apparent to a viewer. Signs of authority and identity, of clan or family, of royal power, of rank and position are all present, although the significance of many details is uncertain at this much later period and without the painted additions that once existed on the carved surfaces.

Most of the images appearing in early Sasanian dynastic art are familiar ones, widely used throughout the eastern Mediterranean and Near Eastern worlds in the centuries before this period. On Sasanian rock reliefs, there are scenes of confronted, equestrian images of a god and king, depictions of the dynastic family, and illustrations of individual, equestrian combats. In early Sasanian paintings and on silver vessels hunting scenes and medallion "portraits" of the king and nobility are the common motifs. "Portrait" busts also appear on early Sasanian coins and seals, and on stucco relief plaques and wall paintings. All of these subjects appear in reliefs and paintings at Dura-Europos, Palmyra and Hatra in the preceding Parthian period, but at the hands of early Sasanian artisans the motifs assumed a standard form and became familiar icons that were easily recognized references to Sasanian power and authority.[4]

Outside the early Sasanian dynastic centres the images that have survived are more varied and less stereotyped than those appearing in the dynastic court productions and are comparable, in this sense, to the rich imagery employed by artists in the Greco-Iranian, late Parthian world. A rescue dig by Massoud Azarnoush of a partially bulldozed, fourth- or possibly fifth-century complex at Hajiabad in Fars provides a rare glimpse of this richer and more fluid imagery as it was utilized by a local landowning authority.[5] In section C, Room 114, an area designated by the excavator as having cult or religious associations, the walls were decorated with stucco figural and plant motifs. Medallion portraits, clothed and nude females and nude youths holding grapes are also subjects represented. These are the same themes seen in casual drawings, the graffiti and dipinti, of the west Parthian world at Dura-Europos in Syria and Hatra in Mesopotamia where the meaning of the figural motifs is also unclear.[6] Closer geographically to southern Iran and Hajiabad are the remains found at a manor or fortress off the Khurasan road in central western Iran at Qaleh-i Yazdgird.[7] This was the residence of an independent, late Parthian border lord. Excavations by Edward Keall at the site in the 1970s were never completed because of the deteriorating political situation in Iran at the time, but the stucco and painted images remind us of Hajiabad: medallion portraits, an assortment of Dionysiac imagery including nude females and Eros-like figures standing and, in some examples, playing with monstrous animals among grape vines. There are small nude hunters, their backs turned to the viewer to give a sense of movement in space (Fig. 1), and an eclectic array of Greco-Iranian monsters. All the stucco designs at Qaleh-i Yazdgird were once garishly painted and the decorated spaces must have had the dramatic appearance of a stage setting, a background thought to be appropriate for a landholder of position and wealth. The remains at Qaleh-i Yazdgird and those unearthed at early Sasanian Hajiabad provide an insight into the courtly lives of lords and nobles. We are reminded of the inscription left by the early Sasanian official, Apasay, who erected a columnar monument at Bishapur in the third century which bore an image of Shapur I.[8] In the inscription on the monument, Apasay, who was from Carrhae on the west Sasanian border, records how the king rewarded him with silver and gold, slaves, women, a garden and lands, a courtly environment for a man of position and favour who might well have lived in palatial buildings not unlike those at Hajiabad and Qaleh-i Yazdgird.[9]

Fig. 1. Drawing of scenes decorating an engaged column. Qaleh-i Yazdgird, Iran. Herrmann 1977a:70.

Azarnoush suggests that the hand-carved over life-size, stucco busts, found at the base of engaged columns at the entrance to *aivan* 149 in reception area A, were attached to these columns, a supposition that seems reasonable considering the position in which the pieces fell and the fact that the heads are turned slightly downward (Fig. 2).[10] These significant images are, therefore, comparable to the columnar monument erected by Apasay and bearing an image of Shapur I.[11] A more elaborate pre-Sasanian monument is the columned street at Palmyra where statues of important officials and personages were mounted high on the shafts of the columns.

The hand-carved large-scale busts at Hajiabad have an iconic, static appearance, a characteristic they share with the medium-sized busts found in section C in room 114.[12] In that room, among the varied stucco figural images, geometric designs and plant motifs are high-relief busts of significant persons, placed on circular background plates (Fig 3). What is notable is that the figures are individualized solely by the distinctive arrangement of the hair above the brow, by the headdress if there is one or by the insignia worn on the headdress. Otherwise the busts of the different individuals are identical, apparently made from a single model or mould. Rika Gyselen writing about the standardization of the busts carved on personal seals of high Sasanian functionaries, has suggested that the artists who fashioned the seals were following one of two models distinguished by specific features or details (a Parthian tiara or rounded cap; plain neck band or beaded necklet).[13] From the evidence of the stucco busts at Hajiabad, it is apparent that images of significant persons were similarly standardized there in early Sasanian times and defined the rank or position of the personage in society.

The Hajiabad male "portraits", large and medium, provide illustrations for a text inscribed in the early fourth century on the walls of Persepolis.[14] The newly appointed ruler in Sakastan, Shapur, journeying from Istakhr to take up his position, describes his entourage in an inscription listing the persons who accompanied him by rank and authority: handarzbed, magus, satrap, scribe, the Persian and Saka nobles as well as Zarangians and delegates and ambassadors from the provinces. The various personages portrayed on the walls of the buildings at Hajiabad probably fall into one or another of these categories. A prayer for the king, Shapur II (309–379 CE), the leader under whom the Saka king, Shapur, held authority, comes at

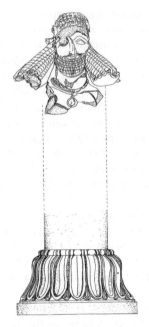

Fig. 2. Reconstruction of an engaged column and stucco male head. Hajiabad, Iran. Azarnoush 1994: fig. 143

Fig. 3. Drawing of a stucco plaque having a medium-sized male bust. Hajiabad, Iran. Tracing by the author from Azarnoush 1994: pl. xi.

the end of the Persepolis inscription and, at Hajiabad, "portrait" busts of Shapur II may have supplied a similar point of reference.

The different hair arrangements of figures at Hajiabad are hard to interpret but surely have some meaning related to rank, family, clan or ethnicity. North and far to the east of Hajiabad, in the gorge of Kal-i Jangal, near Birjand in southern Khurasan, is a rock-cut representation of a lion hunter grasping and spearing his quarry (Fig. 4).[15] The scene is not a crudely executed design but a rather skilful and careful, if somewhat confusing, image. A Parthian inscription accompanying the image was read by Henning, who suggested a date between 200 and 250 CE for the monument. The text gives the name of a prefect/satrap in a small area, Gar Ardashir. An unusual detail in the Kal-i Jangal drawing is the treatment of the hair of the hunter.

From the forehead rise full and bouffant parallel strands or braids. This arrangement of the hair is comparable to the hairstyle of one of the medium-sized busts found at Hajiabad (Fig. 3), a personage who may, at a later date, have shared the same rank or have been from the same region.[16]

Other features of the Kal-i Jangal scene are also noteworthy (Fig. 4). Henning commented on the awkward position of the arm of the hunter holding the weapon, bent at the elbow and tucked in by the body. This stylized pose is intended to underscore the sense of action and force behind the thrust of the weapon and follows more naturalistic models that were common in the art of the Greco-Roman

Fig. 4. Drawing of a rock-carved hunting scene. Kal-i Jangal, Iran. Tracing by the author from Henning 1953: pl. v

world. The force of the hunter is further emphasized by his bent leg as he presses forward toward his quarry. The image at Kal-i Jangal is active and "real" if not actually realistic, an impression underscored by the pose of the hunter and by the fact that his back is turned to the viewer (the spine and shoulder blades are defined). This pose, derived from the naturalistic imagery of the Greco-Roman and Parthian worlds, rarely occurs in early Sasanian representations but appears, as noted above, at late Parthian Qaleh-i Yazdgird (Fig. 1).

Adding to the sense of drama in the Kal-i Jangal scene is the fact that the second arm of the hunter is outstretched as he grasps the ear of the lion with his hand. Scholars have commented on the antiquity of the motif of the hunter who, in superhuman, heroic fashion, grasps the ear of his quarry.[17] In royal inscriptions of the seventh century BCE, the Assyrian monarch, Ashurbanipal, states that he grasped his feline quarry by the ear or tail, fearless royal deeds that were also represented on his reliefs and that were part of a visual, literary and presumably oral tradition inherited from the Assyrian dynasts by the Achaemenid kings. On the reliefs at Persepolis, visible in Parthian and Sasanian times, standing royal/heroic slayers of animals and monsters hold bulls by the horn, and lions and leonine creatures by the ruff or ear.

A contrast to the active and vibrant nature of the Kal-i Jangal hunt is provided by a worn and battered image, in low relief, of a lion slayer carved on a boulder at Tang-i Sarvak in Elymais (Fig. 5).[18] That frontal figure, probably carved in the second century CE, wears a tall tiara and stands almost immobile, with his weight on his right leg. With his right arm he reaches out and grasps with one hand the head or neck of his quarry, effortlessly subduing him. His bent left arm rests on his sword. As at Kal-i Jangal, an inscription identifies the hunter and his position: "This is the image of ... assuming the throne". The hunt theme on the two monuments, at Kal-i Jangal and Tang-i Sarvak, is the same but different artistic traditions in the two widely separated regions influenced the appearance of the scenes.

The array of personages depicted in painting and stucco at Hajiabad, including the Sasanian king, Shapur II, leads to thoughts about the geographical area in which this site lies: Fars, ancient Persis, a region that had some autonomy in the Seleucid and Arsacid periods. Rulers minted their own coins and exercised considerable authority.[19] This was the homeland of the Sasanian dynasty and a centre of the Zoroastrian faith. The proximity of the Persian Gulf ports and the

Fig. 5. Drawing of a low-relief hunting scene. Tangi-i Sarvak, Iran. Tracing by the author from Mathiesen 1992: II, fig. 21.

importance of Indian Ocean trade, at a time when the Han Dynasty in China had collapsed (220 CE) and the great northern land routes became — for a time — less secure, must have contributed to the prosperity of Persis. The first moves of Ardashir after he assumed control were to establish his rule in Kerman and in southern Mesopotamia, in a newly created province of Meshan, which incorporated Characene and Mesene. The Palmyrene traders who had settled in the Gulf region went home as the Sasanians took control and began to handle the lucrative trade between the Persian Gulf and the mouth of the Indus to the detriment of Palmyrene, Roman and Egyptian interests. Later, in the first half of the fourth century, Shapur II was to fight battles on the east coast of Arabia to protect the southern shore of Iran on the Persian Gulf from Arab incursions into Fars.[20] Viable ports, Rishahr, Siraf and undoubtedly others, existed along the east coast of the Persian Gulf. Roads from Persis to Sakastan were used in the early fourth century CE by Shapur, the Saka king mentioned above, and Seleukos, a judge from Kabul, who added his comments to Shapur's inscription at Persepolis. Other roads also led north. The wealth of graffiti near Birjand may indicate that that area was a crossroads of well-travelled routes. At present, roads run north and south through Birjand to Mashad and Zahedan and south-west to Kerman. As the late Parthian lord flourished at Qaleh-i Yazdgird on his hilltop near the Khurasan road, so the noble at Hajiabad, near well-travelled roads and having access to the Persian Gulf, must have had varied contacts and connections.

The existence of graffiti depictions of prominent figures at Persepolis is an example, on a small scale, of Sasanian imagery in the region of Persis at the time of the rise of the dynasty.[21] On a much larger scale is another monument found in the region, a damaged sculpture in the round of a male head wearing a tiara or headdress. This impressive work of art, more than twice

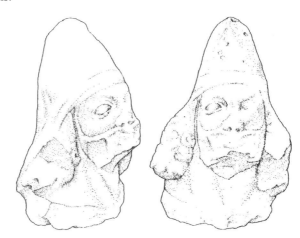

Figs. 6 a & b. Drawing of a monumental sculpture of a male head. Qaleh-i Now, Iran. From Kawami 1987: Figures 31, 32.

life-size, was a chance find by an expedition of the University of Pennsylvania at Tepe Ahmad Shahi or Qaleh-i Now, a site near Malyan (Figs. 6a, b). Identified as a king or a prince because of the tiara and dated by various scholars to the early third century, the head has not been given the attention it deserves in the context of early Sasanian dynastic imagery.[22] Three important points to consider are the appearance, including the immense size, of the Qaleh-i Now head, the fact that it is a sculpture in the round and, finally, that it was found in the region of ancient Persis. The figure is described in publications as wearing a tall tiara complete with ear and neck flaps and bound with a diadem but details are hard to detect in illustrations because of the worn and battered condition of the sculpture. Curling locks of long hair fall beside the face. There is no evidence of ears, presumably hidden by the ear flaps of the tiara. The face has a somewhat frozen and iconic appearance, which is particularly noticeable if the sculpture is compared to another monumental stone head in the round found at Hamadan, perhaps a depiction of the Arsacid ruler, Mithradates II (123–88 BCE).[23] In the Hamadan sculpture, the artist has depicted the aging ruler with some sensitivity and naturalism. Closer comparisons for the Qaleh-i Now head are a few coin images of Ardashir (later

Ardashir I of the Sasanian dynasty), as king of Persis, wearing the same headdress as on the Qaleh-i Now head and having a long beard and long hair falling in wavy locks.[24]

When Ardashir I became king of kings in 224 CE, he initiated a major programme of dynastic imagery on his coinage and on over life-size rock reliefs, showing his victory in battle and defining his role as supreme monarch under the great Zoroastrian god, Ohrmazd. His son, Shapur I, continued to commission rock reliefs and is the subject of an over life-size sculpture in the round in the cave at Bishapur. It is possible, perhaps probable, that Ardashir, following his Arsacid predecessors, also commissioned this over life-size image of himself in the round, to mark or celebrate the initiation of the new dynasty. Because of the size and attributes of the sculpture found in Fars it seems likely that this is an image of the already powerful ruler, Ardashir, the king of Persis, as he moved to assume the title of king of kings of Iran.

Only a small portion of what may have been an extensive sculptural programme initiated by the first Sasanian kings has survived. Few images in metal exist, and other stone sculptures such as the image of Shapur I mentioned in association with the column at Bishapur and a fragmentary, over life-size relief showing part of a clothed female figure found at Istakhr are tantalizing reminders that much is lost.[25]

To turn from early Sasanian works in stone to decorated silver vessels is to find that the images used were once again universal ones, known and familiar in the late Roman and Parthian worlds. However, in contrast to the variety that exists in the shape and decoration of silver vessels made within the Roman Empire, the Sasanian production is remarkably restricted in form, subject matter and design. "Portraits" of significant personages and elite equestrian hunters are the only subjects documented on the earliest vessels, and these vessels are primarily in the shape of open plates and bowls.[26]

The earliest royal image appears on a unique silver cup found at Sargveshi in Georgia and is a medallion "portrait" of the Sasanian king, Bahram II (276–293 CE), depicted, as on his coins, with personages who probably include his wife and son.[27] As early as this image of Bahram II and contemporary with some of the vessels on which medallion images of high officials and members of the royal clan appear, are scenes on silver plates of equestrian hunters.[28] The persons depicted, according to their dress and equipment, are high-authority figures (but not the king of kings), and Lukonin argued decades ago that they were princes of the Sasanian royal family, sons and grandsons of Shapur I (240–272 CE) identified in his inscriptions as rulers (under the great king) in Armenia, Meshan, Guilan, Kerman, and Sakastan, Turan and Hind up to the sea.[29] Some of the earliest vessels illustrating hunting scenes have been found in the western lands of the new empire, in modern Azerbaijan, Georgia and in Abkhazia. A large plate, c. 28 cm in diameter, found at Shemakha in Azerbaijan, and now in the Museum of the History of Azerbaijan in Baku, must be one of the earliest as the image is not yet standardized.[30] Features that appear here and are never repeated include the back view of the hunter astride his horse, a rather naturalistic detail, reminiscent of the images at Qaleh-i Yazdgird (Fig. 1) and Kal-i Jangal (Fig. 4). The horse is in a flying gallop and the hunter, his head turned in left profile, wears a princely headdress on which a broad, leaf-like fan of folds rises above the head. Drawing his weapon, a bow, he shoots at a single animal. The scene fits within the circular frame of the plate and no scenery elements are included.

Another plate (diam. 28 cm) from Krasnoya Polyana in Abkhazia, now in the Abkhazian State Museum in Sukhumi, may be of slightly later date.[31] It is certainly a more sophisticated and accomplished work, more closely comparable to the controlled court products that became canonical later, in the reign of Shapur II (309–379 CE). The hunter, his upper body full-face and his profile head turned to the viewer's left, rides a horse that is outstretched in a flying gallop to the viewer's right. Turning towards the rear, the hunter lassoes one bear, still alive, while a second bear lies dead beneath the horse. The headdress of the hunter is not a crown seen on Sasanian coins. Balanced and iconic, the composition has none of the action or urgency of a real hunt. No landscape elements that might have contributed to the naturalism of the scene are included.

On the reverse of this plate the name Bahram is inscribed and Lukonin suggested that the hunter was the princely son of that name who later became Bahram I, king of Iran.[32] A related hunting scene appears in one of the late Parthian paintings in Building A, room S15 at Arab Hatra (Fig. 7).[33] There, the hunter is a turbaned figure, his upper body full front and his head in three-quarters profile, riding a horse outstretched in a flying

Fig. 7. Hunting scene on a wall in Building A. Hatra, Iraq. From Venco Ricciardi 1996: fig. 7.

gallop. His quarry is a boar, and a second boar, perhaps dead, lies beneath the first. No scenery is represented, and Roberta Venco Ricciardi notes that additions of scenery appear to have been avoided by the Hatrene artists. In these details and in the stereotyped rather static nature of the hunting scenes in S15, the Hatrene images are comparable to some of the royal hunts of the earliest Sasanian period and to the canonical hunts of the central Sasanian court silver vessels from the time of Shapur II.

Rather different in appearance are scenes on mid-third-century mosaics found by the Polish expedition at Palmyra in the western sector of the old city immediately north of the great columned street.[34] One panel shows a helmeted

Belerophon, astride a leaping and flying Pegasus, spearing a chimera (Fig. 8). The pose of the horse, with his two hind legs drawn under his body, is more exaggerated than the rearing posture, which was the preferred pose for horses in Greco-Roman scenes of hunting or battle. In the Hellenized West, the more static, flying gallop was never a favoured motif. While some sense of action pervades the scene, the hunter, his head turned in three-quarters view, spears the fantastic animal almost effortlessly. In the field above the hunt two eagles hold a wreath and a diadem.

Fig. 8. Drawing of a mosaic pavement showing Bellerophon and Pegasus. Palmyra, Syria. Tracing by the author from Gawlikowski 2005: fig. 37.

In the second hunting scene in the mosaic pavement, a helmeted rider on a horse rearing up from the ground shoots with a bow and arrow at a tiger springing up at the horse. A second animal, apparently dead, lies beneath the horse (Fig. 9). The heads of the hunter and his horse are turned slightly toward the viewer of the scene. In the field above is a diadem-bearing eagle. Both hunters in these mosaics wear the Iranian style, Palmyrene dress including tunic and trousers. The only scenery element included in the mosaic scenes is the undulating ground surface represented beneath the horse and the fallen tiger.

The images at Hatra and Palmyra illustrate the popularity of two slightly different types of hunting scene current in the arts of eastern Mediterranean lands in the early third century, before the subject was adopted and given Sasanian royal/dynastic, iconic form. One approach to the theme, seen at Hatra, is stereotyped and unreal; the horses are extended in a flying gallop. The other type, seen at Palmyra, follows, in a modified

Fig. 9. Drawing of a mosaic pavement showing a tiger hunt. Palmyra, Syria. Tracing by the author from Gawlikowski 2005: fig. 38.

form, the more active and naturalistic style preferred in the arts of the Greco-Roman world. As the silver vessels of the Sasanian period illustrate, both pictorial approaches persisted in different parts of the early Sasanian world, the stereotyped Hatrene model in the central Sasanian court productions and the more Hellenized style seen at Palmyra in the east Sasanian lands.

East of Iran in Marv and Balkh, members of the family of Shapur I were sent to represent Sasanian authority, becoming at first prince governors under the Sasanian king in former Kushan territories and, in time, assuming considerable independence, as Kushano-Sasanian rulers who minted their own coins and wore individualized crowns differing from Sasanian types. The artisans working in the Hellenized lands east of Iran followed Greco-Roman models more closely than craftsmen in the Sasanian dynastic centres in Iran. This is apparent in the vibrant and naturalistic hunting scenes that appear on provincial Sasanian silver vessels and commonly include rearing horses and lush scenery elements. In the third and fourth centuries, the production of court silver vessels in the lands on the eastern borders of the Sasanian

Fig. 10. Rubbing from a silver plate found in the tomb of Feng Hetu. Datong, Shanxi Province, China. From WenWu 1983.8

realm is a separate and distinctive expression of regional authority and provides a contrast to the central Sasanian dynastic works of art.[35]

The earliest of the silver plates relating to the presence of Sasanian authority in the lands in the east may well be a small deep plate (diam. 18 cm) found in China in the tomb of Feng Hetu, a provincial Sasanian work perhaps of the mid-third century CE (Fig. 10).[36] As on the early plates found in Iran and in the west Sasanian lands, the hunter represented is recognizable by his dress and regalia as a high-authority figure but he does not wear a crown known from Sasanian coins. A long diadem surrounds his head and two balls of hair rise above it. The body of the standing hunter is in a frontal position; his legs are in right profile and his head is turned back to look at an attacking boar behind him. The hunter is in an improbably dangerous, heroic position, warding off three wild boars emerging from a huge thicket of reeds before and behind him. The appearance of the scene is not unlike the hunting scene cut onto the rock at Kal-i Jangal where a hunter also performs heroically on foot, his arms in a similar pose suggesting force. The body of the boars on the silver plate is partly cut off by a circular moulding on the interior of the vessel.

Probably somewhat later in date than the plate found in the tomb of Feng Hetu and quite different in decoration, is a large plate (diam. 28 cm) in a Japanese private collection published by Katsume Tanabe who identified the hunter as a Kushano-Sasanian provincial ruler of the second half of the third century, Peroz I Kushanshah (Fig. 11).[37] On this plate the scene is arranged skilfully to fit within the frame of the plate; the heroic hunter, in right profile, is astride a rearing horse moving to the viewer's left. The horseman turns back to stab his quarry, a tiger springing up behind the horse. A second tiger apparently dead, lies beneath the horse. The heroic nature of the scene is underscored by the action of the hunter who stabs the tiger with his sword and reaches out with his left hand to grasp the ear of the animal. Huge scenery elements are arranged around the circumference of the scene and provide a natural setting for the hunt. While some features of

Fig. 11. Drawing of a tiger hunt on a silver plate. Japanese private collection. From Tanabe 1998: fig. 1.

the composition are comparable to early Sasanian court products, the activity and tension in the scene are notable differences between this vessel and works made in Sasanian dynastic centres.

The headdress of the hunter on the plate in the Japanese private collection is not a Sasanian royal crown but a flat cap bound by a long diadem. Parallels for this type of flat cap exist among the stucco busts at Hajiabad and the representations on Kushano-Sasanian coins. The latter images influenced Tanabe in his identification of the figure, at first as either Ardashir (I, II) Kushanshah or Peroz I Kushanshah and, subsequently, as Peroz I Kushanshah. However, the main detail on the rim of the headdress depicted on the plate is a series of curvilinear volute forms (Fig. 12, top), and this detail appears to me to make the identification with the Kushano-Sasanian ruler Ardashir Kushanshah more likely (Fig. 13). Following the dates suggested by Martha Carter for the Kushano-Sasanian rulers, Ardashir, the first in the Kushano-Sasanian series, ruled in western Bactria, Marv and Balkh, from 270–285 CE.[38]

Fig. 12. Above: Drawing by the author of a crown detail on Fig. 11. Japanese private collection.

Below: Drawing by the author of the bud device on the reverse of Fig. 11. Japanese private collection.

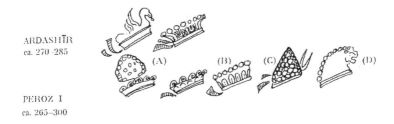

ARDASHIR
ca. 270-285

PEROZ I
ca. 265-300

Fig. 13. Drawing of the crowns of the Kushano-Sasanian rulers Ardeshir and Peroz I. From Carter 1985: 223, table 1.

On the reverse of the plate in Japan, within the foot ring, is a symbol in the form of an opening bud on a stem (Fig. 12, bottom). This symbol or heraldic device is related but not identical in form to a familiar family or clan sign in Sasanian Iran, one that appears on the early Sasanian rock reliefs of Ardashir I, on the cap of his page, and on a relief of the later Sasanian king, Hormizd II (303–309 CE), on the cap of his fallen adversary (Fig. 14).[39] It is perfectly possible that Sasanian princes, identifiable by this bud-like sign or device, were among the rulers, both under Sasanian authority and subsequently independent from it during the third and early fourth century, in the former Kushan East.[40] Whoever the eastern ruler represented on the silver plate is, the scene on the vessel is clearly intended to give expression to an authority distinct from the rulers in Iran.

Fig. 14. Drawing of a detail on the rock relief of Hormizd II (303-309 CE). Naqsh-i Rustam, Iran. From Herrmann 1977b: fig.1.

An important detail on the silver plate in the Japanese collection is the extended arm of the hunter who unrealistically grasps the ear of his quarry with his hand. In this detail, the hunt on the silver plate is linked to the mid-third-century lion hunt at Kal-i Jangal described above (Fig. 4) and to the image on a later provincial Sasanian plate in the Hermitage Museum.[41] On that vessel a royal hunter whose crown resembles, but is not identical, to the crown of Shapur III (383–388 CE) is depicted on foot subduing a leopard by grasping the animal's ear. The plate in the Hermitage Museum was made, in my opinion, when the Sasanian king, Shapur III, was still the overlord of some territory east of Iran. The replacement of the canonical plant element on the Sasanian crown with triple-dot astral symbols as well as the depiction of the heroic, ear-grasping hunt on foot are important details intended to transform a canonical central Sasanian image into an icon meaningful in an eastern region, perhaps around Kabul, where Sasanian authority still held.[42]

The silver vessels described above, as well as others, illustrate variations in the works of artisans outside the Sasanian court centres. From the earliest times in the third century, the products of east Iranian workshops were separate and distinct in appearance from the central Sasanian works. By the beginning of the fourth century a central Sasanian court model was established and rigidly followed in court workshops within Iran but at the same time, in various eastern territories around Marv and Balkh, in lands held and lost by the Sasanians, other more vigorous and heroic types of hunting scenes continued to be favoured by local authorities who commissioned silver vessels.

It is evident from this review of the art of the early Sasanian period that the establishment and codification of a central Sasanian dynastic imagery in the Iranian and Mesopotamian kingdom occurred rapidly at the start of the period in the third century.[43] As soon as the borderlands in eastern Iran came under the authority of Sasanian princes, a related but distinct imagery arose there, in composition and design more reliant on artistic traditions in the Greco-Roman world and, in the primacy of epic/heroic themes, reflecting cultural traditions in the east Iranian world.

In the past the differences between the dynastic arts of the Sasanian court centres in Iran and Mesopotamia and the art of the eastern borderlands were observable chiefly in the prestigious court silver vessels of which a relatively large number have survived. However, the discovery of an immense, third-century rock relief at Shamarq (Baghlan Province), in northern Afghanistan provides added evidence of the cultural division between the two realms already apparent in the silver vessels.[44] Typologically comparable to and influenced by the early Sasanian dynastic reliefs, the subject matter and composition of the Shamarq relief, called locally Rag-i Bibi, are distinctive. The complex scene, replete with multiple figures, landscape elements, rearing horses and fierce animal quarry, share on a much grander scale features characteristic of the east Iranian silver vessels.

The dynastic art of the Sasanian heartlands, given a stereotyped and distinctive form at an early period, was a visual expression of Sasanian power and authority. The corpus of motifs and designs utilized by Sasanian artisans was selectively drawn from the art of the contemporary Roman and Parthian worlds but ancient, significant themes and images, some going back to Achaemenid times, were not forgotten.[45]

The early successes, both military and socio-political, of the Sasanian rulers, led to a broad recognition of their supremacy and their position among contemporary powers. Not surprisingly, Sasanian dynastic icons were soon adopted and adapted beyond the borders of the kingdom. At first, in newly acquired territories on the eastern borders of the Sasanian realm, a different but related imagery, based on Sasanian patterns, was created by rulers intent on expressing their regional authority. Eventually the prestige of the Sasanian dynasty, the extent of the empire, and the long duration of the period in which the kings held power led to a much more widespread transfer of Sasanian motifs and icons. In lands beyond the Near East, both to the east and to the west, the art of the Sasanian court became synonymous with world rule and imperial aspirations, influencing the cultures of other political centres, not only during the period of Sasanian hegemony but also in the centuries following the collapse of the dynasty.

Notes:

1. Garrison 1991: 1–30; Invernizzi 2001: 133–157.
2. For the Parthian reliefs at Tang-i Sarvak see Mathiesen 1992: I 57–70; II 130–149; for the development of relief sculpture under Ardashir I, see Herrmann 1969: 63–88.
3. Mackintosh 1973: 181–203.
4. For Palmyra and bibliography, see Schmidt-Colinet 2005; for Dura-Europos, see Goldman 1985: 279-300; Goldman 1999: 19-106; Gignoux 1983: 101-118.
5. Azarnoush 1994.
6. See note 4 above.
7. Herrmann 1977a: 67–72; Mathiesen 1992: I 70; II 177 ff., cat. nos 99–134. Mathiesen dates the erection of the palace in the 220s CE and states that it remained in use in Sasanian times.
8. Ghirshman 1971: 10, 12, 18, 29, 36, 177, pl. XL.
9. Back 1978: 378–383.
10. Azarnoush 1994: 105–107, 136, pl. VIII, figs 22, 83, 86, 143.
11. It seems likely that the stucco busts of Shapur II at Kish were mounted on the engaged columns there. See Watelin 1967: fig. 172.
12. Azarnoush 1994: 110–115, cat. nos 21–25, pls. IX–XVI.
13. Gyselen 1989: 153–154.
14. Back 1978: 492–494.
15. Henning 1953: 132–136, pl. V.
16. Azarnoush 1994: pls 11, 16. The bouffant hairstyle over the forehead also appears on another medium-sized bust but the hair, in that case, is in tight curls rather than single strands (Figs 99–101).
17. Gignoux, Ph 1983: 101–118.
18. Mathiesen 1992: II, 138–139, fig. 21.
19. Differences of opinion exist about the extent of the independence of the kings of Persis at various times. See Wiesehöfer 2007: 37–49.
20. Bosworth 1983: 603.
21. For a recent discussion of the date and identity of the graffiti figures see Razmjou 2005: 315–341. For illustration of the graffiti in this volume, see D. Huff: 33, fig.1.
22. I have never had a chance to see the actual sculpture, which is in Tehran. Kawami 1987: 138 ff., 222, cat. no. 62, figs 31, 32; Mathiesen 1992: I 65; II 170, cat. no. 90. See also Curtis 1998: 65, pl. IV c-d.
23. The sculpture is correctly dated, I believe, to the first half of the first century BCE by Kawami 1987: 51ff., 167 ff., cat. no. 6, pls 8–9, figs 4–5 and Mathiesen 1992: I 22; II 177, cat. no. 98. A date in the second to third century CE is suggested by Ghirshman 1962: fig. 52 B and Colledge 1977: 86.
24. Lukonin 1968: 106–117; Göbl 1971: pl.1, nos 1, 2; Mitchiner 1978: 130, nos 755–756.
25. The Istakhr block was evidently part of a much larger architectural relief: Bier 1983: 307–326, pls 25–30.
26. Harper and Meyers 1981: 48–57.
27. Harper and Meyers 1981: 25, pl. 2.
28. Harper and Meyers 1981: pls. 8–11.
29. Lukonin 1961: 58–59; 1969: Genealogical Tables I–IV.
30. Harper and Meyers 1981: 30, 48–50, pl. 8.
31. Harper and Meyers 1981: 29–30, 50–52, pl. 9.

32. Lukonin's opinion initially was that the hunter was the future Sasanian king Bahram II. Later he revised this opinion and identified the hunter as the future king Bahram I. See Harper and Meyers 1981: 29, footnotes 21, 22.

33. Venco Ricciardi 1996: 147–165, fig. 7.

34. Gawlikowski 2005: 29–31, figs 36–38.

35. For a fuller description of this style see Harper and Meyers 1981: 88–94, Table I.

36. Harper 1990: 51–59; Watt 2004: cat. no. 62.

37. Tanabe 1998: 93–102; 2001: 167–186. Tanabe follows Cribb's Kushano-Sasanian chronology and dates Peroz I Kushanshah to 245–270 CE: Cribb 1990: 151–193.

38. Carter 1985: 215–281, pls 47–52. In Carter's rough sketch in her article (223, Table1, and Fig. 13 here) the volute-like curvilinear elements on the flat-topped crown are visible and topped by pearls. On the photograph of the copper coin it is clear that the volutes are part of a repeated palmette design (pl. 47, 3). While the design of the headdresses on the silver plate and the Kushano-Sasanian coin are similar, they are certainly not identical. Carter dates Peroz I Kushanshah between 265 and 300 CE.

39. The lower rim of the cap of the fallen enemy on the relief of Hormizd II has a floral design, which is another point of comparison between the Hajiabad bust, the crown on the silver plate and the coins of Ardashir Kushanshah. Hinz 1969: 215, pl. 133A; Herrmann 1977b: 5–9, fig. 1. Von Gall warns that without colour it is impossible to state that the bud devices on the reliefs from Ardashir to Hormizd are all identical: von Gall 1990: 30–31, pl. 9.

40. For a historical review of the period see Carter 1985 in note 38 above.

41. Harper and Meyers 1981: 129–130, pl. 24.

42. See Carter 1985 in footnote 38 above. In a personal communication, Martha Carter expressed her opinion that the triple-dot motif on some Parthian, Sasanian and Kushan works of art had astral significance, a subject on which she is preparing a future publication.

43. As in the Parthian period, stylistic variations exist within the kingdom in different geographical regions as the differences between the fourth-century rock reliefs at Taq-i Bustan and the reliefs in the south of Iran illustrate.

44. I have only seen the images and read the descriptions of this relief on the Internet (Rag-i Bibi, Shamarq) and have not heard F. Grenet speak on the subject. The site is apparently on an ancient road linking Bactria and northwest India. A unique feature of the relief is the addition, when necessary, of pieces of stone to complete higher relief parts of the design. These additions have fallen away but the technique is comparable to the practice of silversmiths in the Sasanian period, who produced high-relief parts of their designs by attaching additional pieces of silver to the background shell of the plate. "Ed. note" For a recent publication of the Sasanian relief of Rag-i Bibi, see Grent, Lee, Martinez and Ory 2007: 243–267, figs. 2–7, 9–11, pl. 6.

45. Harper 2006: 1–55.

6

The Sasanians in the East

A Bactrian archive from northern Afghanistan

Nicholas Sims-Williams
(School of Oriental and African Studies, University of London)

Bactrian, which belongs to the Iranian branch of the Indo-European language family, was the principal administrative language of the region now known as Afghanistan during most of the first millennium of our era. After its first appearance in the poorly preserved Dasht-e Nāvūr inscription of the Kushan king Vima Taktu, which probably dates from the end of the first century CE, the Bactrian language begins to be better attested from the time of his grandson Kanishka, the first of the Kushan dynasty to use Bactrian on his coinage. While the coins of Kanishka and his immediate successors are mostly inscribed in an easily legible, monumental form of the Greek script, those of later rulers of Afghanistan — Sasanians, Kidarites, Hephthalites, Turks and others — use a cursive variety of the same script which has proved extremely difficult to decipher. The main problem has been the lack of extended texts written in the cursive script: until the 1990s, the only available sources other than the coin legends were equally short inscriptions on seals, a few graffiti, and scraps of manuscripts from the Turfan oasis in Xinjiang.

During the last two decades, however, the discovery of more than 150 Bactrian documents written in cursive Greek script has at last made it possible to complete the decipherment of the script and to obtain a fuller understanding of the language itself, as well as providing an invaluable new source for the history of Afghanistan and the adjacent regions.[1] Most of the new documents are written on leather or parchment, a few on cloth or on wooden sticks. They include letters, legal contracts, economic documents such as receipts and tallies, and even a few Buddhist texts. Many of them name the places where they were written, mostly in the principality of Rōb, modern Rūī in the northern Hindukush, a smaller number in Gōzgān, in the extreme north-west of what is now Afghanistan (see Fig. 1).

About forty documents bear dates written in Greek numerical letters. These dates range from the year 110 to the year 549 of an era which is not named in the texts but whose starting point has recently been convincingly identified as

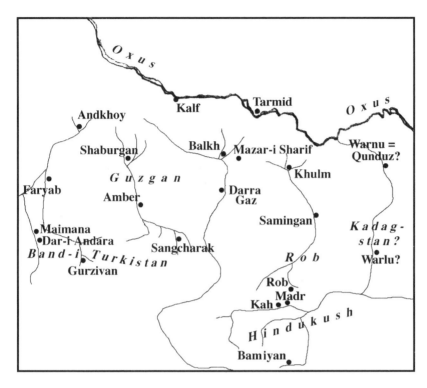

Fig. 1. Sketch-map of north-central Afghanistan, showing places mentioned in the Bactrian documents.

223/4 CE, the year of the accession of Ardashir and the inauguration of the Sasanian dynasty.[2]

Naturally, the Bactrian documents contain a huge amount of information on the political, social and economic history of the eastern Iranian lands. Since it would be impossible to cover everything which is worthy of notice within the limits of a single paper, on this occasion I shall concentrate on chronology and political history, which provide the basic framework within which everything else has to be understood.

To put the new information into context, let me first try to outline the history of Bactria during the Sasanian period, as it appears from the sources previously known:[3]

The end of the Parthian Empire in Iran and that of the Kushan Empire in Bactria seem to have been nearly simultaneous. In 224 CE, Ardashir I defeated the last Parthian king and founded the Sasanian dynasty; and within a few years, perhaps already during the reign of Ardashir,[4] the Sasanians had also established their rule in Bactria. For a while Bactria may have been under the direct rule of the Sasanian king of kings, though this has been disputed; but at some point, at the latest in the early fourth century, the rule was assigned to viceroys who called themselves "Kushan-shah" and who issued their own extensive coinage (the so-called "Kushano-Sasanian" series). In 350, Shapur II was obliged to abandon military operations against the Romans in the west in order to defend his north-eastern borders against the Chionites or Huns, who had recently established themselves in Transoxiana. Within a few years, Shapur made a treaty with the Chionites, some of whom, under their chief Grumbates, fought on the Persian side at the siege of Amida in 359.[5] The rule of the Kushan-shahs in Bactria seems to have come to an end soon afterwards, but it is not entirely clear whether they were displaced by the Chionites as they migrated southwards towards Kapisa and Gandhara, or whether the Sasanians succeeded in re-establishing direct rule for a time. This uncertainty is connected with the vexed problem of the Kidarites, the next people to appear on the Bactrian scene, who some scholars regard as identical with the Chionites, while others see them rather as restorers of the previous order and successors to the Kushan-shahs.[6]

Be that as it may, by the middle of the fifth century another wave of invaders from the north-east had arrived in eastern Bactria. These were the Hephthalites, who were soon to play an important part in Sasanian affairs. After the death of Yazdgird II in 457, his sons Peroz and Hormizd fought over the succession, and it was only with Hephthalite support that Peroz was able to defeat Hormizd and take control of the empire. Subsequently, Peroz seems to have decided that the Hephthalites had become too powerful and undertook several campaigns against his former allies, each of which ended in disaster for Peroz, the last of them with his death in 484. After this debacle, the Sasanians left the Hephthalites in control of Bactria until the middle of the next century, when the arrival of the Western Turks in Sogdiana provided the opportunity for a strategic alliance. In about 560 the Hephthalites in Bactria were crushed by the combined forces of the Sasanians under Khusrau I and the Turks under a leader named Silziboulos or Sinjibu. To begin with, the victors may have divided their areas of influence along the Oxus, but at some point the Turks seem to have made themselves masters of Bactria as well as Sogdiana. Finally, in 657–659, not long after the fall of the Sasanian Empire to the Arabs, the Western Turks too were subjugated, in their case by the Tang dynasty of China.

The earliest dated Bactrian document is a marriage contract written in Rōb on the tenth day of the second month of the year 110, which should correspond to 13 October 332 CE.[7] No authority higher than the "district chief" is mentioned directly, but the fine for a breach of the contract is payable to "the royal treasury", which seems to imply the overlordship of a king. This could be the Sasanian king of kings (at this time Shapur II) or more likely the Kushan-shah. The fine is payable in "gold dinars", which probably refers to the scyphate or "dish-shaped" gold coinage issued by the Kushan-shahs. Some of the more important persons involved as witnesses bear Middle Persian names such as Warāz-ōhrmuzd Khwasrawagān, whose patronymic means "son of Khusrau"; Sasanian personal names of this kind remain common in the later documents.[8] But the use of the local month-name Ahrēzhn, rather than the Middle Persian name Ardwahisht, shows a certain cultural independence from Iran, as does the fact that the contract involves the marriage of two brothers to the same woman simultaneously. Polyandry is mentioned in Chinese sources as characteristic of this region,[9] but was unknown in Sasanian Iran.

Another early, though unfortunately undated, document is a letter from a princess named Dukht-anōsh.[10] It concerns a complaint made by the eunuch Dathsh-marēg, probably a servant of the princess, against certain shepherds who had allegedly allowed their sheep to eat and trample his corn and had then attacked his brother and nephew. The princess, Dukht-anōsh, bears a Middle Persian name and may well have been a member of the Sasanian royal house.[11] But the most important person named in this letter is the Kushan-shah Warahrān, who sends the letter jointly with, or on behalf of, the princess.

At least one Kushan-shah named Warahrān or Bahram is known from the Kushano-Sasanian coins. Although opinions on the dating of the Kushano-Sasanian series differ strongly, most numismatists believe that it came to an end some time between the 350s and the 380s and that the coins bearing this name belong near the end of the series.[12] If they are right, this document should be placed around the middle or third quarter of the fourth century, during the latter part of the reign of Shapur II (309–379).

The letter of Dukht-anōsh is addressed to a certain Khwadēw-wanind, who is evidently a high official, though lower in status than the princess and the Kushan-shah. He is probably the same person who is referred to in several other undated letters as "Khwadēw-wanind the fortress-commander" or as "Khwadēw-wanind Khāragān" — in the latter case with a family name which indicates that he belongs to the dynasty of local princes who bore the title *khāhr* or *khār*, i.e. "ruler".[13] One of these letters is concerned with a dispute over the ownership of a meadow in Rizm (a district which seems to have included the towns of Kah and perhaps Malr, immediately to the south of Rōb, in the foothills of the Hindukush):

> "Khwadēw-wanind Khāragān has appealed to your lordship (saying) that in Rizm, in the meadow (named) Yukhsh-wirl, there was a stream, and then the stream was blocked from the meadow, and he — (namely) Khwadēw-bandag the satrap — gave the land where the stream was to Khwadēw-wanind, and then you would not recognize (it as) his property; and then your lordship in your goodness heard the request (submitted) by Khwadēw-wanind ...".[14]

The letter from which this extract is taken may contain a further reference to the Kushan-shah, but unfortunately the reading is uncertain and the context broken. More important is the mention of a "satrap" (*šahrab* or *šarab*), a term which suggests an appointee of the Sasanian king of kings. In fact, another document of about this period refers specifically to a "Persian satrap" (*pārsā-šarab*).[15] The use of such terms seems to imply a resumption of direct rule from

Iran at the end of the period of the Kushan-shahs, under Shapur II or one of his immediate successors.

The history of the meadow Yukhsh-wirl is continued in another letter,[16] in which the meadow is assigned to another member of the Khāragān family, namely, Nāwāz Khāragān, the sender or addressee of a number of surviving letters, who appears to have been active in the latter half of the fourth century.

The most interesting feature of this group of letters is a series of allusions to enemies, hostages, horsemen, fortresses, all implying a state of war. The most specific is a letter that refers to the fall of the fortress of Bamiyan:

> "Sang-khird's close family (and) extended family (and) clan have been the king's servants, and they have been true and [loyal (?)]. Consequently, in as much as the fortress Bamiyan had been captured, he went from (one) person to another person, (and) now he is returning thither (to you), to his own fortress. So, (if) it should please your lordship in your goodness, receive him there (with you)".[17]

On the other hand, these letters also contain much discussion of comparatively trivial and unwarlike matters — the ownership of the meadow Yukhsh-wirl, obtaining linen shirts from Balkh, sending a dog as a present, exchanging a mule for a concubine — so the fighting cannot have been all-consuming or continuous throughout the career of Nāwāz.

Who are the enemies? The most obvious candidates are the Chionites. As has already been mentioned, the Chionites had occupied Sogdiana by 350 and were then confronted by Shapur II. This confrontation ended with a peace treaty in 358, after which Chionite troops fought on the Persian side at the siege of Amida. During the next decades, according to Chinese sources, the Chionites overran Bactria, gradually moving south to Kapisa and Gandhara by a route that would very likely have included both the Rōb kingdom and Bamiyan. On the other hand, one should also consider the possibility that the enemies were the Sasanians, who may have invaded this region in order to re-establish their control at the end of the period of the Kushan-shahs.[18]

We have already noted the references to a "satrap" or a "Persian satrap" in two undated documents from the late fourth century. Other Bactrian documents strongly support the idea of a renewed Sasanian domination from about this period. Two of the next dated documents are a deed of gift and a letter, which were both written in the year 157, in the eleventh and twelfth months respectively, i.e. in the summer of 380 CE, the first year of the reign of Ardashir II.[19] While the deed of gift still uses a local month-name, the letter is the first document to employ a month-name borrowed from the Middle Persian calendar of Sasanian Iran. Thereafter, Middle Persian month-names are used in almost all Bactrian documents for the next 100 years.[20] The same letter also contains the first occurrence of the title *kadag-bid* "lord of the house", in practice something like "steward" or "governor", which is found frequently from this time on. These changes suggest a new regime, or at least a new administrative structure, which, to judge from the Middle Persian month-names, must have been closely linked with Sasanian Iran.

This "new administrative structure" appears to have been quite stable. The *kadag-bid* in 380 CE, who is named Kēraw Ōrmuzdān, was still in office forty years later, in the next group of dated Bactrian documents,[21] and the position of *kadag-bid* is still attested 100 years later in documents from the time of Peroz. Here his function as a subordinate of the king of kings is made clear, though he himself also bears a royal title (which will be discussed in the Appendix below): "Mēyam, the king of the Kadagān, the *kadag-bid* of the famous (and) prosperous Pirōz Shahan-shah".[22] It is also at the time of Peroz that we find in our documents the specifically Sasanian title *kanārang*, the Persian equivalent of the Kushan title *karālrang* "margrave" or "lord of the borderlands".[23] All these features are most easily explained by supposing that Sasanian authority over the area to the north of the Hindukush was re-established in the last years of Shapur II and maintained thereafter for about a century.

It does not of course follow that the Chionites played no part in the wars which led to the establishment of this new order: Rōb and Bamiyan may well have been invaded both by the Chionites and by the Persians. We do in fact have a slight indication in our documents of the Chionite presence: two letters, both of which can probably be assigned to a date between the 420s and the 460s, name a certain Gurambād Kērawān "Gurambād son of Kēraw" or Gurambād Khwadēwān "Gurambād of the family of the lords".[24] As is indicated by his patronymic Kērawān (together with the general context), he may well be the son of the *kadag-bid* Kēraw Ōrmuzdān; but his personal name echoes that of Grumbates, the Chionite leader at the siege of Amida, suggesting that by this time the local aristocracy had come to incorporate a Hunnish element. Similarly, a recently published seal impression names a Hunnish ruler of Samarkand who is described both as "king of the Huns" and as "Kushan-shah", thus claiming a connexion with the former rulers of Bactria — whether the Kushano-Sasanians or the Kushans themselves — and with the Chionites or Huns.[25]

The next important events reflected in the Bactrian documents are connected with the coming of the Hephthalites, another nomadic people from the north-east who had taken up residence in eastern Bactria, at the latest during the reign of Yazdgird II. On the death of Yazdgird in 457, a dispute broke out between his sons Hormizd and Peroz, each of whom claimed the throne. According to Tabari, Hormizd was the first to gain power, while Peroz took refuge with the Hephthalites; a couple of years later, with Hephthalite aid, Peroz succeeded in defeating Hormizd and making himself Shahan-shah. Although the historicity of Tabari's account may be questionable in some respects,[26] there seems to be no reason to doubt the reality of the war between Hormizd and Peroz during the years 457–459 CE.

Three Bactrian letters can plausibly be assigned to the period of this war or to the years immediately following. All three mention a certain Kirdīr-warahrān: in one he bears the old Kushan title *hasht-wālg* (of unknown meaning) and the honorific "true to Parōz"; in the other two he is described as the *khāhr* of Rōb, with the honorific title "glorious through Ōhrmuzd".[27] Despite these differences, there is little doubt that all three letters refer to the same man, who may have sided first with one brother and then with the other, and received honorific titles from both.

In passing it is worth mentioning that one of these letters contains the earliest datable reference to the Afghan people, about half a century before they are mentioned in a Sanskrit astrological treatise and half a millennium before the first reference in any Islamic text. Here they are contrasted with the locals, the "men of Rōb", each group apparently accusing the other of stealing some horses.[28]

The existence of a group of Bactrian documents bearing dates that fall within the reign of Peroz has already been mentioned. In addition to the two letters which seem to name the Shahan-shah Peroz, these include a deed of manumission, three receipts and two land-transfer documents.[29] Some of the persons named in these documents are also mentioned in undated letters, giving us altogether more than a dozen documents which can definitely be assigned to this period. Perhaps surprisingly, these documents do not contain the slightest hint of the wars against the Hephthalites which occupied much of the reign of Peroz and which ended with his death in battle. Even the name of the Hephthalites is not mentioned until the year 260, i.e. 483 CE, a year before the final defeat of Peroz, when the two land-transfer documents refer for the first time to the payment of taxes to the Hephthalites. It was probably soon afterwards that the *kadag-bid* transferred his allegiance from the Shahan-shah to the Hephthalite *yabghu*, as we see from an undated letter whose sender describes himself as "the king of the Kadagān, the *kadag-bid* of the famous (and) prosperous *yabghu* of Hephthal".[30] In another undated letter the ruler of Rōb is actually identified as a Hephthalite *yabghu*, though he has an Iranian patronymic and appears to be a member of the local dynasty: "Sārt Khudēwbandān the glorious *yabghu* of Hephthal, the *khār* of Rōb, the scribe of the Hephthalite lord (or lords), the judge of Tukharistan (and) Gharchistan".[31]

Under Peroz, the Sasanians were probably more directly engaged in Bactria than ever before. Peroz even issued coins, following the pattern of the Kushano-Sasanian scyphate gold dinars, with his name and title in Bactrian, as is demonstrated by the unique (and previously unpublished) specimen illustrated in Figure 2. However, the defeat and death of Peroz brought an end to Sasanian influence in Bactria for many decades. Under his son Kavad I, the Persians had to pay an immense annual tribute to the Hephthalites, and Sasanian silver drachms — often referred to in the later Bactrian documents as "drachms of Kavad" — eventually replaced gold dinars as a money of account and standard of purity. The rupture in tradition around this time is also marked by the disappearance of the Middle Persian month-names in favour of the local names that had been in use before.

Fig. 2. Scyphate gold dinar of Peroz with legend πιρωζο þα—
υανοþαυο = pirōzo šauanošauo *"Pirōz Shahan-shah". Collection of
Aman ur Rahman, Islamabad/Dubai.*

Until the arrival of the Western Turks in the middle of the sixth century, the
Hephthalites remained unchallenged. We have only one Bactrian legal
document from the period of the Hephthalite supremacy, but it is a remarkable
one. A masterpiece of calligraphy and probably the most magnificent of all the
surviving documents, it was found with the upper copy still rolled up and
sealed with five clay sealings.[32] The text is a contract for the purchase of a plot
of land and was written in Siwan 295, i.e. Nov./Dec. 517, at the court of the
ruler of Malr. Although the document refers to the payment of taxes to the
"Hephthalite lord (or lords)", and introduces a term of Indian origin for "royal
tribunal",[33] in most respects it follows the local tradition: in particular, both the
price of the land and the penalty for breaking the contract are stated in gold
dinars, which by this time must be merely conventional. The vendors are
described as "servants of the king" and the buyers as "servants of Shābūr

Shābūrān". Shābūr Shābūrān may have been the ruler of Rōb, though the text does not indicate this specifically; at any rate, it is likely that he was a member of the Shābūrān family, known from many documents and sealings, which provided the hereditary rulers of Rōb during the following centuries.

In about 560, before the time of the next dated Bactrian document, the Hephthalites were forced to submit to the allied armies of the Western Turks and the Sasanians under Khusrau I.[34] One document which is likely to belong to this period, or to the following decades of intermittent hostilities between the Sasanians and the remnants of the Hephthalites, is a sort of memorandum of expenditure drawn up by a local lord who seems to have found himself squeezed between the warring factions, paying a so-called "allowance" (rōtsīg, literally a "daily payment") both to the Hephthalites and to the Persians, as well as various other forms of levy or compensation:

"Then every month (I) gave five drachms (as) an allowance for the Hephthalites and for the Persians ... And when the governor of the city drank wine, then I [again] paid two drachms. And I gave to the ... and to [the] scriptorium two drachms. And I gave, when ... drank wine here in the city, eight dinars. And I [gave], (as) an offering and (mark of) ho[nour] for Wirishtmish the lord, two dinars ... And I [gave towards] the Hephthalite levy, for the vessels of ... [and for] those of silver, and for the offerings, and for fod[der for] the sheep, eight dinars. And a horse belonging to the Hephthalites died [in] the city: then I paid five drachms. And [I gave] two dinars to the ... And I gave [every] month, for the Hephthalite lord or the king ...".[35]

It is interesting to note that it is not the Turks but the Persians who appear here as the opponents of the Hephthalites in the northern Hindukush. If the present document does indeed belong to this period, it may be added to the evidence recently gathered by Rika Gyselen for a significant Sasanian presence in the "Iranian East" in the years following the military successes of Khusrau.[36] In addition to coins of Hormizd IV and Bahram VI issued by the mint of Balkh in the years 587–591, this evidence includes a series of bullae impressed with the seals of officials in the Sasanian administration reconstituted at this time.[37] One of these officials is the āmārgar or "accountant" of Marv-rud and Balkh.[38] Another, whose seal is illustrated in Figure 3, is the ōstāndār or "provincial administrator" of Kadagistān, a region which is also mentioned in the Bactrian documents and which may have lain immediately to the east to the kingdom of Rōb, in the valley of the Qunduz-āb (see the Appendix below).

After this period the Hephthalites cease to be mentioned by name in the Bactrian documents: certainly not because they had been displaced, let alone extermi-nated, but rather because those who had adopted a sedentary life-style and settled in the kingdom of Rōb had largely merged with the local population, like the Chionites before them. A pointer in this direction is the name Tōrmān Aspandagān, which occurs in a document written in Warnu (probably to be identified with the later Warwāliz, modern Qunduz) in 602 CE.[39]

As in the earlier case of Gurambād Kērawān, the patronymic or family name of Tōrmān Aspandagān indicates that he was of local origin, but his personal name alludes to a former chieftain of the nomadic invaders — in this case Toramāṇa, the famous "Hunnish" ruler of North India, who appears to have flourished about a century earlier.[40]

Although the Hephthalites fade from the scene, no dated text refers to the new overlords,

Fig. 3. Seal with the Pahlavi legends KTK "Kadag" and ktkst'n 'wst'nd'l "provincial administrator of Kadagistān" (after Gyselen 2002: 222, fig. 43).

whether Persian or Turkish, until 629. In this year, a document written in Samingan describes the khār of Rob as the iltebir of the qaghan, using the title regularly given to local rulers who had submitted to the Western Turks.[41] By this time, Sasanian power had evidently waned once again and control of the region had passed to the Turks.

Thirty years later, in 659, a document written in Guzgan refers for the first and only time to the payment of taxes to the Turkish qaghan;[42] but by this time the Western Turks themselves were on the point of capitulating to the Tang Chinese, and of course the Sasanian period had already come to an end with the death of Yazdgird III in 651. The later Bactrian documents, which continue for more than a century after this time, are therefore irrelevant to the topic of this paper.

Appendix: The Sasanian province of Kadagistān

The existence of a Sasanian province named Kadagistān first became known from the bulla illustrated in Figure 3 above, which bears an impression of the *ōstāndār* of Kadagistān. When publishing this bulla in 2002, Rika Gyselen drew attention to the Bactrian form Kadagstān (spelled *kadagostano*) in two late Bactrian documents,[43] which I had understood as a common noun meaning "(royal) household", rightly pointing out that the contexts in which the Bactrian word occurs would favour its interpretation as a place name.[44] In a review of Gyselen's book, Frantz Grenet drew attention to the fact that both of these Bactrian documents also refer to a people named Warlugān or Wargun and argued that Kadagstān may have lain just to the east of the kingdom of Rōb, in the valley of the Qunduz-āb, the likely location of the city *Warlu, Chinese Huolu 活路 (Early Middle Chinese γwat-lɔʰ), from which the Warlugān people presumably took their name.[45]

The evidence of the bullae indicates that Kadagistān was a Sasanian province under the control of an *ōstāndār*, though perhaps only for a quite limited period after Khusrau's reconquest of the area in the late sixth century. On the other hand, Bactrian documents from both earlier and later than this period, some of which have already been cited above, refer to a "king of the Kadagān":[46]

> "Mēyam, the king of the Kadagān, the *kadag-bid* of the famous (and) prosperous Pirōz Shahan-shah" (Document ea, dated Sharēwar 239 = Dec. 461/Jan. 462, and Document ed, dated Mihr 242 or 252, i.e. Jan./Feb. 465 or 475);
>
> "Kilman, the king of the Kadagān, the *kadag-bid* of the famous (and) prosperous *yabghu* of Hephthal" (Document ja, Hephthalite period);
>
> "Kēra-tonga Tonga-spara, the king of the Kadgān, the *kadag-bid* of the famous *qaghan*, prosperous in glory" ... "the lord *sēr*, the king of the Kadgān" (Document Y, lines 1–3, 11, dated in the year 549 = 771/2 CE).

There can be little doubt that the Kadagān or Kadgān, i.e. the "people of Kadag", are the inhabitants of Kadagstān. Apart from the fact that the two names are formed from the same element Kadag, both are connected with a place (unfortunately unidentified) named Kurwād or Kurād, the "accountant" or "treasurer" of which appears both in Document Y, a letter issued by the "king of the Kadgān", and in Document X, a contract drawn up in the presence of "the lord of the Wargun people, the general of Kadagstān".[47] Moreover, it is noteworthy that all the documents which refer to the "king of the Kadagān" also entitle him *kadag-bid*, literally "lord of the house". This is hardly a matter of chance. In all likelihood the place-name Kadag is in origin the same as the common noun *kadag* "house", used in the special sense "(royal) house". The *kadag-bid*, the "lord of the (royal) household", would have acted as a steward or governor of a royal demesne on behalf of the Shahan-shah, the Hephthalite *yabghu* or, eventually, the Turkish *qaghan*; at the same time he was evidently regarded as a king in his own right, rather like the Sasanian Kushan-shahs.

In this connection it is worth pointing out that the earliest known "king of the Kadagān", the *kadag-bid* Mēyam named in the Bactrian documents from the time of Peroz, may well be the same person as the king whose name is written in Brahmi script as Mehama.[48] A king of this name is known from coins[49] and also from a very important copper scroll inscription, tentatively dated to the year 492/3 CE, in which he appears as a contemporary of the famous Hunnish or Hephthalite rulers Khiṅgila and Toramāṇa and as the ruler of an area which probably included Ṭālaqān, to the east of Qunduz.[50] The close coincidence in name, dating and localization between the Mēyam of the Bactrian documents and the Mehama of the copper scroll inscription seems too striking to be due to chance.

Notes:

1. The majority of these documents are edited in the two volumes of my *Bactrian Documents from Northern Afghanistan* (Sims-Williams 2001 and 2007, henceforth cited as BD1 and BD2 respectively). See also Sims-Williams 2005a and Sims-Williams and de Blois 2006: 185–187 (Document Aa). A more detailed description of the contents of the documents is given in Sims-Williams 1997 (in some respects outdated as a result of the steadily increasing amount of material available).
2. See de Blois forthcoming.
3. For a fuller summary see Bivar 1983: 209–216.
4. The narrative of Tabari (Nöldeke 1879: 17–18; Bosworth 1999: 15) has generally been understood as indicating that the Kushan king submitted to Ardashir, but this interpretation is energetically disputed by Göbl 1993: 53–55.
5. Ammianus Marcellinus: 19, 1, 7–19, 2, 6.
6. See for instance the contrasting views of Bivar 1983: 212 and Grenet 2002: 205–209.
7. Document A, in BD1: 32–35. I would like to express my thanks to François de Blois for calculating precise Julian dates for this and other documents referred to below.
8. The Pahlavi spelling of the name Warāz-ōhrmuzd (*wr'c'whrmzdy*) is attested on a seal in the Hermitage, see Gignoux 1986: 174, no. 942.
9. Enoki 1959: 51.
10. Document ba, in BD2.
11. The Pahlavi spelling of this name (*dwht'nwš*) is attested on a seal in Paris, see Gignoux 1986: 78, no. 326.
12. For a variety of views on the dating of the Kushan-shahs see (amongst others) Bivar 1979; Cribb 1990; Göbl 1984: 79–86; Nikitin 1999; Schindel 2005.
13. On this title see Sims-Williams 1997: 15–16.
14. Document bg, lines 5–10, in BD2.
15. Document xr, in BD2, a fragmentary letter, which cannot be very much later than this on linguistic grounds. The title "Persian satrap" also occurs in Document xn (of unknown date) and much later in Document ag (where it may be used as a personal name as suggested by Tremblay 2003: 122).
16. Document ci, in BD2.
17. Document cg, lines 4–11, in BD2.
18. According to Cribb 1990, esp. p. 178, Shapur II issued coins in Gandhara as a successor to the Kushano-Sasanians. Differently Göbl 1984: 85.
19. Document C, in BD1: 38–41 (month Drēmatigān = June/July); Document cr, in BD2 (month Spandarmid = July/August).
20. See Sims-Williams and de Blois 1998: 153; 2006: 189–190. (The recently discovered Document cr shows that the use of the Middle Persian month-names in Bactrian began several decades earlier than we had known at the time of writing these articles.)
21. Document D (year 195 = 417/418 CE), in BD1: 42–43, and Documents da–de, in BD2, three of which are dated in the years 198–199, i.e. 421–422 CE.
22. Document ea, lines 1–2, in BD2. The date of this letter is the month Sharēwar of the year 239, i.e. Dec. 461/Jan. 462. Identical wording is found in a badly preserved letter (Document ed) dated Mihr 242 or 252, i.e. Jan./Feb. 465 or 475. At a lower level, the continuity of the administration is also illustrated by the fact that a certain Mir-bandag, who "authorizes" Document ea on behalf of the *kadag-bid*, seems to carry out the same function in another letter of almost exactly 40 years earlier

(Document de, in BD2, dated Ab 199, i.e. March/April 422 C.E.).

23. Documents G (dated Drēmatigān 249 = May/June 472) and H (dated Ardēyushtug 250 = Aug./Sept. 472), both in BD1: 48–49.

24. Documents dg (where the name is partly restored) and eb, both in BD2.

25. Aman ur Rahman, Grenet and Sims-Williams 2006.

26. Schindel 2004: 388–9, 411–19, gives reasons for believing that Hormizd never succeeded in obtaining the throne and that Peroz came to power already in 457 CE.

27. Documents ck–cm, in BD2. For further discussion see Sims-Williams 2005b: 340–341.

28. Document cm, lines 6, 9. The name appears in the form *abagano*, i.e. Abagān or Avagān, plural *abaganano*, i.e. Abagānān or Avagānān; cf. Sanskrit Avagāṇa in the *Bṛhat-saṃhitā* of Varāhamihira.

29. Documents ea and ed, in BD2 (see n. 22); E–I and Ii, all in BD1: 42–53.

30. Document ja, lines 1–2, in BD2.

31. Document jb, lines 1–3, in BD2.

32. Document J, in BD1: 54–61.

33. Bactrian *razogolo* (lines 24, 28) from Sanskrit *rājakula*.

34. Grignaschi 1984 takes a sceptical view of the tradition underlying Tabari's account, according to which Khusrau "penetrated to Balkh and what lies beyond it" (Bosworth 1999: 160; cf. Nöldeke 1879: 167) and conquered a region stretching from Sind to Tukharistan, but the basic fact of the defeat of the Hephthalites by the Western Turks and the Sasanians is not in doubt.

35. Document al, lines 5–6, 14–25, in BD1: 162–163. In Sims-Williams 1999: 255 this document was assigned to the period of Peroz, but the use of a triangular letter "⊿" to represent the sound [d] is typical of much later documents and is therefore more easily compatible with the dating proposed here (see BD2: 38–39).

36. Gyselen 2003.

37. Gyselen 2002. On the dating of the bullae see ibid. 23–24; Gyselen 2003: 165–166.

38. Gyselen 2002: 138.

39. Document L (dated Āb 379 = Jan./Feb. 602 CE), in BD1: 64–71. For the possible derivation of the medieval name Warwāliz from *War(a)wā(ng)-liz "the fortress of Warnu" see Sims-Williams 1997: 16 n. 28.

40. See Melzer 2006: 260–261.

41. Document N, in BD1: 74–79. The date is given as the 26th day (Ashtād) of the fifth month (Khandig) of the year 407, i.e. 9 Nov. 629.

42. Document Nn, in Sims-Williams 2005a: 12–13, 22–24. The document is dated on the 22nd day (Wād) of the eighth month (Āb) of the year 436, which should correspond to 27 January 659. ("Year 416" in my edition is a regrettable misreading.)

43. Documents T (dated Bidīnōsard 478 = June/July 700) and X (dated Drēmitagān 527 = March/April 750), in BD1: 98–105 and 136–143 respectively. A variant *kadgostaggo*, i.e. Kadg-stāng, may occur in a much earlier document (de, dated Āb 199 = March/April 422 CE, to be published in BD2), but the reading and context are both unclear.

44. Gyselen 2002: 152.

45. Grenet 2006: 147–148, referring to Yoshida's identification of Bactrian *Warlu with the Chinese Huolu (Yoshida 2003: 158).

46. Wrongly translated "ruler of the houses" in BD1: 144.

47. In the light of this phrase, which identifies the "lord of the Wargun people" as "the general of Kadagstān", my previous translation of the final phrase of Document T

(BD1: 104) needs to be corrected. I suggest: "And may Baralbag, the commander of the army of Kadagstān, the lord of the Warlugān (people), be the enforcer (of this contract)". This interpretation of *list-lēr(a)g* as "(person in) authority, enforcer" (rather than "helper, assistant") also suits the final phrase of Document Y (BD1: 144–145): "And the enforcer in respect of this agreement (is) Oz, the treasurer of Kurwād". Other Bactrian legal documents conclude by expressing a wish that the contract may be accepted as authoritative, but without naming a particular person who has the power or right to enforce it.

48. In any case the name Mēyam (*mēiamo*), which is quite common in the Bactrian documents, is probably a variant of Mēham (*mēuamo*), which is now attested in this spelling on an unpublished Bactrian sealing in the collection of Aman ur Rahman. See Sims-Williams in Melzer 2006: 262 n. 83.

49. According to the new reading of NumH 71 and NumH 73–74 proposed by Melzer 2006: 262. The related issues NumH 62–63 may bear the Bactrian legend μηο = *mēo*, which could be an abbreviated spelling of the name of the same king as suggested by Göbl 1967, I: 73–74.

50. See Melzer 2006: 256 (on the localization of the inscription), 258–261 (on Khiṅgila and Toramāṇa), 262–264 (on the ruler Mehama and the dating of the inscription).

7

Religion in the late Sasanian Period: Eran, Aneran, and other Religious Designations

Shaul Shaked
(The Hebrew University, Jerusalem)

There used to be an established common view among scholars that the advent of the Sasanian dynasty marked a strong new identification with the Zoroastrian religion, perhaps in contrast to the situation that was prevalent under the Arsacids.[1] This image of the early Sasanians is reinforced by the pious utterances in the rock inscriptions of the early Sasanian kings and particularly by the inscriptions of Kirdēr the high priest under four Sasanian monarchs.[2] The religious phraseology, mixed with well-chosen political slogans and catchwords, is strongly present in the early Sasanian royal inscriptions. I am quoting from the inscription of Shapur I (240–272):

> I am the Mazda-worshipping god Shapur, king of kings of Eran and Aneran, whose origin is from the gods, son of the Mazda-worshipping god Ardashir, king of kings of Eran, whose origin is from the gods, grandson of the god Papak — I am the ruler of the kingdom of Eran.[3]

The wording makes it clear that the king claims some kind of genetic association with the gods for himself and his forbears; that he asserts his position as a Mazda worshipper; and that he uses the terminology of "king of kings" of the two-fold division of the world, "Eran and Aneran", which should mean Iranian as against non-Iranian lands. The assertion that he and his father were both "Mazda worshippers" (but not his grandfather Papak, if we stick to the carefully chosen wording!) should be significant for our discussion.

By describing himself as "Mazda worshipper" the king no doubt wishes to place his kingship in a position of religious and political correctness. This however does not necessarily makes him a person who is filled with religious zeal, and it does not forcibly suggest that his kingdom has behind it a religious drive. The main ambition that may lie behind his words may be said to relate to the use of the terminology "Eran and Aneran", in other words, to the question as to the extent to which his kingdom stretches beyond Iranian lands and how much of "Aneran" it includes.

Did the early Sasanian kings indeed seek to construct their newly founded empire on a new religious identity, around the Zoroastrian priestly establishment, and on the basis of a Zoroastrian orthodoxy? By presenting the question in these terms I obviously wish to put this view of the Sasanians in doubt.

There certainly are a number of facts in that period that go against the assumption of a tendency to adopt Zoroastrianism as the state religion and to consolidate the kingdom around the Zoroastrian cult. The position of Mani in the court of Shapur I does not entirely support the idea of a pious Zoroastrian king who wishes to align his people around the worship of Ohrmazd.[4] Was the monarch deluded for a brief period into thinking that Mani represented a variety of Zoroastrianism, and did Bahrām I only wake up to the realization that Mani's religion did not exactly tally with orthodox Zoroastrianism? Is it possible that even the priests in the Sasanian court were unable initially to tell that Mani was not a whole-hearted worshipper of Ohrmazd in the Zoroastrian style? This is a proposition that is difficult to accept.

We must assume that the first Sasanian kings either did not regard Mazdaism as their religious emblem, as the bearer of their battle cry around which to rally the populace in support of their kingship, or else that their view of Zoroastrianism may have been lax, that it was not so rigorously defined according to the lines that we are accustomed to draw, even though they may have been devout Zoroastrians by their own faith and practice.

These are questions that we cannot hope to resolve, but which should be kept in mind when we wish to define the attitude of the early Sasanian monarchs towards the religion. Even if they did feel a strong religious urge, it is quite possible that their type of religion was not the same as the one preached and practised by the Zoroastrian clergy as set out in the Pahlavi books. It is true that they kept a chief priest at their court, though perhaps not from the very beginning.[5] At least at a later period the Sasanian kings also kept in the court a chief Christian bishop or Catholicos as well as a prominent leader of the Jews, an exilarch.[6] This does not necessarily mean that they were engaged in the study of comparative religion; it only indicates that they practised the advice given to them in the document known as the *Testament of Ardashir*,[7] according to which the king would do well to have under his control the leaders of the different religions of the empire, so as to ensure that no activity in a field as important as religion go unnoticed and unsupervised. We need hardly be reminded today that when people are assembled together under a religious banner, their association is likely to have serious political implications, and that a growing religious crowd which stands in opposition to the mainstream cult can endanger the structure of the state. This insight was already part of the political science of the Sasanians, and they frequently referred to it.[8] Such Sasanian views as to the importance and relevance of the different religions in the realm are therefore indicative less of the religious zeal of the kings than of their political acumen.

Most of the internal sources concerning the Sasanian period which we have at our disposal, usually written in Middle Persian, came down to us through the channel of the Zoroastrian priesthood. The extant royal chronicles of the period survived mostly thanks to the interest taken in them by compilers who wrote in Arabic. There are great discrepancies between these two types of sources. What we may term the royal Sasanian chronicles, those that were transmitted by writers in Arabic, seldom show any interest in religion. The religious sources, on the other hand, have a great deal to say concerning kingship and its place in the religious scheme of government. By putting them side by side we can imagine the dialogue that may have taken place between Zoroastrian priests and the other members of the Sasanian court, a dialogue that was no doubt often tense, with each party pulling in a different direction.

Both parties subscribed to the adage: "Religion and royalty are twins",[9] but each interpreted it in its own way. For the royal court, religion has to serve the needs of the state and be subservient to the king; for the priests, the function of government, embodied in the person of an ideal and pious king, is to establish the rule of religion.

The priestly literature, when we wish to use it as a source for the social history of the period, has its obvious shortcomings from our point of view. This does not mean that it is less reliable than any other form of tradition. Every historical document bears the marks of those who are responsible for formulating and propagating it. Today's newspaper, or a digital version of it, or an archival document, cannot be used as an objective reflection of the contemporary situation without putting alongside it a variety of other sources. Historical documents are not much different. If we can divine the particular slant or ideology that lies behind the document and its specific interest, and if we have enough knowledge of other types of written documents, we may be able to achieve a more balanced point of view. Otherwise we may find ourselves at the mercy of a one-sided report. All we can do is to try and imagine the missing portions of the picture. We may hit it right, but we are also likely, not infrequently, to get it very wrong.

The tendentious slant of a document is not necessarily a drawback; it also has a certain advantage. Once it is recognized, it allows us to understand the particular point of view of one party in a historical debate. As long as we know who are the authors of a document, and what they are interested in conveying, we may derive a great deal of information from what they tell us.

For the late Sasanian period we have to rely mostly on the Zoroastrian literature in Pahlavi. Most of this literature was put down in writing in the post-Sasanian period, in the ninth century CE. This does not necessarily disqualify them for being used as evidence for understanding Sasanian attitudes, for much of the material is quite likely derived from the late Sasanian period and sometimes can go back to earlier times, but we should be aware of this chronological problem. In some cases, on the other hand, it definitely seems clear that the texts reflect conditions that prevailed under Islam.[10]

The Zoroastrian writers in Middle Persian are fond of playing about with pairs of contrasting epithets. Thus we frequently have an opposition between *hu-dēn* "an upholder of the Good Religion" as against *duš-dēn* "an upholder of the Evil Religion". We also have the very common *weh-dēn* "follower of the Good Religion", which became the most usual designation of a Zoroastrian, and in opposition to it *ag-dēn* "follower of an evil religion", which may mean anything, but essentially means someone whose religion is not what it should be, a religion that we do not approve of. We have the designation *ahlamōg*, which is normally rendered by "heretic", and there again we cannot tell exactly what is meant by this epithet; it probably alludes to someone within the Zoroastrian fold, but who holds views, which the orthodox (i.e. those whose writings we are using) think should be abandoned. Besides all these positive and negative appellations, we have the term *an-ēr*, or in the plural, *an-ērān*, to designate the "non-Iranians", or perhaps those who are "unworthy".

These antithetical notions serve to isolate "us", those who, according to the notions of the authors, hold the correct faith, from the "others", those whose faith is improper and who cannot be counted among the true believers. The last pair mentioned, however, *ēr* as opposed to *an-ēr*, presents a more complex antithesis. It applies apparently to both a religious distinction and to an ethnic difference. The ethnic division alludes presumably to two groups, one of which may have been defined as sharing a common ancestry, perhaps also using a common language,[11] as against another that does not share these characteristics (and may be assumed to derive from diverse origins). At the same time, this opposition is associated with a distinction of religious faith and practice. The Zoroastrians were not the first, and certainly not the last, to use a terminology that combined genetic, linguistic and religious criteria. In this case, the reality represented by the term "Ērān" is much vaguer and less precise than its opposite, "an-ērān". It may be asserted with little exaggeration that the former designation gets its sense and purpose from the latter. Ērān can only be understood by its contrast to that which is more easily defined, namely that which is not Ērān.

There are numerous passages that have this contrast at their core. Assuming that the positive terms for religion, such as *weh-dēn*, are not ambiguous, because they evidently refer to the type of faith and religious practice approved by the speaker, the opposite terms by their nature lack precision and can hardly be taken to refer to one particular religion. Their main function is to delineate, to set apart, the notion of *weh-dēn*. Does *ag-dēn* refer to a specific form of bad religion, or is it a general term, covering any religion to be rejected? One may well argue that this is a term that encompasses any deviation from our notion of good religion. The same dilemma exists with regard to most of the other negative terms that we have mentioned. It has been suggested that *ag-dēn* designates in texts of the Islamic period (such as the *Pursišnīhā*) a Zoroastrian convert to Islam, while *an-ēr* refers to a non-Iranian, generally an Arab.[12] As far as I can see, although this interpretation makes sense, it is not confirmed by any explicit statement. Thus, we can see that *an-ēr* is used in the *Zand* of

Avestan texts, for example in the *Herbedestan*, as a gloss on *dēwēsnān* "demon worshippers",[13] which is normally the opposite of *mazdēsn*, "Mazda worshipper". This seems to demonstrate that the term *an-ēr* was often taken to be a religious designation, not exclusively or predominantly an ethnic one. In the same context we have a distinction between *an-ērān*, *ag-dēnān* and *marg-arzānān*, "adherents of a non-Iranian faith", "adherents of an evil religion" and "guilty of a mortal sin" respectively.[14] The order here seems to be of descending severity, with *an-ēr* apparently indicating the worst type of religious deviation and corruption.

> +*bandag-ē ī ag-dēn ka be ō weh-dēnīh āyēd šāhān-šāh bandag a-š wahāg abāmīhā pad-iš* (*Herb.* 11:7).[15]
>
> An *ag-dēn* slave who comes to the Good Religion becomes the slave of the King of Kings, and his value is as a loan for him (i.e. the owner).

An opposite case is supplied by the passage that follows:

> *bandag ī hu-dēn ka be |ō ag-dēnān frōxt a-š* +*bunīgīh ō radān appār*[16]
>
> If a Zoroastrian slave is sold to *ag-dēns*, then the responsibility (for dealing with this) is transferred to the (religious) authorities.

We have here two parallel and inverse situations. In the one case, a slave who upholds an alien faith and converts to Zoroastrianism, and in the second case, a Zoroastrian slave who is sold to non-Zoroastrians.[17] In both situations the non-Zoroastrians are called *ag-dēn*, "adherents of an evil religion". The text also confirms, what should have been self-evident, that the possibility of conversion to Zoroastrianism was open during the Sasanian period, just as Zoroastrians often converted to another faith.[18] The state authorities were apparently supposed to deal with the danger of a lapse from Zoroastrianism, at least when it concerned a slave. Similar concerns are heard with regard to an *ag-dēn* child.[19] We also have instructions on how to regard the family of a non-Zoroastrian who converts to Zoroastrianism: the children who were born to him are all automatically Zoroastrian, but his wife may stay on in another religion (the underlying assumption is that the other religion is Christianity), and she does not cease to be his wife, although he cannot have intercourse with her.[20] He is obliged to provide for her sustenance, and is not allowed to beat her.[21] An *ag-dēn* woman who converts to Zoroastrianism is still in a state of mortal sin for a year after her conversion.[22] The practical outcome of this situation is that, if she dies within the first year after her conversion, her body cannot be disposed of in the manner accorded to Zoroastrians.[23]

There are some indications that the terminology underwent some changes from the Late Avestan period to that of the Sasanian commentators. This can be seen for example when in the *Herbedestan* the Avestan quotation says: "Can a man study under a priestly teacher who is a demon-worshipper or whose body is forfeit?" The *Zand* to this passage has it: "How is a man to study under a priestly teacher who belongs to the demon-worshippers [gloss: non-Iranians] or *tanāpuhl* sinners …"[24] The Avestan situation envisages a scenario according to which a Zoroastrian acquires knowledge, perhaps even religious knowledge, under the guidance of a demon-worshipper, which can only mean someone who upholds a creed outside the pale of the Zoroastrian religion. The term "demon-worshipper" seems to have been abandoned in the Sasanian period, except when it formed part of a traditional phrase, and is replaced in the present quotation by *an-ēr*, which perhaps refers to someone outside the religious or ethnic definition of an Iranian.

It is difficult to admit under the Sasanians or indeed in the post-Sasanian period the possibility of a Zoroastrian studying under a non-Zoroastrian teacher. The fact that we have this phrase in a Sasanian text can be explained by its being a commentary on an Avestan passage. The solution to this dilemma as given by the Avestan passage, and continued by the Pahlavi *Zand*, advises to avoid giving a real remuneration to the instructor.[25] In the Pahlavi *Zand* we appear to deal with a milder kind of religious deviation than what is conveyed by the epithet "demon-worshipper", one of the worst religious offences known in Zoroastrianism. As long as the teacher does not get proper material remuneration for his work, the relationship is quite acceptable.

The text also discusses the opposite situation, when a pious Zoroastrian is asked to teach a demon-worshipper. The solution given to this question is that this is only permissible when the teacher gets proper remuneration and needs it for his sustenance. The discussion concludes with the statement in the Avestan text, repeated in the Pahlavi: "He who teaches the Sacred Word to a non-believer gives a tongue to a wolf".[26] In a further gloss an anonymous commentator is quoted as saying: "'wolf' denotes a heretic".[27] A heretic presumably alludes to a Zoroastrian who embraces unorthodox views, a status of lesser offence, presumably, than that of "demon-worshipper". It is also said that one should not learn the Sacred Word, the *Avesta* or the religious law, from heretics (*ahlamōg*) and from sinners (*abārōn*):[28]

> If a man of alien faith (*ag-dēn*) or a non-Iranian (*an-ēr*), who in prosperity or otherwise, is an associate with the upholders of the Good Religion (*weh-dēn*), … and he helps the upholders of the Good Religion with resources, is it possible for him to participate in the duty and meritorious deeds and righteousness of the Good Religion, or not? (*Purs*. 46).

The answer to this question is negative. Another question that concerns us is:

> Is it proper to help and to give things to the wicked enemies of the religion, or not? (*Purs*. 50).

This is a question the answer to which is a simple "no". The justification for this is: "because it decreases righteousness".

***

The line of demarcation between members of the Zoroastrian community and those outside it is not so simple as might seem at first sight. There are conflicting standards of definition. The contrast between *ērān* and *an-ērān* seems to be based initially on ethnic, rather than on religious considerations. But even in purely ethnic terms it is not easy to draw the line. Are the Armenians considered part of the notion of Iran? Are adherents of Mazdaism in Babylonia, in the western regions of Sasanian Iran, considered Iranian? Ctesiphon in Babylonia was one of the seats of the Sasanian throne. Are the Arabs, who were partly Iranized in the sixth and early seventh centuries,[29] part of *ērān*? Persian was apparently widely used in Mesopotamia, and Persian deities were part of the popular culture, but it is not certain which of these elements could serve as a criterion for establishing Iranian identity.[30] There must have been a fair amount of mixture of blood between Semites and Iranians in Sasanian Babylonia. This emerges from the study of the Aramaic magic bowls, where one and the same family often has some members carrying personal names of Semitic origin and other members carrying distinctly Iranian names, and the Iranian names considerably outnumber the Semitic ones. The Iranian names used are typically Zoroastrian, with Zoroastrian deities used as theophoric elements in the proper names.[31] How do such cases fit into the pattern of the division between *ērān* and *an-ērān*? Are such families considered to be part of the former, or of the latter? Was Babylonia considered to be part of *ērān*? This is another question to which we have no ready answer.

We have clear instructions as to the manner of dealing with religious distinctions within a family. In other words, we are told how non-Zoroastrian members of a family should be treated, and how children born to Zoroastrian parents who are taken over or adopted by non-Zoroastrians are to be regarded. These situations must have been fairly common in the late Sasanian period, when conversions to Christianity and Manichaeism were not very rare. An example for this is the following:

> *mard ka-š be zan ayāb ān ī an-ērīh dārēd ayāb-eš be aburnāyag ī ō ag-dēnīh šawēd ane frazand nēst stūr ōh gumārišn*

> If a man has no wife, or if he has a wife (who belongs to) an *an-ēr* religion, or if he has no children other than a minor son who has converted to an evil faith (*ag-dēnīh*), a *stūr*[32] must be appointed for him.[33]

Note that the terminology does not seem to distinguish between *an-ērīh* (when there is talk of the wife) and *ag-dēnīh* (when there is talk of the son). Both seem to fall within the same category. The only difference that may exist here is that the religion of the wife is one in which she was born, while that of the son is one to which he converted.

We have a body of polemics between Zoroastrians and Jews as well as between Zoroastrians and Christians. These writings seem quite typical of the late Sasanian period. In one of these texts a definition of the Good Religion as against the Evil Religion is given in *Dēnkard* 3, 227.[34] The two religions are set out in this chapter in a parallel scheme, one against the other, in a rigid antagonism. Whatever the Good Religion says is countered by its exact opposite, which represents the position of the Bad Religion. No attempt is made at an objective representation of a real dispute between two parties. The views of the antagonists are a negative mirror image of those of the Good Religion. This is quite typical of the literary polemics in the Pahlavi books. These books conduct what amounts to an internal discussion, which merely uses an invented and imaginary "other" to present the point of view of the Zoroastrian religion. To a large extent this is also the method employed by authors of other faiths in Late Antiquity and through the Middle Ages when they argue against their opponents. The Zoroastrian claims whole goodness to the Creator Ohrmazd, and denies that any evil can issue from him (*Dk.* 3, 227:2–3). The opposite is true of the adherents of the Evil Religion (§5–6). From §8 the debate becomes more interesting. Yima (Jam) reveals goodness and character to people, he gives them the law of the Right Measure, for Zoroastrianism is founded, in the Zoroastrian theology, on *paymān*, the Right Measure, which abhors excess and deficiency (§8).[35] Without sticking to the Right Measure, the whole structure of the world would crumble. Now there is a public encounter that is initiated by Yima. He convenes the people and the demons to a grand meeting, in which the demons have to answer the question: "Who created the world and who will destroy it?" (§9). The demons claim the power of creation as well as the power of destruction to themselves, and here (§11) Yima can claim his victory in the dispute: it is not possible for one and the same entity to be both a creator and a destroyer. The case of the demons (who represent the evil religion) is therefore untenable, the author concludes.

The principle of the Right Measure is tied up with the institution of the good king, the righteous ruler (§12), which not only establishes the proper order of the world but also pushes away the Adversary who creates havoc. The next section, §13, maintains that there is a succession of power and revelation, which goes directly from Zoroaster to the eschatological period. A parallel negative succession goes on in the evil domain (§14), from Dahāg on, and it is responsible for the disruption of the world order through excess and deficiency, the enemies of the Right Measure, and through corruption to the character of people. All this is a preamble to a theological dispute with the Jews, which follows in the next two sections.[36]

It is important to understand that in this presentation the Good Religion stands in opposition to the Evil Religion, and the prototype of Evil Religion given here is the one preached by the Jews in their holy scripture, the Torah, or as it is called in this text, Orayta, the Aramaic form of the word. The term used is not *an-ēr*, which we might think should be natural for a faith which is clearly non-Iranian, but *ag-dēn* or *duš-dēn*, a purely religious term. Upholding the Zoroastrian faith here is not thought of in terms that make it the faith of Iran, whereas in some of the other texts we quoted, and especially in the legal texts, it seemed that *an-ēr* is more or less the same as *ag-dēn*.

One other point that emerges from this discussion is that this theological passage, like so many other texts which present the priestly point of view, yearns for a kingship which establishes the desirable Good Religion. Assuming that the text goes back to the Sasanian period,[37] this kingship is not necessarily the one that rules the land at the time when the text was composed. In other words, if our assumptions are accepted, we may discern here a covert criticism of the Sasanian dynasty.

**

We have seen how difficult it is to establish a clear line of division between Iranians and non-Iranians in the theological thinking of the Sasanian period, and that the term "non-Iranian" becomes synonymous with people of Bad Religion. The purely religious distinctions are just as blurred. There is no doubt that Manichaeism was a distinct religion in the Sasanian empire, and indeed it had its own church structure, its distinctive ritual and sacred scriptures, and much else which set it apart from Zoroastrianism. But in the short period in which it was accepted in the Sasanian court, did it not pretend to be a reformed kind of Zoroastrian dualism? Can we establish that such a claim would have been regarded as preposterous in the eyes of all Zoroastrians? The case of Manichaeism is indeed peculiar. In a way its relationship to Zoroastrianism seems like a repetition of the relationship between early Christianity and Judaism. We know that Mani aimed quite consciously to reproduce the precedent of Jesus.

The Mazdak movement, or rather the different sectarian groupings that were registered towards the end of the Sasanian period under the general name of Mazdak, were certainly an outcome of Zoroastrianism. They were no doubt presented not only as a reform of the social order but also as a modification of, indeed an improvement on, a dominant ancient religion that needed to be purged of certain elements which were deemed to be corruptions of its original spirit.[38] In a sense they are reminiscent in some respects of the phenomena of Babism and Bahaism. The Bahai faith sprang out of the scholastic Shiʻa schools of pre-modern Iran, and subsequently, following a break with the Shiʻa establishment, it became an independent universal faith and severed its ties with the original Islamic faith.

Even within the official body of Sasanian Zoroastrianism there were divisions, large and small, which may have given rise to recrimination as representing a "bad religion". The myth of Zurvan, a myth of creation which presents an alternative to the official Zoroastrian version, enjoyed great popularity in the Sasanian period, but does not seem to have established itself as a distinct religion or sect, and apparently did not have the structure of a religious community. There is surprisingly little debate and polemic around this myth, despite the enormous efforts made by a succession of modern scholars to discover traces of such polemics in the extant Zoroastrian literature. There was normally no reticence in attacking doctrinal opponents in the Middle Persian literature, but the Zurvanite issue is not a problem that drew much fire. To what extent were the propagators of the Zurvan myth part of the community of adherents of Zoroastrianism? It seems that they were, for we have no evidence of clashes or social recrimination around the issue of Zurvanism,[39] but again our knowledge is rather limited.

There are other important differences between Zoroastrian points of view. From chapter 142 of the Third Book of *Dēnkard* it is possible to deduce that a doctrinal debate raged over the question as to whether darkness should be regarded as a mere absence of light, or as an ontological existence independent of and apart from the light.[40] The latter position became the official doctrine of Zoroastrianism, but the opposite view could claim its origins in the Gathas, and may have been followed by some members of the clergy. This question is connected with the one that concerns the existence or inexistence of the principle of evil itself, of Ahreman. We are told in several places in the Pahlavi literature that Ahreman does not exist.[41] One may well ask whether Zoroastrianism, a religion that is based on a sharp distinction between the two opposing powers, can really survive when it rejects the ontological existence of the principle of evil. The question is only partly resolved by observing that Ahreman does not exist in the material world, in *gētīg*, but that, in contrast, he does exist in the world of mental abstraction, in *mēnōg*. This is another area of real or potential disagreement between two groups of Zoroastrian thinkers.

I have tried to show by these examples some divisions that could lead people to label the holders of a view opposed to them as upholders of an "evil religion". Although the epithet is extremely common in the Zoroastrian religion, it is never described or defined in a way that could help us identify it in precise historical terms, and it seems likely that it could be applied quite freely to opponents within or without the official boundaries of Zoroastrianism. "Un-Iranian" is an epithet which probably carries a graver tone of reprimand, and would not be used, one imagines, for describing bad Zoroastrians, but it does seem to combine two distinct notions, that of someone who is not considered to be ethnically Iranian, and that of someone who worships a religion other than Zoroastrianism. For the kings, especially the early Sasanian kings, it denoted chiefly inhabitants of countries outside those recognized as the Iranian lands. For the theologians, especially in the later period, it denoted primarily someone who is alien from the religious point of view. One must assume that there may have been considerable difference in usage between the priests and theologians as opposed to the king and his entourage when it comes to terminology.

Appendix: Dk 3,227[42]

1   On the principle and effect of the Good Religion and the Bad Religion. Of the teaching of the Good Religion.
2   The principle of the Good Religion is one word, the whole goodness of the Creator, and the effect (is): no evil issues (from him).
3   The road that lies within it (consists of) the whole goodness of the creatures, which is from the initial creation to the Renovation. [...]
4   The principle of the evil religion is one word, the wickedness of the Creator, and the effect is that evil issues from him.
5   The road that lies within it is all the goodness of the creatures, from the original creation to the Renovation. [...]
6   The Mazdean religion and knowledge (says): When, because of the Creator's instruction and command, Yima brought the offspring (?) of character to the creatures, through the law of the Right Measure of the whole goodness and lack of evil of Ohrmazd, the demons stood in that animosity and desired to delude people to a most harsh (belief in) non-existence concerning the principle of all-goodness, and (concerning) the effect of the obedience to the Creator's work, and the poor man (?), so that their character should be corrupted by that; from the corruption of character there would be born in the world excess and deficiency; the law of the Right Measure would be corrupted and Yima would be incapacitated. The immortality of the creatures can be arranged through the law of the Right Measure which is within people. Yima asked people and demons to a convocation in order to remove their deceit from people, and asked the demons: "Who created this world, and who will destroy it?"
7   The demons shrieked in response: "We created, we, and we shall destroy (it), (we) who are demons".
8   Yima replied to the demons saying, "I do not believe in this, you are ignorant demons. For what purpose should those create the world who destroy the world? It is not proper for the two statements to be borne together, for creation and destruction are not derived from one principle". By this speech of a deity the deceit of those demons was annulled, and the immortality of the creatures was established.
9   That law of the Right Measure, the principle of righteousness, the speech of a deity, by which Yima became the character for those who follow the succession (has as its effect) establishing a ruler and a good king, pushing away the adversary from the creatures through it, arranging, cultivating and decorating the country according to the law of the Right Measure.
10   And the same divine principle, the summary of the Iranian law, the foundation of the Mazdean religion, through the greatest law, the supreme good work in the doctrine of the religion, went from Zardušt, of worshipped soul, to the succession of the early believers, and they, through it, established the Mazdean religion among the peoples, enlarged the creation in goodness, and caused it to be bound to the Beneficent and

Victorious one, the great power of the Renovation. A revelation of the Good Religion.

11 That principle, which is the setting up of deceit by the demons, filtered through to Dahāg, of the race of Tāz, the reducer of creation. Dahāg corrupted character through it and put it into action, and generated the tyranny and heresy of excess and deficiency. Through it he caused corruption to the character of people, caused the world to moan, and the creatures to die.

Notes:

1. The chapter dealing with religion in the Sasanian period in Christensen's *L 'Iran sous les Sassanides* carries the significant title "Le zoroastrisme religion d'état" (Christensen 1944: 141). Gnoli, who devoted to this question a detailed and penetrating discussion, holds the opinion that the early Sasanians showed a strong tendency towards "the formation of a national culture and the foundation of a State Church proper" (Gnoli 1989: 138–139; see also p. 140). His arguments are forceful, but the evidence can sometimes be interpreted in more than one way. Wiesehöfer 2001: 211) is more sceptical on this point; cf. also his detailed list of references (Wiesehöfer 2001: 294–298).

2. For the inscriptions of the Sasanian kings, the most accessible edition and translation is by Back 1978; for those of Kirder, Skjærvø 1983; MacKenzie 1989; Gignoux 1991. Kirder served under Shapur I, Hormizd I, Bahram I and Bahram II, whose cumulative reigns go from 240 to 293 CE.

3. From the initial phrase of ŠKZ; cf. Back 1978: 284f.; translation in Wiesehöfer 2001: 155. Abolala Soudavar (2003: 41–48; also 2006) has endeavoured to show that the term *cihr* can never mean "origin, descent", but always "appearance, manifestation". I believe however that it would put a strain on some of the contexts in which this word occurs to translate it otherwise than "origin, descent". In this context in particular the use of the preposition *az* "from" practically excludes any translation except "origin". The title which the king applies to himself, "god", expressed by the heterogram **ALXA** in Parthian, the MP word **bgy**, the Greek θεός, points in the same direction. Like this title, which was never taken literally, so also the phrase "whose seed is from the gods" seems to be a metaphorical hyperbole for the royal majesty. Several occurrences of the word *cihr* and its derivatives or compounds occur in the *WZ* and *Dd*, where the sense of "nature, essence" is imposed.

4. On the early Manichaean period and on the relations of Mani to the Sasanian court see Puech 1949: 44–54; Lieu 1985: 58–59; Gnoli 2003: xxxi–xl.

5. On the status of priests in the Sasanian state a short survey is given in Wiesehöfer 2001: 175–176.

6. No precise information is available on the function of holders of these offices, who may have served already from the third century CE. From the fifth century CE their presence is quite well documented. A thoroughly researched comparative history of the Jewish exilarchate and the Christian function of catholicos is included in Herman 2005.

7. *'Ahd Ardashir*, 'Abbas 1967; Grignaschi 1966; Shaked 1969: 214–219. The composition may be dated to the late Sasanian period.

8. Some notes on the Sasanian doctrine of government can be found in Shaked 1969: 214–219.

9. Cf. Shaked 1984: 31–40.

10. This is evident in some of the legal texts where the presence of Muslims in the background is felt, e.g. in the *Rivāyat ī Ādurfarnbag*, the *Rivāyat ī Ēmēd ī Ašavahištān*, or *Pursišnīhā*. For these texts cf. Boyce 1968b: 46; de Menasce 1975: 544–545, 550–553; Cereti 2001: 154–157.

11. This is a delicate question. Can we assume that there was a kind of *lingua franca*, possibly Middle Persian, which could have marked Iranians from non-Iranians? Parthian and Sogdian were still in use throughout the Sasanian period, as were Choresmian and Bactrian, and we may well wonder whether these and other Iranian

languages could have been felt to be so closely related that they might be lumped together as a single tongue.

12. JamaspAsa and Humbach 1971: 82.
13. *Herb.* 11:1.
14. *Herb.* 11:3. In the gloss of *Herb.* 11:3, giving the child up to those who are in a state of mortal sin or to non-Iranians is singled out as the worst thing to do, akin to giving the child up to be killed. In *Herb.* 12:5 we have the expression *ag-dēn ī an-ēr ī aburnāyag* "one of evil religion, a non-Iranian, who is under age", which shows once again that *ag-dēn* and *an-ēr* are not synonymous.
15. Text and translation according to Kotwal and Kreyenbroek 1992: 60–61.
16. Ibid.
17. Kotwal and Kreyenbroek render *ag-dēn* by "infidel", which does not fall into any of the recognized categories. This choice of an English term probably reflects the authors' inability to make an unambiguous decision as to the nature of the alien religion in question.
18. On the problem of conversion to Zoroastrianism in the Sasanian period, cf. Brody 1990: 52–53. A short discussion of conversion in the Sasanian period, together with texts, can be seen in Shapira 1998: 82–83. For the Muslim period, there is a discussion of various situations in which non-Zoroastrians wish to observe Zoroastrian purity laws, and how one can accommodate that desire; cf. *PersRiv* I: 279, 282, translated in Dhabhar 1932: 273, 276.
19. *Herb.* 11:6.
20. The reason for this ruling has presumably to do with the fear that a non-Zoroastrian woman would not observe the purity laws.
21. *Herb.* 12:3.
22. This again is presumably because of the scruples about menstrual impurity.
23. *Herb.* 12:4.
24. *Herb.* 18:1. A similar gloss is in *Herb.* 19:1.
25. *Herb.* 18:4.
26. *Herb.* 19:6; also *Purs.* §6, JamaspAsa and Humbach 1971: 16f.
27. *Herb.* 19:6.
28. *Purs.* 7, JamaspAsa and Humbach 1971: 16f.
29. On Iranized Arabs see the brief notes in de Jong 2005: 207. There are scattered reports in Arabic literature concerning Arab tribesmen who converted to Zoroastrianism and concerning Zoroastrians who lived in Arabia. Kister 1968: 144–145 quotes an interesting tradition according to which the Sasanian king Qubādh, who was an adherent of Mazdak, ordered al-Ḥārith to impose the Mazdakite faith on the Arabs of Najd and Tihāma, and this faith was also adopted by some people in Mecca. At the advent of Islam there were still some former Mazdakites among the Meccan population.
30. On Semitic-Iranian religious syncretism in Sasanian Babylonia cf. Shaked 1997: 114, with reference to further literature.
31. The names of the clients in the magic bowls from Sasanian Babylonia deserve a special study which has not yet been undertaken on the whole corpus. Some observation on the composition of families may be found in Morony 2003.
32. "Person upon whom is laid the obligation to provide a successor for a dead man who left no male issue", Perikhanian 1997: 387.
33. *MHD* 44: 6–8, translation as in Perikhanian 1997: 119; Macuch 1993: 303, 319.
34. The relevant quotation is given in the Appendix.
35. On this notion cf. Shaked 1987.

36. The Pahlavi text of the whole chapter is given in Shaked 1990: 97–99.
37. This is however uncertain.
38. A recent article by Dan Shapira (2005/6) tries to establish the Zoroastrian scriptural source of Mazdak's religion.
39. On the position of Zurvanism within the Zoroastrian faith, cf. Shaked 1992.
40. Cf. Shaked forthcoming.
41. On the position that Ahreman does not exist see Shaked 1967.
42. Cf. Shaked 1990 for text and translation.

8

State and Society in Late Antique Iran

James Howard-Johnston
(Corpus Christi College, Oxford)

The Sasanian Empire could not match the grandeur of its Achaemenid predecessor. It merely controlled the western approaches to central Asia and the eastern approaches to the Mediterranean. The rich core of the Eurasian continent, to be found beyond the Oxus in the highly urbanised, aristocratic and mercantile world of Sogdiana,[1] lay beyond its political reach, while a good half, the richer half of the Middle East — northern Mesopotamia, Syria, Palestine, Egypt — as well as Asia Minor, all once subject to Achaemenid authority, now formed the heartland of the Roman Empire. Caught between these two outer worlds, Sasanian Iran had to strive unceasingly if it was to sustain its power, let alone to project it further afield. This makes the achievement of rulers and governing elite in late antiquity all the more impressive.

The Sasanian dynasty clawed its way to power, eventually defeating the Arsacid kings of the loosely structured Parthian Empire and gaining control of the milch cow of the further Middle East, Mesopotamia, in a mere twenty years.[2] Ardashir, crowned *shahanshah* probably in Ctesiphon in 226 CE, profited from a virtuous circle in the build-up of power, success adding to his prestige, prestige drawing in additional followers, an enlarged following facilitating further success and so on. It is a familiar process, attested in many other historical contexts — best analysed perhaps with respect to the Normans in the eleventh and early twelfth centuries.[3] Ideology also played a part. Ardashir and his son and successor Shapur I (240–272) demonstrated their Zoroastrian faith, thereby appealing to their subjects. They and their successors also drew inspiration from the visible physical vestiges of a past, only vaguely remembered, when formidable rulers had bestridden the world. Hence the choice of Naqsh-i Rustam as the principal site for the monumental commemorations of their feats.[4]

One great problem faces the historian of Sasanian Iran — a paucity of trustworthy sources.[5] There are some: first and foremost, the monumental inscriptions of the third century, which, beside their principal functions of commemorating achievements of individual rulers and stressing their promotion of the true faith, provide invaluable incidental information about the political organisation and social order of the empire in its earliest phase of development. Key figures and major episodes are also visually recorded in great rock-cut reliefs dating from the third and fourth centuries. Thereafter this direct Sasanian documentary record fails us, apart from papyri dating from the ten-year occupation of Egypt (619–629) by the armies of Khusrau II (the cursive script, however, acts as a virtually impenetrable code, so that even the most persistent of scholars can do little more than decipher the opening and closing formulae) and one unfinished set of rock reliefs, commissioned by Khusrau II.

The only continuous indigenous historical narrative to have survived, the *Khwadaynamag* ("Book of Lords"), is a written version of a set of orally transmitted stories about the Iranian past which were intended as much to edify and to entertain as to recall vanished times. It dates from late in the Sasanian era, probably from the reign of Khusrau I who may have commissioned it, and was subsequently revised and extended under Khusrau II and Yazdgird III. The oral tradition fixed in writing, which had been adapted to changing circumstances in the past, bore a strong Sasanian impress. It is at its fullest on the recent past, the events of the three generations preceding the time of recording – back to the much embroidered feats of Bahram V (420–438) in the steppes – and on the much elaborated story of the foundation of the dynasty by Ardashir I. This Sasanian history is itself prefaced by a much longer account of the deep past, a past transmuted from historical reality, in which a legendary dynasty, the Kayanians, supplants the Achaemenids as the great champion of sedentary civilisation against the forces of Turan. The accounts of the Parthian period and of the two centuries separating the death of Ardashir (239/240) from the accession of Bahram V (420) are remarkably skimpy and garbled.[6] There is a further problem. While some texts evidently drew on sixth and early seventh century sources, and survive in Pahlavi — notably the *Letter of Tansar*[7] and the *Book of a Thousand Judgements*[8] — the *Khwadaynamag* is not among them. It reaches us, inevitably somewhat transformed, chiefly in different versions retailed by later Muslim sources, which drew on Arabic translations of the Pahlavi original, and in a Persian version, the yet later *Shahnama* of Ferdowsi, who embellished it greatly and lifted it up on to a grand epic plane.[9]

The history of Sasanian Iran cannot be written on the basis of Sasanian documentary or narrative sources, without leaving some very large blanks in the bare narrative of events. It is also difficult to gain a proper understanding of the institutional, social and economic structures which gave stability and durability to state and culture in late antiquity, in the crucial middle phase extending from the end of the third century to the accession of Khusrau I in 531. Thereafter a general reform programme instituted by Khusrau, or at least those aspects of it which affected state institutions, primarily the fiscal system and the army, is reported in considerable detail by the *Khwadaynamag*, which stresses the element of theatre involved in its formal introduction, and by a free-standing text, the *Sirat Anushirwan*, likewise transmitted in an Arabic version (by Ibn Miskawayh), which itemises, with remarkable precision, later measures taken to ensure full implementation of the programme in the provinces.[10] So, with only a modest leap of faith, it is possible to sketch the main structural features of the Sasanian Empire in the final phase of its evolution.

What can be added to this limited stock of Iranian material about the Sasanian period? External observers, foremost among them Romans and Armenians, covered international relations in the west, paying particular attention, in the long-established tradition of classical historical writing, to periods of armed conflict. A great historian from Antioch, Ammianus Marcellinus, who had direct experience on the Persian front but allowed too much antiquarian material taken from books to intrude into his work, provides an invaluable account of a period of prolonged discord in the middle decades of the fourth century.[11] Łazar P'arpec'i, an Armenian who witnessed at first hand the large-scale rebellion of his compatriots against Persian rule in 482–484 and had access to good sources of information about an earlier rising in 450–451, provides the best information about foreign affairs in the fifth century as well as considerable insight into the workings of Sasanian government, both at the centre and in the provinces of the north-west.[12] The sixth and early seventh centuries are well covered by Roman texts, several of which make use of official sources of information.[13] It is a great pity, though, that there is no Armenian work to complement them before the history attributed to Sebeos comes on stream, from the outbreak of the penultimate war between the great powers in 572–573.[14]

Authors writing in Syriac and belonging to the dyophysite (Nestorian) church, which achieved something close to established status in the early fifth century, supply additional bits and pieces of information about court and society in Mesopotamia, but there is relatively little to be extracted from texts emanating from the no less important Jewish community.[15] Much, much more important is the cumulative contribution of archaeological work, both excavations of individual sites and large-scale surveys, subject always to the proviso that the material evidence should not be placed within a framework of interpretation based on conclusions drawn from written sources.[16] Finally, mention should be made of those small material objects, which bear inscriptions and which, when studied in aggregate, yield useful information: coins, principally silver drachms which were minted in large quantities to a high standard throughout the Sasanian era (a vital source of information about the fiscal system and the symbolic representation of royalty); and seal stones and clay sealings which have survived in large quantities, especially from the last century of Sasanian rule, and which, on being subjected to proper scrutiny, yield fascinating information about administrative systems.[17]

It is possible then to piece together the domestic history of the Sasanian Empire in outline. The sequence of kings and the lengths of their reigns can be established, coins providing invaluable corroboration for the *Khwadaynamag*. Political crises can be picked out when different Sasanian claimants competed for the throne, although the coverage of the *Khwadaynamag* is poor for the disturbed period of the late third century (but luckily this deficiency is made good, for the seizure of power by Narseh in 293, by the Paikuli inscription). Several bouts of religious repression are also recorded, each time in response to the spread of dangerous rivals to the officially sponsored Zoroastrianism of the state: (1) Manichaeism, successfully suppressed in the fourth century after the crown abandoned its initially complaisant attitude;[18] (2) Christianity which was too deeply embedded in Mesopotamia and Armenia to be rooted out but which was persecuted at times of acute tension with the Romans in the fourth and early fifth century;[19] and, most serious of all, (3) Mazdakism which was generated within the Zoroastrian tradition and swiftly grew into a widespread movement pressing for religious reform and radical social change in troubled times after a catastrophic defeat at the hands of Turan in 484.[20]

There is rather more material to hand about foreign relations, especially with the Romans. The changing diplomatic positions of the two sides are recorded, behind which may be discerned their underlying ideological stances.[21] Several military campaigns are described in great detail, the best single narrative probably being Pseudo-Joshua the Stylite's extraordinary detailed and lucid account of the massive mobilisation and carefully co-ordinated operations extending over two years (503–504) with which the Romans responded to the fall of Amida, taken after a sudden, unprovoked Persian attack in force in autumn 502.[22] It is much harder to construct a connected history of Persian relations with the peoples of central Asia, but the rise and fall of the principal nomad powers of Turan is just detectable.[23] As regards relations with the Indian subcontinent, we hear only of occasional attempts to project power over the arid, wind-scarred south-east into the Indus basin and of the reception of some Indian texts.[24]

So it is just possible to take a global view of international relations in western Eurasia in late antiquity. An initial phase of warfare in the west, actual or suspended, lasted from the first, fierce Sasanian thrusts toward the Mediterranean and into Asia Minor (230–260) to the late fourth century. It was followed by a century of peaceful symbiosis (interrupted by two fleeting crises), once both great sedentary powers had taken proper stock of the enhanced striking power of the Huns, east Asian nomads who brought to the west Eurasian steppes an advanced level of governmental capability developed in the course of centuries of interaction with China. Finally, there was a steady deterioration in Persian-Roman relations through the sixth and early seventh centuries, as each empire in turn took advantage of the temporary weakness or distraction of the other to launch large-scale attacks, each eventually going so far as to seek nomad allies against the other.[25]

I turn now to the question of the Sasanian state. Historians have long acknowledged that the new dynasty refurbished the organs of government and, with time, pulled the variegated component parts of the empire together to form a more cohesive whole than its Parthian predecessor. Together with certain military considerations (ease of access to tempting targets in the Roman Levant), this largely explains the increased political prominence of Mesopotamia under the Sasanians.[26] As the binary capital of the empire, Ctesiphon on the left bank of the Tigris and Veh Ardashir on the right, increased in size, *qua* administrative centre and principal residence of the court, Mesopotamia grew both in population and in wealth. Iran proper remained central to the Sasanian world-view — that was where the dynasty's roots lay, that was where it displayed its triumphs — but it was sidelined by the new metropolitan region in Mesopotamia when it came to the everyday management of practical affairs.

It has proved hard to escape from the gravitational field of the *Khwadaynamag*. This naturally focuses attention on the figure of the *shahanshah*, who gives a morally uplifting address at his accession, however little else may be recorded about his reign. Domestic politics are largely confined to the court, set against a background of assemblies, feasts and hunting expeditions. Warfare is only covered properly if the king is in command and, even so, it may be neglected.[27] Historians writing in the Greco-Roman tradition do not provide an antidote, as they tend to personalise history, none more so than Procopius, our best Roman informant about internal Sasanian politics.[28] So it should cause little surprise that a well-established, virtually universal scholarly consensus views the Sasanian Empire as underdeveloped bureaucratically in comparison to the Roman, as, in a loose sense, a huge proto-feudal state, with royal and aristocratic power being grounded in landownership rather than office-holding.[29]

But how on earth can such a view be reconciled with what we know of the performance of the Sasanian state in late antiquity? Perhaps the extraordinary level of success achieved by Ardashir I and Shapur I may be put down to the *élan* of a militaristic power in an early phase of particularly dynamic growth, as well as to the problems facing the Romans on other fronts. But what of the middle decades of the fourth century, when the Sasanians clearly had the better of their Roman adversaries? Or of their recovery after Peroz's death and the destruction of a large expeditionary force at the hands of the Hephthalites in 484, or, despite all the problems created by the Mazdakites, the effectiveness of the attack launched by Kavad on the Romans in autumn 502?[30] As one proceeds through the sixth century, the achievements mount up. A long-planned Roman *riposte* to the attack of 502 which took the form of a northern offensive involving three armies in 528, ended early in disaster in Lazica, before they had joined forces,[31] to be followed, after a year of fruitless attempts by Kavad to negotiate peace, with formidable and simultaneous displays of Persian military power in the Armenian and north Mesopotamian theatres of war in 530 and a psychologically important victory at Callinicum in 531. After that, Justinian had no option but to negotiate peace from a position of weakness, at heavy cost, and to seek to recuperate lost prestige in the west.[32]

There can be no denying the military power generated by the Sasanians from a resource base that was considerably inferior to that of the Romans. But it is the cohesion of a naturally fissiparous continental empire and the resilience shown in crises, which most impress the modern observer. Those peoples who belonged to the world of Iran, even the Armenians at times of great religious and political tension in the fifth century, did not conceive of breaking away. Nor is there evidence of regional rebellions associated with Mazdakism, which seems rather to have engaged with orthodox Zoroastrianism throughout Iran. As for resilience, the most striking example comes in 573, when the Roman regime of Justinian's nephew and successor, Justin II, initiated a war on the largest possible scale. For Sasanian Iran it was an *annus nefastus*, when it was attacked from all sides. The Persarmenians had rebelled in 572, and, with Roman help, had prevailed, driving out the Sasanian authorities. Turan, which now took the form of the transcontinental Turkish khaganate, had agreed, in the course of direct negotiations with the Romans, to attack in concert with a major Roman offensive targeted on Nisibis in northern Mesopotamia.[33] The crisis, much transmuted and repositioned some fifteen years later, has left its mark on the *Khwadaynamag*.[34]

The Persians rose to the challenge. They cut their losses in the north, temporarily abandoning Persarmenia. Nothing is recorded of operations in the east, but the defences in Gorgan seem to have held in 573 and there is no evidence of Turkish penetration through the narrow passage between the Elburz mountains and the salt desert commanded by Nishapur, which leads west along the northern edge of the plateau. In the south they succeeded in trumping Roman diplomacy, first by taking direct control of Yemen (in 570/571) and then by suborning the Ghassan-led nexus of Arab tribes who served the Romans. This opened the way for a devastating counterstroke. Deprived of intelligence from their Arab clients, the Romans laid siege to Nisibis and remained unaware of a Persian army's swift advance up the Euphrates to its junction with the Khabur, where the main force, commanded by Khusrau himself, turned north to attack the Romans in the rear. Taken by surprise, the Romans fled in panic, leaving Khusrau free to attack Dara with the siege equipment left outside Nisibis.[35]

Dara fell six months later, and within two years Persarmenia was once again under firm Persian control. The fighting continued for more than a decade, with the initiative lying very much with the Persians. Having settled their accounts with both Romans and Armenians, they demonstrated their ability to use Armenia as a platform for attacking Asia Minor and northern Syria in 576 and 578, and seem then to have turned their attention to central Asia where they embarked on a successful war of revenge against the Turks. Even so they proved stubborn and effective opponents on the north Mesopotamian front, containing Roman attacks without great difficulty and limiting their gains to a very few forts (either captured or constructed). By 588 they had broken the Roman army's offensive spirit, and, having brought the war against the Turks to a victorious conclusion, were in a position to initiate large-scale offensive action in the west. The Romans were only saved from defeat or diplomatic humiliation by the rebellion of Bahram Chubin, the victor over the Turks, who resented what he took to be grudging acknowledgement of his achievement on the part of the *shahanshah* Hormizd IV.[36]

The Sasanian military and political record can surely leave us in no doubt about the efficiency and effectiveness of the state. It is inconceivable that the army, which took on and defeated the forces of Turan in the east and the Roman army in the west, was nothing more than a feudal host, immeasurably enlarged. An agglomeration of local levies, looking up to the lords who raised them, lords who looked up in turn to regional aristocrats and, beyond, to great court magnates, any army of this sort would not have been amenable to the central direction which was vital if Iran was to cope with dangers as they materialised on different fronts. Equally certainly it could not have carried out sustained operations in distant theatres of war — as Sasanian forces did on many occasions both in the east and the west.[37] It is plain that the *shahanshah* could call on the services of a large professional fighting force, funded from taxation and probably paid, on the analogy with the late Roman army, in cash and kind. This is indeed the picture presented of the late Sasanian army in the *Khwadaynamag*. Khusrau I seems to have limited himself to improving its discipline and equipment.[38]

Massive infrastructure projects, both civil and military, provide equally unequivocal testimony to the organisational capability of the Sasanian state.[39] Century by century, under successive imperial dynasties, lower Mesopotamia was gradually reshaped by man. It is generally agreed that the acme came in the late Sasanian period, with the implementation of a grand scheme to transform the Diyala plains on the left bank of the Tigris into a vast breadbasket, and simultaneously to endow Ctesiphon with impregnable water defences (a northern extension of the Nahravan Canal, known as the Cut of Khusrau). By the middle of the sixth century at the latest, the whole of the Mesopotamian alluvium together with adjoining lands in Khuzistan, was criss-crossed by trunk canals (which doubled as transport routes and lines of defence) and irrigation canals. As a result the metropolitan region became self-sufficient in food, grain being shipped in by river and canal from its immediate hinterlands.[40] Other schemes helped develop large areas of the interior of Iran into productive and well-populated agricultural zones — around Isfahan, for example, on the Marvdasht plain by Istakhr, and in the lower part of the desiccated Helmand basin.[41]

The scale of capital investment in military infrastructure was no less impressive. Sasanian cities, like their Roman counterparts, were normally fortified. A few, which commanded strategic routes leading from the frontier to the interior, were endowed with unusually strong defences and large garrisons so as to deter an enemy from penetrating into Sasanian territory. This role of acting as a strongpoint on an exposed frontier is known to have been played by Nisibis in the west and Nishapur in the east. Dvin probably performed the same function in Transcaucasia. On several frontiers, nature's defences needed relatively little reinforcement by man — the Caucasus, the Kopet Dagh behind Khurasan, the near desert of Sistan in the far south-east, and the lower Euphrates. But powerful linear defences were required to secure two weak points in the north, through which Turan could threaten Iran: (1) the easy passage (known as the Caspian Gates) between the eastern end of the Caucasus and the Caspian shore; and (2) the wide Gorgan plain (classical Hyrcania) which pushes south between the eastern shore of the Caspian and the north-western end of the Kopet Dagh. Two stone-built long walls, with interval towers, and three earth ramparts blocked the Caspian Gates. The principal line of defence, the northern wall, abutted onto the Caspian at the heavily fortified port of Derbend, was doubled as it crossed the plain, and continued for some 34 km into the mountains.[42] But this Derbend wall, in its final phase of development (attributable to Khusrau I) pales into insignificance when it is compared to the 196 Km brick wall securing the southern Gorgan plain, which seems to have been constructed in a single phase, datable it seems, to the reign of Peroz (459-484), and which was garrisoned by troops barracked in 36 regularly spaced forts.[43]

Any remaining doubts about the organisational development of the Sasanian Empire can be dispelled by glancing at what is known of the administrative and financial systems. Different branches of government were separately represented in the localities. There was a justice system, headed at the level of the province (*shahr*) by a Defender of the Poor and Judge (*driyōshan-jādaggōw ud dādwar*), a tax system managed at a higher, regional level by an accountant (*āmārgar*), and, of course, a general civil administration, headed normally by a governor (*shahrab*). The Zoroastrian priesthood formed a parallel hierarchy, the priest in charge of a locality (*mōgh*) being answerable to the provincial chief priest (*mōbed*).[44] Cash, the only efficient way of funding a ramified apparatus of government, raised from taxation and paid out in salaries, was available in abundance, thanks to an empire-wide system of mints which issued drachms of a uniform type to a consistently high standard and which continued to function after the destruction of the empire by the Arabs.[45]

The Sasanian Empire can thus be classified as an advanced state, which, by gearing itself to war, was able to project its power far afield and to ward off formidable adversaries in the west and north-east. The general features of its social organisation can be discerned. Two texts, both written or, at any rate, thoroughly revised in the sixth century when memories of the long Mazdakite crisis were still fresh, the *Letter of Tansar* and the *Testament of Ardashir*, are particularly informative. Both stress the importance of maintaining a stable and deferential social order, presided over by the *shahanshah*. The guiding principles are hierarchy and heredity. Status is to be preserved from generation to generation. Everyone has their place in society — clergy, soldiers, state servants, members of the professions, peasants, artisans and traders.[46] It was expected that the crown would aid an aristocratic family which fell on hard times, as Khusrau I is reported to have done in many cases.[47]

There were evidently several tiers to the aristocracy, the highest consisting of magnates with direct access to the *shahanshah* and first claim on the great offices of state. The crown gave its support to the existing hierarchy of aristocratic families, which reciprocated by accepting the ruling dynasty's hereditary right to the throne. It is not known, however, how many tiers of aristocracy there were or what terminology was used after the first century of Sasanian rule. A Roman author, Theophylact Simocatta, writing in the 620s, notes, in an aside, that there were seven great families, each of which, he thinks, had a hereditary right to a specific high office.[48] It is just possible, by scouring the extant sources to come up with their surnames: Suren, Waraz, Karen, Aspahbadh, Spandiyadh, Mihran and Zik. Although they did not monopolise particular posts, as Simocatta supposed, they regularly figured in the army high command or in charge of major departments of state.[49] Below them, we may postulate several gradations of status — say, (1) a high aristocracy, with widely dispersed estates; (2) regional and (3) provincial aristocracies; and, at the base, (4) something akin to local gentry. But it is only the lowest tier which is attested in the sources, if, as is probable, the heads of localities (*dehganan / dihqanan*) who figure in accounts of the Arab conquests were drawn from it.[50]

So the middle echelons of the stratified elite who ran the Sasanian Empire remain invisible to us. Prosopography, the study of politics in terms of the careers and connections of individual participants, has no future in Sasanians studies. Nor is there any prospect of producing a regionally differentiated history, nor indeed of understanding how status was sustained in the localities (or, to put it in other words, what degree of lordship was exercised over the peasantry, whether providing agricultural labour or residing in nearby villages). The dearth of relevant evidence is deeply frustrating, especially for those who regard social systems as key determinants of political and economic change. Even material evidence fails us in this respect. Only two high-status residences have been discovered, a villa at Bandiyan on the edge of the Turkmen steppes in northeastern Iran with fine stucco reliefs, and a substantial house at Hajiabad in southern Iran. Religious complexes are associated with both, a fire chamber and ossuary integrated into the secular building at Bandiyan, and a free-standing *chahar taq* at Hajiabad. But there is nothing to indicate whether the owners were gentry or belonged to a higher, aristocratic stratum.[51]

In whatever direction we turn, we come up against blank walls. There simply is no useful evidence about social power away from the court. It is not even certain that the Sasanian aristocracy was rooted in the country, their standing reflected in the grandeur of their houses and the lavishness of their hospitality. For we know very little about city life in the Sasanian era outside Mesopotamia. Once Muslim geographical texts come on stream from the late ninth century, Iran can be seen to be highly urbanised, its cities manufacturing products which are traded all over the caliphate. By the tenth century it has a good claim to being the economic heartland of the caliphate.[52] But this urban, mercantile world may not have been a creation of the Muslim era. It may simply have become visible then for the first time. There was undoubtedly significant economic growth in the context of the Islamic single market, but the cities themselves may have existed and indeed flourished under the Sasanians. So we should not close our minds to the possibility that aristocrats had town houses as well as country estates, that they may have regarded the town as the principal forum for the exercise and display of power, and that they may have co-existed in greater or lesser harmony with city notables whose wealth came from trade and manufacture rather than from land.

The merchant seldom appears in Sasanian sources. But there can be no doubt of his importance, given what can be learned of long-distance commerce. The long battle for hegemony in the Indian Ocean between Romans and Sasanians had been won by the latter by the middle of the sixth century. The evidence comes from Cosmas Indicopleustes, a Roman trader with intellectual pretensions, who, in his idiosyncratic work on the cosmos, refers in passing to the dominance achieved by Persian merchants in Sri Lanka.[53] By land too, it is evident that the Sasanian empire was a major trading power and regarded Sogdian competition as an affront. Hence the extraordinary action, taken in the late 560s, of publicly burning a whole consignment of Chinese silk brought by a Sogdian-Turkish embassy. It was this trade dispute which prompted the Turks to send a first exploratory mission to Constantinople, and, in due course, to agree a joint plan of action against Iran.[54]

It is not as if Iranian manufactured products — most notably glass, silver plate and silk — do not turn up abroad, nor as if a commercial ethos was not making advances in the sixth century. A changed atmosphere and growing social flux at the time of writing, as well as memories of Mazdakism, would explain the extreme reactionary stance of the author of the *Letter of Tansar*, who seems to be trying to conserve an idealised, ultra-stable social order against all change. A telling passage inveighs against the young who abandon an aristocratic way of life and "busy themselves like tradesmen with the earning of money, and neglect to garner fair fame".[55] No weight whatsoever should be attached to the silence of most sources about merchants and commerce, nor to the dearth of evidence about cities. The Sasanian Empire of the sixth century may have been far more dynamic in the economic field than we have supposed. As a result the balance of power between regions within the empire may have been changing, Transcaucasia, say, gaining at the expense of the old political heartland in the Zagros, Khurasan suffering while southern Mesopotamia and the Gulf coast boomed. It is also not beyond the bounds of possibility that development schemes began to realise the agricultural potential of the Caspian lowlands in the sixth century, under the stimulus of the demand generated by the forces manning the Gorgan wall.[56]

Significant economic growth overall and increasing flexibility in the social system would help us understand the extraordinary achievements of the *shahanshah* Khusrau II in the first two decades of the seventh century. He managed, in effect, to destroy the Roman Empire, first breaking its military power in a long war of attrition and then taking over all its rich Middle Eastern provinces, including Egypt. The only substantial territories left untouched were Asia Minor and Greece, and both were all too exposed to attack by Khusrau's forces and those of his Avar allies in the Balkans. Failure in the 620s can be attributed mainly to renewed intervention in the west by the Turks at the apogee of their power and a sudden, vertiginous drop in Persian morale at the prospect of a much extended and much tougher war on two fronts.[57]

The old aristocratic social order, manifest in court on great ceremonial occasions, had not, however, been seriously damaged, save in hyper-anxious minds. What gave great tensile strength to the state was the involvement of the elite at all levels and in all branches of government. Individuals had legitimate expectations of gaining offices appropriate to the status of their families. It was obviously in the interests of the monarchy and the provincial authorities to retain a degree of discretion about individual appointments, thereby both generating competition for preferment and directing the aristocracy's attention towards those with offices in their gift. But the claims of different grades in the aristocracy had to be met with offers of suitable posts, from the highest to the lowest, from magnates at the apex of the empire to *dihqanan* in the localities. The Sasanian aristocracy was an aristocracy of service, with a firm base in landownership.

As long as his prestige was sustained, a *shahanshah* would have relatively little difficulty in upholding his authority. The idea of Iran, first formulated as a coherent religious-political ideology in the third century, co-opted the whole people into a cosmic enterprise of battling evil, represented on earth by the wilderness and Turan.[58] Ruler and aristocracy worked together for a common, higher cause, strict ethical standards being inculcated by speeches and slogans at all levels of the administration. Royal authority was underpinned by great landed wealth, the principal crown estates (each managed by an *ostandar*, who seems also to have been in charge of the local province) being concentrated in two strategically important peripheral regions, Transcaucasia and the north-eastern Marches.[59] It was not challenged, although at times of crisis a rival candidate from within the Sasanian family might be put forward. The only exception came late in the sixth century, when, in 588–589, a member of one of the leading magnate families, Bahram Chobin, buoyed up by a historic victory over Turan, rebelled against Hormizd IV whose mother was Turkish, perhaps justifying this unprecedented move (but this is pure speculation) by arguing that Turanian tyranny must be rooted out at the centre.[60]

Despite the terrible disappointment of ultimate failure in Khusrau II's Roman war (a failure for which he paid with his life, on 28th February 628) and a subsequent period of political turbulence (628–632), the Sasanian Empire demonstrated impressive powers of resistance when it came under attack from the forces of Islam from 636. The initial successes of the Arabs were reversed in 637 by a counteroffensive that drove them out of Mesopotamia. Defeat at al-Qadisiyya on 6th January 638 was not followed by a collapse. Ctesiphon held out for many months under siege, and hard fighting was required for the Arabs to gain control of Khuzistan and to seize a bridgehead on the plateau. Later, when they first appeared in force on the Anatolian plateau in 654, the whole population were ready to submit. Not so on the Iranian plateau and in the surrounding highlands in 642. There the fighting lasted for ten years and only ended in victory for the Arabs, when they succeeded in neutralising the army of Media and concentrating their forces against Yazdgird III, the last *shahanshah*, in Khurasan in 652.[61]

Sasanian Iran, bound together by a shared ideology, its social order meshed into its governmental system, proved a formidable military and political power in late antiquity. It loomed large on the stage of west Eurasian international relations, despite restricted resources and manpower. This achievement is attributable ultimately to the efficiency of its government, the commitment of its aristocracy and the dynamism of its ideology.

Notes:

1. De la Vaissière 2002.
2. Schippmann 1990: 10–17.
3. Le Patourel 1976.
4. Herrmann 1977a: 85–94; Wiesehöfer 2005: 134–136, 141–142.
5. Wiesehöfer 2001: 153–164 and 2008.
6. Wiesehöfer 2005: 138–147.
7. Boyce 1968a.
8. Macuch 1976.
9. Rubin 1995; Wiesehöfer 2005: 138–147.
10. Rubin 1995.
11. Drijvers 2006.
12. Thomson 1991.
13. See, for example, Greatrex 1998; Börm 2007; Whitby 1988.
14. Thomson and Howard-Johnston 1999.
15. Brock 1979/1980.
16. Howard-Johnston 1995.
17. Alram and Gyselen 2003; Gyselen 1989; 2002.
18. Wiesehöfer 2001: 205–208; Lieu 1994: 1–21.
19. Brock 1982.
20. Klíma 1957; Crone 1991.
21. Rubin 1986: Blockley 1992.
22. Trombley and Watt 2000.
23. De la Vaissière 2002: 102–118, 197–207.
24. Wiesehöfer 2001: 216–221; Gignoux 2006.
25. Dodgeon and Lieu 1991; Greatrex and Lieu 2002.
26. A point emphasised by Gray 1973.
27. For example, the western wars of Shapur II and Khusrau II, both of whom took the field themselves.
28. Börm 2007.
29. Altheim and Stiehl 1954; Widengren 1969.
30. Greatrex 1998: 5–119.
31. Malalas, 18.4, tr. Jeffreys, Jeffreys and Scott 1986.
32. Greatrex 1998: 139–223.
33. Whitby 1988: 250–257.
34. Al-Tabarī, tr. Bosworth 1999: 298–301.
35. Whitby 1988: 252, 257–258.
36. Whitby 1988: 258–292; Thomson and Howard-Johnston 1999: 162–169.
37. To the example given above of the war of 573–588 may be added an earlier notable one, from the reign of Shapur II — the five years' campaigning in the east required to secure Iran's position *vis à vis* the Huns (353–357), while desultory fighting continued in the west — Dodgeon and Lieu 1991: 211–212.
38. Al-Tabarī, tr. Bosworth 1999: 262–263.
39. Howard-Johnston 1995.
40. Adams 1965; 1981; 2008; Northedge 2008.
41. Christensen 1993: 117–243.
42. Howard-Johnston 1995: 188–197.
43. Nokandeh, Sauer, Rekavandi *et al.* 2006.
44. Gyselen 1989; 2002.

45. Mint identifications: Gyselen and Kalus 1983: 143–155, and Malek 1993: 86–90.
46. Boyce 1968a; Grignaschi 1966: 68–83.
47. Al-Tabarī, tr. Bosworth 1999: 154–157.
48. Simocatta, iii.18.6–10, tr. Whitby and Whitby 1986.
49. Rubin 2004.
50. Morony 1984: *dahaqin*.
51. Rahbar 2008; Azarnoush 1994.
52. Lombard 1971.
53. Cosmas Indicopleustes, xi.13–19, tr. Wolska-Conus 1968–1973.
54. Menander, fr.10.1, ed. & tr. Blockley 1985.
55. Boyce 1968a: 44.
56. Virtually nothing is known of the Caspian lowlands before the Islamic conquest, as they lay beyond the horizon of vision of Romans, Armenians and Syrians.
57. Howard-Johnston 1999.
58. Gnoli 1989.
59. Gyselen 2002: 69–75, 117–119.
60. Whitby 1988: 292–297; Thomson and Howard-Johnston 1999: 168–170.
61. Thomson and Howard-Johnston 1999: 243–246, 251–253, 264–266; *cf.* Kennedy 2007: 98–138, 169–199.

9

Prices and Drachms in the Late Sasanian Period

Philippe Gignoux
(École Pratique des Hautes Études, Paris)

conomic data for the Sasanian period are particularly rare, "even more
rare" than for preceding periods. Philip Huyse affirms this in a recent
work wherein he goes no further than to state that a pater familias
"received everyday three-fifths of a drachm for food as well as a sum for
clothing".[1] This corresponds, according to another text,[2] to a monthly salary of
4 stēr, equal to 16 drachms. It is in my opinion possible to learn a little more
with a view to estimating the price of things, by consulting two types of
sources:[3] first, Pahlavi literature, albeit written at a much later date (ninth and
tenth centuries), evokes in legal texts the cost of living at the end of the
Sasanian period, or a little later; and to this must now be added new documents
written in Bactrian and published by Nicholas Sims-Williams,[4] and those
written on leather and linen held in the Pahlavi Archive at the Bancroft Library,
Berkeley, which, albeit slightly later than the fall of the Sasanians, give us a
more reliable idea of economic realities in the second half of the seventh
century. I would like to show how these data scattered through Pahlavi
literature may be confirmed, in part only, by those of the Berkeley documents.[5]

I. Pahlavi literature

Two types of text give us data associated with figures: legal texts that
include contracts and define fines to be paid in case of breach, the glosses in
Pahlavi from the Vendidad and other texts concerned with more practical
matters. Elsewhere, there is little to be found in religious texts. It must be noted
that in the first century of our era, an Avroman parchment estimated the price
of half of a vine called *Asmak*, bought in 33 CE, to be 65 drachms.[6]

In the Mādayān ī hazār dādestān,[7] the lawyer Mardag states that 500
drachms is to be given as security, a sum that corresponds to the price of a slave
who does not fulfil his service. But elsewhere in the same work, the price of
several child slaves rises to 200 drachms; however, upon reaching adulthood,
each of them is worth the same sum.[8] In inheritance matters,[9] the *Mādayān ī*

hazār dādestān tells us that an estate worth 75 drachms of a father having two sons and one daughter, was shared as follows: 30 drachms for each son and only 15 for the daughter. This is proof, should it be needed, of the inferior condition of the latter.

Illicit unions were heavily penalized: unauthorized intercourse with a woman (*a-pādixšāy*) carried a fine of 300 stērs, i.e. 1200 drachms![10] The abduction of a woman with whom a man has illegal relations was punished with a fine of 500 drachms for the abduction and 700 drachms for the copulation, i.e. the same sum as in the preceding case.[11] And if some person abducted a minor child, he would be liable for 600 drachms.[12] These measures were part of a legal system organized, no doubt, by the magi and by religious commentators, but it is not known whether they were actually applied.

Elsewhere, the *Mādayān ī hazār dādestān* speaks of a *xwāstag* whose estimated worth was 200 drachms.[13] Maria Macuch translated the word in this context as "Sache", which is very vague but, as we know, it is difficult to discern its precise meaning, which is often defined as "possession or property".[14] The Berkeley documents lead me to think that it may sometimes refer to a soil or cultivable field.[15]

In another field, that of trial by ordeal, the verdict does not seem to be very costly: it amounts to 3 drachms and 2 dāngs, i.e. 3.5 drachms, to be shared between both parties. On the other hand, recourse to trial by ordeal was not possible if the dispute involved a sum of less than 48 drachms. If we compare these two data, we may suppose that the percentage levied by legal authorities did not exceed 10 per cent.[16]

The price of animals, medicine and meat

According to the glosses in the Vendidad 4.2,[17] a sheep was worth 3 stērs, a bullock of poor quality four times as much, i.e. 12 stērs, a man 125 stērs[18] and land over 500 drachms.

In the Vendidad 7.41,[19] a physician charged a scale of fees according to the social condition of the patient: the head of a household (mān) was required to pay 12 stērs, the head of a village (vis) 221 stērs, the head of a district (zand) 30 stērs, the head of a region (šahr) 70 stērs. The last figure was equivalent to the price of a quadriga: however, according to a Bactrian document,[20] a horse was worth 10 dinars which may have corresponded, as we shall see, to 50 drachms. If this is the case, four horses would have cost 200 drachms and 80 drachms would have been left over to pay for the chariot and harness, which is plausible enough.[21]

With regard to an ingenious explanation of the expression *sēnag masāy ud bāzā masāy*, which until 1990 had not been understood, Maria Macuch has highlighted the price of meat: 30 pieces of mutton (*gōspand*), i.e. fifteen from the fore part of the beast and fifteen from the rear, were worth 12 drachms.[22] As the daily ration of an adult man was two pieces, the price of one piece came to three fifths of a drachm, according to the *Frahang ī Ōim*, or 24 drachms for the month, which does correspond to two pieces of meat per day. Alternatively, according to the *Rivāyat ī Ēmēd ī Ašavahištān*, compensation amounted to only 18 drachms, or according to the *Dādestān ī dēnīg*, just 16 drachms, which was also the salary of a head of the household (*dūdag-sālār*), but it is not clear whether this was added to the equivalent of the meat mentioned. However, in view of the moderate price of corn, these values seem to be credible enough. Indeed, according to the *Dādestān ī dēnīg* 51,[23] eight *kabīz* of wheat were worth 1 drachm.

The cost of ceremonies

Chaper 87 of the *Dādestān ī dēnīg* certainly refers to the Islamic period when the living conditions of priests became difficult. It contains a discussion on the price of a *hamāgdēn* ceremony, which in Fars amounted to 350 to 400 drachms, a seemingly considerable sum. According to archives, the price of 350 drachms was normal in Ardaxšir-Xwarrah. The writer goes on to explain that the price was enough to celebrate two *hamāgdēn*, and even in this period, which corresponds to the ninth century, it was possible to organize the celebration for 150 or even 120 drachms, excluding the zōhr. This indicates an obvious impoverishment of the upper classes as probably only they could afford to offer themselves such rituals.

II. Bactrian data

The texts published by N. Sims-Williams in *Bactrian Documents I* are for the most part contracts that incurred fines if they were breached. As most of them are dated, I will only retain those that relate to the later period. In general, an identical fine was to be paid to both the authorities and the opposing party. Thus, in the case of a breach of a marriage contract, 40 dinars were to be paid.[24] A much later document, dated 723 CE, allows us to estimate the value of a silver drachm in relation to a golden dinar because the text speaks of a fine of 100 dinars to be paid to the *bredag* and 500 drachms to the opposing party. As these sums were in normal circumstances identical, we are able to deduce that 1 dinar is equivalent to 5 drachms. This is quite different from the value attributed to the dinar in western Iran, i.e. 11.2 drachms, as indicated in the *Frahang ī Pahlavīg*.[25] We can only infer that money in gold had a higher value there than elsewhere.

According to document "J", dated 528 CE, a property of 7 lukhs was worth 8 dinars. The fine was the same, that is 40 dinars, but in document "L" dated CE 612, a property sold for 20 dinars incurred twice the fine, i.e. 80 dinars. A palimpsest, and therefore earlier than text "M" dated 621, tells us that a vine cost 17 dinars.[26] Document "P" dated 679 gives us the selling price of a boy to be only 3 drachms. Document "Q" is very interesting because, although of a later date, CE 682, it does allow us to estimate the price of borrowing money: for 40 Kavad drachms, interest rates were as high as 2 drachms a month, which represents a cost of 5 %. In the case of default, the fine would have been very high: 80 drachms multiplied by two, thus amounting to four times the capital!

III. The Pahlavi archive at Berkeley

The most legible documents of this archive, dating from the second half of the seventh century, constitute for my purpose the most authentic and reliable source. But contrary to what we may expect from these accounting documents, there are very few that link wares to prices because the great majority only mention the quantity of the wares and the unit of measurement used. However, two documents[27] give us a few ware prices.

   a.   Document 46: 8 *dōlag*s of *šuftag*, which could mean "whey", but this is far from clear. Should we compare it to the Persian *šaft* meaning "drupe",[28] but the associated measure is for liquid, so perhaps fruit juice, or should we turn to the Parthian *šyft* meaning "milk"?[29] On the other hand, since the word is placed in document 97 between "wine" (*may*) and "must" (*bādag*), we may suppose that it indicates another grape-based product such as "grape juice" or "sweet wine". Whatever it may be, the price of 1 *dōlag* was 1 drachm.

   b.   Oil or butter (*rōyn*): 1 *dōlag* cost 2 drachms, this is confirmed in document 97.14.

   c.   Honey (*angubēn*): a *dōlag* was worth 3 drachms, but in document 97.12–13, it cost 2 drachms; however, if my interpretation is correct, the information therein is followed by the word *mayān* to indicate that it relates to an "average" price. It is not surprising that honey was relatively expensive; since ancient times it had been a multi-purpose product and was essential in a sugarless society. Hippocrates[30] has already told us that wine was used for preserving meat and other things, as was snow, honey, vinegar and salt according to ms. Syriac 423.[31]

   d.   Mutton (*gōspand*) cost 4 drachms, according to both documents 46 and 97. The price given in the *Vendidad*, i.e. 12 drachms, was higher. This allows us to believe in the relative reliability of the prices mentioned in the glosses of the *Vendidad*. We may suppose that a goat cost more or less the same as a sheep, and for proof we can turn to accounts given in the treatise called *Draxt ī āsūrīg*:

>   ka buz ō wāzār barēnd ud pad wahāg dārēnd har kē dah drahm nē dārēd frāz ō buz nē āyēd

>   "When one takes a goat to market, and one considers it valuable,[32] all those who do not possess ten drachms, will not approach the goat..."

   e.   Wine and its by-products: wine (*may*), along with its by-products must (*bādag*) and perhaps *šuftag*, is mentioned in a great number of documents, thus attesting its constant use. However it was not recognized for its cost, but rather for its quantity. Probably the reason for this was that it was a common consumer item and perhaps cheap, much like cereals and products for animals such as straw, alfalfa and barley. However, according to document 49, 6 *dōlag*s of wine cost apparently 1 stēr and 1 drachm, i.e. 5 drachms, which seems to be a logical price when compared to those of other wares.

f. Clothing: document 154 was able to enlighten us, subject to legibility, as to the price of two children's shirts (MP *pīrāhan*), which cost 18 stērs, i.e. 72 drachms, or for one shirt 30 drachms. This may seem high, but document 15 tells us that to manufacture two items of clothing (*kabāh*, Arabic *qabā* "robe d'homme à manches" according to Al-Faraid 1955: 615; Lazard 1990: 314 "vêtement long, ouvert devant et porté par les hommes"), 4 *man*s of cotton were required, but unfortunately the price of this textile remains unknown.

g. Wood (*ēzm*): according to document 46.6, wood in the quantity of 2 *hlw'l* cost 1 drachm, in document 97.11–12 the cost of each quantity is precisely 1 drachm. The word spellt *hlw'l* should be read *xarvār*, which is a measurement of weight equivalent to approximately 300 kg, recently explained by Thiesen[33] as a "donkey load". This wood was probably used as firewood, mostly for cooking. It was much more abundant at this time than it is today, after centuries of deforestation.

IV. An incursion into the Islamic era

By way of conclusion, I feel it would be interesting to present some data found in early Arabo-Persian literature relating to the drachm. The *Kitāb al-tāj*, attributed to Ĝahiz, paints a colourful picture of life at the Sasanian court. The sums given in drachms are extraordinarily high, on an altogether different scale to those that we have seen for the seventh century, and denote, even if we take into account exaggeration by the author, inflation during the first few centuries of Islam comparable to that seen by Germany in the period between the two World Wars. For the Sasanian era, the author clearly commits some anachronisms that cannot give us any information on the real cost of living. Thus, under Harun al-Rashid, a singer such as the famous Ibrahim, received from the Sultan 200,000 drachms![34] The drachm appears to have become so devalued that by the ninth century the *badra* was introduced, being the equivalent to 10,000 drachms and always worth more than 1000 drachms. The cleaning of a garment required the sum of 30 *badra*s. It was said that courtiers received from the Sasanian king 10,000 drachms a month for expenses relating to receptions, expenditure and other needs. The value of a royal gift could be as much as 10,000 drachms, but in such cases it would have to have been recorded in the *diwān* of the court.

The small treatise *Xusrō ud rēdag*[35] also relates that an exceptionally talented young boy was given 12,000 drachms, as a kind of capital in my opinion, since the text goes on to say that the king ordered him to be given 4 dinars per day, which is more in keeping with the group of prices that we have already looked at.

The *Tarīx-e Boxārā* corroborates the Book of the Crown since it affirms that a pearl, at the end of the ninth century, cost 70,000 drachms.[36] And finally in the *Tarīx-e Tabaristān*, at the end of the eight century, under Harun al-Rashid, the price of a plot of land for the construction of the Great Mosque of Amul was 8032 dinars, and the construction itself cost 47,340 dinars. Similarly the Ispahbed presented to the Amir of Hilla horses, coats, belts, helmets and so on, and 10,000 dinars in gold.[37] The revenue of Tabaristān under the Tahirid dynasty, from 820 to 872 CE, amounted to 6,003,000 drachms![38]

Notes:

1. See Huyse 2005:109, and also Gyselen 1997.
2. Not quoted in the work.
3. Gyselen 1997: 104, who did not mention the sources, has pointed out their rarity: "There is a serious absence of contemporary evidence, both textual (excepting only Syriac texts and the Talmud) and archaeological", but it is true that she does not refer to the late Sasanian period.
4. Sims-Williams 2000.
5. In a paper delivered at the Colloquium of the Societas Iranologica Europaea held in Rome (September 2005), I mentioned these latter data very briefly.
6. See Mackenzie 1987.
7. MHD 12.7; Macuch 1993: 116; Perikhanian 1974: 312.
8. MHD 54.12; Macuch 1993: 374 & 382.
9. MHD 81.11–17; Macuch 1993: 529–530.
10. MHD 73.7; Macuch 1993: 489.
11. MHD 73.8–9; Macuch 1993: 489.
12. MHD 73.10; Macuch 1993: 489.
13. MHD 54.12 & 66.6–8; Macuch 1993: 374 & 446.
14. Sometimes the word can also mean "money", see Safa-Isfehani 1980: 128.
15. So in document 243.6 where I read: *jorab xwāstag*, which can mean "70 acres of (arable) soil".
16. See Perikhanian 1979: 192.
17. Jamasp 1907: I.105.
18. See Darmesteter 1960: II.53 note 7, who thinks that the only figure 500 refers to drachms rather than to tetradrachms.
19. Jamasp 1907: I.267–268.
20. See Sims-Williams 2000: 160, but this document is not dated.
21. For curing the woman of these different heads of household, the number of drachms is not mentioned, but the price does correspond, according to the same hierarchical order, to a she-ass, a cow, a mare and a she-camel. This seems to be an estimation suitable to nomadic life, in which the camel is the most prized animal.
22. Macuch 1990: 140. It is interesting to note that in the Berkeley archive (in document 48), pieces of meat (*kardag*) are counted either with a figure of 15 or with one of 30.
23. This chapter relates to the inflation of the corn's price, but it shows that purchase at a lower price is lawful.
24. See document A, p. 34, dated 343 CE.
25. Chap. 29.12, where half a dinar = 3 *dāng*. One drachm = 4 *dāng*, see Mirza 1954: 9; Utas 1988: 109.
26. This price is almost equivalent to that of the Asmak vine, but the latter does not belong to the same period.
27. I have already briefly used the contents of these documents at the Colloquium in Rome in 2005, but here I present them more completely.
28. See Lazard 1990: 259.
29. Boyce 1977: 85.
30. Gignoux 1999: 45.
31. Page 139; see Gignoux 1999: 45. On a Berkeley document to be published by Dieter Weber, is attested the word *namak-sūd* "salted". I warmly thank him for this information.

32. The translation of this sentence by Mirza (1954: 8) "and offer it for sale" is not correct. That would be pleonastic, since if somebody goes to the market, it is of course for selling (the goat)!
33. See Thiesen 2005: 215.
34. See Pellat 1954: 70.
35. See Unvala 1921.
36. Frye 1954: 91.
37. See Browne 1905: 60; quoted by Gignoux 1990: 14 note 48.
38. Browne 1905: 29.

10

Late Sasanian Society between Orality and Literacy

Philip Huyse
(École Pratique des Hautes Études, Paris)

In the past few years, a whole range of studies has been devoted to the theme of orality and literacy (in its widest sense) during the pre-Islamic period in Iran.[1] Such matters as the historical dating of Zoroaster,[2] the Kayanid character of Iranian history in late Sasanian times,[3] or the possible reminiscence of the Achaemenids by the early Sasanian rulers[4] have been debated with much diligence and probably even more passion, while still other research papers are concerned with the genesis of the Old Persian script[5] and the possible invention date of the Avestan script.[6] Many of these studies have ultimately been triggered by Walter Bruno Henning's masterful lecture *Zoroaster. Politician or Witch-doctor?* (Oxford, 1951) or Ehsan Yarshater's brilliant chapter — actually a sound monograph — in the third volume of the *Cambridge History of Iran*, entitled "Iranian National History" (Cambridge, 1983, 359–477). All of these papers have in common that their authors vigorously speak up for often diametrically opposed positions, the most extreme illustration of this phenomenon certainly being that of the recent argument between Gherardo Gnoli[7] and Jean Kellens[8] on the historicity of the person of Zoroaster: while the latter altogether rejects the historic character of a real Zoroaster, the former, taking up an earlier suggestion of Henning's, considers the precise traditional date provided by the *Bundahišn* and other sources (Masʿudi, Biruni, etc.) that placed Zoroaster 258 years before Alexander to be an "immutable quantity".[9]

As we all know, Iranian pre-Islamic historiography suffers greatly from the qualitative and quantitative paucity of the sources. Since the historian does not, unfortunately, have a choice of sources, it is thus of the utmost importance that he questions them in the right way, since the sources can of course only reveal the answers they contain. Rigour in method and a precise terminology are therefore absolutely indispensable, and in this respect, it is really astounding how little attention has been paid up to now to the consequences of the introduction of writing into social life at all levels of Iranian society. Historians of other ancient civilisations have long recognized that the transition from an oral to a literate society did not take place at once, but that it was the result of a long and slow development. Even after the introduction of writing and script, an oral society continues to function as such for several centuries before literacy spreads on a wider scale. Facts and other pieces of information are not transmitted in the same way in oral and literate (or semi-literate) societies. For this reason, it is highly relevant to find out in what circumstances data were transmitted. It should be kept in mind that the term "oral tradition" encompasses both the transmission process — of foremost concern for sociologists, linguists and folklorists — and its end products,[10] which are mainly of three kinds:[11] the first category of sources can be defined as "oral literature" (either in prose or in verse) and includes popular songs and epics, religious hymns, panegyrics, etc. The two other categories comprise personal memories and oral history. Ethnologists collect personal memories from contemporaneous auricular or ocular witnesses and are of no concern to us here. In the second part of the present paper, our interest will turn to oral history, which is to be considered as verbal (spoken or sung) messages testifying of the past and produced by people belonging to a generation anterior to the present one.[12]

Given the scantiness of reliable and historically relevant sources for Ancient Iran, it seems highly useful to compare the Iranian situation with that of other extinct societies similarly involved in the transition process from orality to literacy. For example the Greco-Roman world in its earliest stages (according to recent estimations, the degree of literacy among the masculine population in Athens of the fifth–fourth centuries BCE would not have exceeded 10 % and there are reasons to believe that the situation would have been very similar in second-century BCE Rome);[13] or medieval Europe around the thirteenth century (which saw the beginnings of historical literature, although history was not yet taught in the first European universities and there was no other historical genre than that of universal chronicles and hagiographies), as well as that of contemporaneous African societies examined in the recent past by anthropologists and cultural historians. In this respect, we should all be alarmed by the following statement by Moses I. Finley (1912–1986), one of the best social historians of Ancient Greece and one of the finest methodologists of his time. In an important book, published one year before his death, he wrote: "Few anthropologists view the invariable oral traditions of the people they study with the faith shown by many ancient historians".[14] The passage continues: "The verbal transmittal over many generations of detailed information about past events or institutions that are no longer essential or even meaningful in contemporary life invariably entails considerable and irrecoverable losses of data, or conflation of data, manipulation and invention, sometimes without visible reason, often for reasons that are perfectly intelligible. With the passage of time, it becomes absolutely impossible to control anything that has been transmitted when there is nothing in writing against which to match statements about the past. Again we suspect the presence of the unexpressed view that the traditions of Greeks and Romans are somehow privileged, though no one has yet demonstrated a plausible mechanism for the oral transmission of accurate information over a period of centuries (e.g. from archaic Greece to Pausanias in the second century CE, or from the Rome of the kings to Livy and Dionysius of Halicarnassus in the late first century BCE). After all, it was in an era of literacy that the Roman nobility successfully paraded fraudulent genealogies at the end of the Republic, or that Tacitus, Suetonius, and Dio Cassius, all of whom had access to contemporary writing, confused the account of the great fire in Rome in 64 CE so effectively that no one has been able to unscramble it satisfactorily".[15]

*****

That Iranian society in its earliest stages was an oral society becomes obvious when we take a closer look at the vocabulary in the oldest languages of Old and Middle Iranian, even if one needs to keep in mind that the text corpus still available is often small. Of course, no one would expect a word for "writing" in Avestan, but it remains striking that the language contains so many different verbs and nouns related to "memory", both in Old and Young Avestan — the same holds good for the Middle Iranian languages — (e.g. Y. Av. [2]*drang-* "to learn by heart, to recite (prayers) in murmuring" [*AirWb*. 772f.], O. Av. *mand-* "[1]to memorize; [2]to remember" [*AirWb*. 1136], to quote but two examples among many). Numerous words also bear relation to the different ways of reciting the prayers, either silently/in murmuring, as in Y. Av. *fra-maraθra-* (*AirWb*. 987), or on the contrary, aloud, as in Y. Av. *fra-sraoθra-* and *fra-sraošiia-* (*AirWb*. 1003f.). Finally, the study of the sacred texts was clearly based on the *hearing* of spoken texts rather than on their reading,[16] as in Y. Av. *aiβiiåŋhā-* (*AirWb*. 99) and its opposite *anaiβišti-* (*AirWb*. 117f., in spite of Bartholomae's erroneous translation "failure to read"), or in Y. Av. *naskō.frasa-*, meaning "related to the study of the *nask*s (i.e. the books of the Avesta)" (*AirWb*. 1060), which shows that the study of texts was obviously to be understood as a "questioning" of recited texts that the student had been listening to (O./Y. Av. *fras-* "to ask, examine, question" [*AirWb*. 997ff.]; to this one should compare OP *pati-pᵣsa-* "[1]to question (thoroughly); [2]to read (used both in the sense of German "(still) lesen" as well as "(laut) vorlesen", all of which is continued in inscr. MP *ptpwls't* /pahipursād/ "to read (silently)"— with variants — and man. MP *phypwrs-* /pahipurs-/ "to read aloud"). Even more surprising is the fact that Old Persian does not have a proper word for "inscription", which it needs to borrow from Elam. *tup-pi* (OP *dipī*; in Bactrian, the same word λιβο takes the sense of "document, copy"). More striking yet is the fact that the consonantal group -*št-* in the past participle *nipišta-* of the verb OP *nipaiθ-* "to engrave, write upon" indicates that the term was borrowed from the Medes; the same verb later lives on in man. MP *nbys-* /nibēs-/ "to write",[17] BPahl. *npštn'*, inscr. MP *npštny* /nibištan, nibēs-/ "to write" (*CPD* 59), and its many derivative nouns.

As a matter of fact, Iranians remained very sceptical about writing until the Islamic period and they demonstrated the same ambiguity in this matter as Plato in the fourth century BCE with his critical attitude towards writing in his

Phaedrus (275c–279b) or in the seventh *Letter*, even though all of his philosophical work was written down, unlike that of his master Socrates. No doubt this should be seen as a perceptible sign of a semi-literate society on its way to a higher level of literacy. Only thus can it be explained that the Mazdaeans of the first post-Sasanian centuries attribute the writing down of the *Avesta* to Zoroaster, as is the case in the *Šahrestānīhā ī Ērān* (*ŠĒ*) 4, a geographical work written in the eighth or ninth century (there exist of course other variants of the same legend): "Then Zoroaster brought the Religion. By the order of King Wištāsp 1200 chapters in the script of religious scripture were engraved [MP *kand*] on golden tablets and written [MP *nibišt*] and deposited in the treasury of that fire [i.e. the fire Bahram in Samarkand]". In the fifth book of the *Dēnkard* (V 3, 4 = *DkM* 437.18), another ninth-century work, the writing of the *Avesta* (and of Zand) was attributed to Jāmāsp, "according to the instructions of Zoroaster" (MP *az ān ī Zardušt hammōg*). On the other hand, the apocalyptic book *Ardā Wīrāz Nāmag*, a work hard to date but whose origins no doubt go back to the period of Khusrau I in the sixth century and with an even older core quite close to the inscriptions of the early Sasanian high priest Kirder in the third century, does not explicitly attribute the writing down of the *Avesta* to Zoroaster. This discrepancy between late Sasanian and early post-Sasanian writings might just be an indication that Iranian society had undergone a change at that time and that it was henceforth quite tempting to ascribe the introduction of writing to Zoroaster himself. After the arrival of Islam and yet another Religion of the Book, Mazdaean priests may just have felt the need to affirm the great age of a written *Avesta*. And how could they have done better than by attributing its redaction to Zoroaster or, even better, to his disciples, in order to keep Zoroaster out of the matter. At any rate, the perspicuous manoeuvre seems hardly to have impressed the Muslims, since they simply did not consider the Mazdaeans to be a "people of the Book".[18]

On the other hand, the Mazdaeans seem not to have had an extraordinary faith in the written word and attribute a superior rank to memorised texts, as can be learned from *Dēnkard* V 24, 13 (= *DkM* 459.8ff.): "the legitimacy of oral tradition [MP *wāz-gōwišnīh*] is thus in many respects greater [MP *wasīhā*] than that of writing [MP *nibēsišnīg*]. And it is logical, for many other reasons as well, to consider the living and oral Word as more essential [MP *mādagwartar*] than the written one". In the same spirit, the first of the *Letters of Manuščihr* 1.4.11 praises the *dastwar* "who most resembles Zoroaster" [MP *zardušttom*, Av. *zaraθuštrō.təma-*] having learnt by heart all of the *Avesta* and Zand". Even Khusrau's page in the Middle Persian work of the same name (par. 9) is proud of "having memorized [MP *warm kerd*] the *Yašt*, the *Hādōxt (Nask)*, the *Yasna* and the *Wīdēwdād* like a *herbed* and of having listened [MP *niyōšīd*] to the Zand, passage by passage". It is therefore not surprising that bad memory was severely punished (*Ṣad-dar naθr* 28). Several Arabic authors, as well as Mazdaean tradition itself (in particular, *Aogəmadaēčā* par. 92 and *Dādestān ī Mēnōg ī Xrad* chap. 27, 23) mention the introduction of seven writing systems by the mythical king Taxmōrub (Av. Taxma Urupi). As was already pointed out by Henning,[19] it is no doubt futile to try to identify each of these writing systems with one of the known variants of the Pahlavi script, but there are indeed good chances that the so-called *dēn-dibīrīh* (*ŠĒ* 3) might well be identical to the Avestan script. Following a suggestion by Werner Sundermann,[20] there are good reasons to believe that the Mazdaeans would have wanted to claim the introduction of all known script variants in the Sasanian Empire for their own community.

*****

As far as the Avestan script is concerned, we know better today: its extreme phonetic exactness (with 53 signs for 16 vowels and 37 consonants) surely indicates that it was an erudite and deliberate ad hoc invention,[21] in order to preserve the text as precisely as possible in its pronunciation at the time of the creation of the script. In recent times, two detailed studies by Jean Kellens[22] and Alberto Cantera[23] have been dealing with the matter of the invention of the Avestan script and of the writing down of the *Avesta* in the form as we know it from the *Dēnkard* (which, on the one hand, is surely only a small part of the original *Avesta* orally transmitted over many centuries, and on the other hand, included at least a partial Middle Persian version). Both scholars agree, as would — I think — most colleagues nowadays, that Karl Hoffmann in his book on the Sasanian archetype[24] proposed an analysis of the question that is in many ways decisive and final. Among other things, Hoffmann established that thirteen of the signs in the Avestan script (*a, i, k, x ͮ, t, p, b, n, m, r, s, z, š*) were borrowed from the cursive Pahlavi script with the same phonemic values, and five more signs (*ā, e, ē, o, ō*) were in one way or another "inspired" by the cursive script. On this basis, he concluded that the signs could only have been borrowed once the Pahlavi cursive had reached its final forms and characteristics. He believed that this last stage of development was attained as early as the late fourth or early fifth century CE; his assumption was based on the evidence of a Christian epitaph on a sarcophagus discovered on a site in Istanbul and which the first editor of the inscription[25] had wrongly dated before 430 CE on false archaeological premises. On the further — actually baseless and purely gratuitous — prejudice that the creation of a new script could only have taken place during the peaceful period of a long reign, Hoffmann concluded that the canonised *Avesta* must have been written down during the reign of Shapur II (309–379 CE). Thanks to the convincing demonstration by François De Blois[26] on the basis of evidence regarding the language, contents and orthography of the inscription, we now know the Istanbul epitaph to be dated rather to the ninth or tenth century CE.

Hoffmann's dating of the creation of the Avestan script thus needs revision: for Kellens, "in the actual state of our documentation",[27] the first irrefutable evidence for the Pahlavi cursive in its final shape is to be found in the Pahlavi papyri related to the brief Sasanian occupation in Egypt from 619–629. He therefore believes that the Avestan script was at best created during the final years of the reign of Khusrau II (590–629 CE), if not simply in post-Sasanian times (after 651 CE).[28] I agree with Cantera that Kellens's position is too sceptical and that it must be refined. Before I come to my own arguments, which differ from Cantera's (though with similar results), I will briefly summarize Cantera's conclusions: after a thorough examination[29] of all the scattered pieces of information on the transmission and writing down of the *Avesta* in Pahlavi literature for the pre-Sasanian period, the third century CE, the fourth century CE, and the fifth and sixth centuries CE, Cantera concludes that most passages, with very few exceptions (such as the information on a Sogdian tradition of the *Avesta*), related to the pre-Sasanian period are unreliable, either because of their entirely fantastic character or because they show anachronistic features and lead to an incorrect dating of the writing down of the *Avesta*. The information from Sasanian times, especially of later Sasanian times, is all in all far more trustworthy, even though it contains many discrepancies and inconsistencies. None of our Pahlavi sources mentions a precise date for the writing down of the *Avesta*, but the *Zand ī Wahman Yasn* 2.1–4 gives a detailed account of a council against Mazdak (presumably in 528/529), in which a certain Wehšābuhr played an important role; the first of the letters of Manuščihr says that the *Avesta* was divided into twenty-one nasks at the time of Khusrau I; and the fourth book of the *Dēnkard* seems to suggest that a canonical Pahlavi translation of the *Avesta* was established during his reign. Cantera's final conclusion is very careful and balanced: "We cannot tell much on the creation of the Avestan script and the writing down of the Sasanian archetype, since on the one hand the Pahlavi sources are mute on this matter and since on the other hand there is a total lack of material for a palaeographic examination between the fourth and seventh centuries CE. Both the Book Pahlavi and the script of the Psalter reached their final stages of development at some point between the fifth and seventh centuries (the fourth century seems far less likely, but there is no sure evidence against such a date). All in all, the Avestan script may have been invented at some point between the fifth and seventh centuries that cannot be nearer determined".[30]

As far as I am concerned, I subscribe to this hypothesis for the most part, and yet I believe that there are strong indications, though admittedly no hard evidence, that the Avestan script might have been invented during the reign of Khusrau I (CE 531–579). What exactly do we know about the characteristics of Pahlavi cursive script during the Sasanian period? At the lower end, we know for sure that the cursive had reached its final features by the seventh century: this is shown not only by the previously mentioned Pahlavi papyri related to the brief Sasanian occupation in Egypt, but also by several epitaphs in the province of Fārs, written in a script palaeographically close to Book Pahlavi. At the higher end, we do not know much about what cursive script really looked like in the third century, but we do have two small Middle Persian parchment fragments from the synagogue in Doura-Europos. One is too small from which to draw any reliable conclusions, but the other one (with a text written on both recto and verso) contains a few lines of a badly damaged letter.[31] In spite of its fragmentary state, enough remains to deduce that the letters have not yet reached their final shape, but some of them come quite close to it; the handwriting is fluid and there is a clear tendency for linking letters with one another. Even if one leaves out the so-called "Letter of Tansar" (the date of which is disputed), there are further (indirect) indications for the existence of a cursïve Pahlavi script in the early third century, for example when the high priest Kirder in his inscriptions speaks of many "documents, charters and records" (MP *gitt, pādixšīr ud mādayān*) that were written in his time.[32] Furthermore, in my edition of the Shapur inscription on the Kaʿba-i Zardusht, I already presumed that a number of mistakes in the Middle Persian version, especially in the spelling of foreign (Roman and other) names, seem only explicable if we assume that they were the result of a misreading of a manuscript written in a script relatively close to Book Pahlavi.[33] What else do we know about the cursive script for the period in between the higher and lower ends of the Sasanian period? From the inscription of Mihr-Narseh at Fīrūzābād, datable to the fifth century, and a few other inscriptions (attributed with less certainty to the fifth century), we know that its script differs little from the monumental style used in third- and fourth-century inscriptions. The script of the sixth century is known as well, thanks to the inscriptions from Darbend: they can be dated with precision to the mid-sixth century, since they are all related to the reinforcement and reconstruction works of the Sasanian fortifications in the Caucasus against the invaders from the north at the time of Khusrau I. Their style is much closer to the cursive Pahlavi script. The inscriptions thus seem to suggest that there was a change somewhere around the turning of the fifth to the sixth century.[34]

This hypothesis is corroborated by yet another piece of evidence. As Karl Hoffmann has also shown, at least one sign of the Avestan alphabet (δ) was borrowed from an alphabet as it was used in the Pahlavi Psalter fragment from Bulayïq. The manuscript itself, containing a Middle Persian translation of the Psalms of David, can probably be dated to the seventh century, since the accentuation system that was used both in it and in the Syriac fragments found alongside, did not come into vogue in Syriac manuscripts before that time.[35] Carl Friedrich Andreas[36] has already pointed out that the manuscript can not be dated before the sixth century, since it contains references to canons attributed to Mār Abhā, the head of the Syriac church from 540–552 CE. On the other hand, the Middle Persian translation of the Syriac original contains a number of archaic forms that seem to suggest that it was much older. In a monograph on the final *yōd* in Middle Persian inscriptions,[37] I have tried to show that the otiose stroke at the end of many words in Book Pahlavi is palaeographically issued from this mute sign of the third-century inscriptions, but with a change of function over the centuries. While the writing or non-writing of the sign (surely a remnant of the gen. sg. and maybe also of other cases of the *a*-declension) was governed by a rhythmic law in the inscriptions from the early Sasanian period, the final stroke of Book Pahlavi is only written after letters that cannot be linked to the left, in order to mark unambiguously the end of a word.[38] In the inscriptions, the transition from one system to another can be observed around the turn of the fourth to the fifth century, and the reason why I mention this, is that the Pahlavi Psalter fragment also occupies an intermediate position between the two systems.[39] From a palaeographical point of view, the final sign is a clear *yōd* (with its characteristic semi-circular form), not a simple stroke, and in most cases, its writing still follows the rules of Rhythmic Law in the third-century inscriptions, with two notable exceptions: the final *yōd* is almost systematically written in past participles and there is a new tendency for writing *yōd* in polysyllables with a long vowel in the final syllable, which end in one of the six signs that cannot be linked to the left. Summing up the palaeographic and linguistic evidence, we may safely conclude that the alphabet of the Pahlavi Psalter had reached its final form by the middle of the sixth century and that it surely already existed in the fifth century.[40] The fourth century seems unlikely for the origin of the Psalter alphabet: though it cannot definitely be excluded from a linguistic and palaeographic point of view, the persecutions of the Christians, especially of the clergy (much less so of the ordinary believers), during the long reign of Shapur II (309–379) after the conversion of the Roman emperor Constantine, make it less plausible.

The combined evidence of the borrowing of a number of signs from Book Pahlavi and the Pahlavi Psalter into the Avestan script would thus seem to narrow the time margin for the creation of the new alphabet to the fifth and sixth centuries, with a clear preference for the latter date. What then could have moved the Mazdaean mowbeds to give up a century-old tradition of oral transmission of the Avestan and to replace it with a written text? It cannot simply have been the wish to possess a written corpus of sacred texts like the Jews, Christians and Manichaeans and become a "People of the Book", since such a wish could have manifested itself at any moment during the Sasanian period, whatever the conditions for the Mazdaean community. Something surely must have happened in the sixth century: if it was not a particular event, then at least the general climate must have changed at such a point that the priests suddenly felt the urgent need to write things down. In the third century, there were no outer compelling circumstances: admittedly, Mānī had written down a summary of his own ideas in his *Šābuhragān*, his only work in Middle Persian, but the Manichaean and Christian missionary movements on Iranian soil had not yet taken the weight they would have two centuries later. I presume that writing down was mainly carried out for the purpose of facilitating reading the work aloud (suffice it to say that the script is close to the actual pronunciation of the Middle Persian language in the third century) and much less the silent lecture in solitude; the fact that Mānī used his own alphabet, rather than the Pahlavi cursive, was by no means fortuitous and will certainly not have pleased the mowbeds. By the fourth and fifth centuries the situation had changed, but remained comfortable for the Mazdaeans. Christianity and Nestorianism (after the separation of their western co-religionists in 484), as well as Manichaeism certainly enjoyed an ever-increasing influence in Iran, but

the systematic persecutions of the Christian clergy from the reign of Shapur II
(309–379) onwards until — with intervals — the reign of Pērōz (459–484) and
the mutual denunciations of Christians and Manichaeans (equally persecuted
during Shapur's reign) only strengthened the position of the Mazdaeans. The
Babylonian Jews for their part had largely escaped the persecutions at the time
of Shapur II since they had preferred to adapt a neutral attitude with regard to
the Sasanian rulers, but in the fifth century they too suffered from persecutions
at the time of Yazdgird II (439–457) and Pērōz (459–484).

This advantageous quietude for the Mazdaeans came to an end with
Khusrau I (531–579): in his open-mindedness with regard to religious and
metaphysical questions, this ruler invited to the Sasanian court a number of
Western philosophers after the closure of their school in Athens in 529.[41] He
furthermore accorded liberty of cult to the Christians in the context of a
renewed peace with Byzantium in 561, and in the face of the anti-Manichaean
legislation of the Roman emperors Justin and Justinian he showed pragmatic
clemency towards the Manichaeans. It is presumably only with the loss of
influence of the Mazdaean priests on Sasanian politics that the permanent
rivalry with Manichaeans, Christians and Jews made them realize that they no
longer occupied privileged rank among the religious authorities and that the
absence of written sacred texts put them in an inferior position. Moreover, the
yearning for a return to the orthodox faith after the Mazdakite rebellion may
also have accelerated the writing of the *Avesta* and its translation, in order to
avoid future conflicts. Rather than as an innovative step, the writing down
should therefore probably be considered as a conservative act to "freeze" the
tradition and save it from further deterioration.

I would like to emphasise that, starting from linguistic and palaeographic
premises I am only trying to say that it is tempting from a historical point of
view to place the writing down of the *Avesta* in Khusrau's reign (as Henning,
Bailey and many others did for other reasons). It is during his reign that
literature began to flourish and the fictive page in the well-known text on
"Xusrō and his page" (XR 8–10) showed that young priests at that time were
not only trained in memorising and reciting the nasks, but also in the skill of
accurate and quick writing (MP *xūb nibēg ud ray nibēg*).[42]

*****

A more widespread use of writing also has a serious influence on the way
people see their own history. Memory does not play the same role in an oral
society as in a written society. As long as writing remained the privilege of a
minority of priests and scribes at the service of the ruling class, the art of
singing and storytelling flourished. Evidence of singers and bards who praise
the kings of old can be found as early as Median and Achaemenid times (cf.
Hdt. I 95; Xen., *Cyrop.* I 2, 1; Athen. quoting from Dinon's *Persika* XIV 633d–
e). From Parthian times, we know the case of the *gōsān*, so thoroughly
examined by Mary Boyce.[43] The word is attested only once in Parthian in a
Manichaean fragment that cannot be dated, but the correct use of grammar

would seem to suggest a date in the fourth or fifth century. It is very interesting in that it gives us a kind of definition of what his function was: *cw'gwn gws'n ky hsyng'n šhrd'r'n 'wd kw'n hwnr wyfr'syd 'wd wxd 'ywyc ny kyrd* /čawāgōn gōsān kē hasēnagān šahrdārān ud kawān hunar wifrāsēd ud xwad ēwiž nē karēd/ "like a *gōsān*, who instructs of the virtue of kings and heroes of old and does not realize anything himself".[44] In other words, he was a singer like the medieval ambulant minstrels, rather than a poet-composer like the troubadours. Similarly, the *rāmišgar* (litt. "merrymaker, one who procures pleasure") and *huniyāgar* of the Sasanian courts (the latter term is again attested in XR 60) were in the first place entertainers and musicians, i.e. performers and not composers. After the arrival of Islam, their art lost much of its popularity, because it no longer met the taste and expectations of the public, who now preferred to read poetry rather than to hear it. If Middle Persian did not have a word for the poet-composer, it might simply mean that the practice was not widespread.

Throughout Iranian pre-Islamic history, we find numerous references to or other material evidence for the existence of archives, although very few texts refer to the existence of *royal* archives. I leave aside here allusions to the Achaemenid archives, which constitute a problem of their own, and would like to take a closer look at the archives mentioned by the Byzantine historian Agathias on three occasions when he speaks of the "royal parchments" (II 27, 8 βασιλικαὶ διφθέραι), the "Persian books" (IV 30, 2 Περσικοὶ βίβλοι) and the "royal annals" (IV 30, 3 βασιλικὰ ἀπομνημονεύματα). Agathias claims to have had indirect access to them by way of his Syrian interpreter Sergius. The interpretation of Agathias' words on the royal archives varies widely: while Pierre Briant[45] considers them to be nothing but a literary *topos* and is extremely sceptical about their very existence, Averil Cameron[46] (and others) believe that Agathias' writings were based on real documents, sometimes completed with information from other sources and occasionally abridged from a longer story. According to Agathias "when Sergius the interpreter went there he asked the officials in charge of the Royal Annals to give him access to the records (for I had often urged him to do this). He added his reason — that his sole purpose in wanting this was so that their affairs could be recorded by us also and become known and honoured. They agreed at once — rightly — thinking the idea a good one. It would actually bring credit to their kings they thought, if the Romans too knew what they were like and how many they were, and how the succession of their dynasty had been preserved. So Sergius extracted the names, the chronology and the most important happenings in their time (λαβὼν ... τά τε ὀνόματα καὶ τοὺς χρόνους καὶ τῶν ἐπ' αὐτοῖς γεγενημένων τὰ καιριώτερα), and translated all this most skilfully into Greek" (IV 30, 4). Agathias would seem to suggest that Sergius abbreviated the material himself from a fuller account. But was that really so? I can see no particular reason why the documents of the Sasanian royal archives pertaining to the "history" of the dynasty would not have contained exactly that, namely the names of the Sasanian kings in the right chronological order, with the dates of their respective reigns and a reference to some key events. Nothing more and nothing less. Apart from that, they may well have contained notes taken by the private scribes of the reigning king (for whom we find occasional references in literature), or duplicates of the official royal correspondence, or copies of the kind of "documents, charters and records" mentioned above in the inscriptions of the high priest Kirder (peace treaties, etc.).

Before examining this assumption, it should be remembered that Agathias (c. 536–c. 581) was contemporary with Khusrau I (531–579). With his *Histories* his aim was to continue the work of Procopius, which had covered the previous period of Justinian's reign up to 552. Taking up the story, Agathias gives a very detailed account of the years 552/3–558/9 and interrupts it at some point for a "complete chronological report" (IV 25,1–30, 2) of the Sasanian rulers up to his time, and according to his own words, his own report on the time immediately preceding the reign of Kavad (488–496; 499–531) is to be preferred to that of Procopius, whenever it differs, since his is founded on the Persian chroniclers (IV 30, 5 τοῖς Περσικοῖς χρονογράφοις). Agathias' account can be divided in two parts: the first one (IV 24,1 – 26,2) goes from Ardashir I (226–240) to Bahram IV (388–399) and covers almost 175 years and the reigns of twelve kings. The second part (IV 26,3 – 29,5) deals with the period from Yazdgird I (399–421) up to Khusrau I succeeding his father Kavad in 531, i.e. a period of 230 years for eight kings. Even though the second part seems hardly more detailed, the difference between the two parts is not insignificant: the order in which the kings appear is correct and the dates for their reigns are "precise" (which is not necessarily synonymous with "exact"), in the sense that they give the number of years, months, and sometimes even days. This holds true for the entire list from Ardashir I up to Khusrau. However, the account of the crucial facts for their reigns is totally different: of Ardashir I (226–240), Agathias knows nothing else but his legendary ancestry; of his son Shapur I (240–272), he only knows that he did much harm to the Romans and he knows the name of Odainath of Palmyra; up to Shapur II (309–379), he knows nothing more than that Bahram III, who reigned for four months in 293, bore the title of Segānšāh "for a special reason, in accordance with an old traditional custom" (IV 24, 6). Of the long reign of Shapur II, all he knows is a legend on his birth and he has heard of Shapur's captivity during a war with the Romans, an event he does not develop any further since all this "has been recorded already by many earlier historians" (IV 25, 8). The reader has to wait until the account on the reign of Yazdgird I (399–421) to get some more details, but these are not necessarily more reliable. It is not until the reign of Kavad I (488–496; 499–531), interrupted by a brief episode under Jāmāsp (496–498) that we learn things beyond the domain of legend.

At this point, I would like to interrupt my demonstration for a digression on the style of Agathias in the *Annals* of the historian Tabari (born in 839 in Āmul in the province of Tabaristān, died in Bagdad in 923). As a historian, Tabari cannot be judged according to modern criteria, but there is no doubt that his work outclasses that of his predecessors and contemporaries in his effort to separate the legendary from the real. His superiority can easily be measured if one compares the original with the abridged translation of it made by Abū ʿAlī Balʿamī later on in the tenth century. Wherever the latter furnishes details not be found in the work of the former, he turns to the legendary. Without going into details, it must be said that the dates for the reigns given by both Agathias and Tabari are close, though not identical, and at least more realistic than the totally erroneous numbers given by oral tradition as we find it with the Armenian authors or in the *Shahnama*. If one compares the factual details given by Tabari with those given by Agathias, it is quite striking that we find the same scheme. Not much information is given for the Sasanian rulers of the first centuries: Shapur I is called Sābūr al-Junūd "Šābuhr of the armies",[47] which is of course reminiscent of his campaigns against the Romans. His reign is discussed at length,[48] but many details are legendary and there are few hard facts. The discussion on the following rulers is extremely summary and hardly exceeds a few lines;[49] the only detail on Bahram III is moreover exactly the same as was given by Agathias, namely on the title Seganšāh. Concerning Shapur II, Tabari dishes up a fantastic story on the king having disguised himself in order to remain unseen when intruding into the Roman camp.[50] He also speaks of his capture.[51] The details on Yazdgird do not inspire any more confidence.[52] It is only from Kavad/Qobād I onward that the report gets more developed, and we obtain some rare historical information on Mazdak, the conflict with the Hephtalites and Jāmāsp's interregnum.[53] The reign of Khusrau Anūšarwān/ Khusrau I is described in great detail, interrupted on two occasions by long digressions on Yemen and the Arabs.[54] The same abundance of details is encountered for the reigns of the last kings of the Sasanian dynasty.[55]

Surely it is not mere chance that we find the same division in the works of the two historians. It obviously reflects the same state of knowledge: up to the middle of the fifth century, historical awareness of the Sasanians is mostly limited to the simple names and dates of the reigning years of the kings. It is no mere chance either that that period coincides with a radical change of Sasanian royal titles in coin legends. The usual title of "X, the Mazdaean lord, king of kings of Ērān and non-Ērān, of the race of the gods" was slightly modified under Yazdgird I (399–421) and underwent more radical changes from Yazdgird II (439–457) onwards, when the word *kdy* "Kayanid" made its first appearance. It seems likely that the Sasanians started collecting legends of old, transmitted over many centuries by singers (MP *gōsanān*) and collective memory, in order to establish a canon which finally led to a first written redaction, perhaps under Khusrau I, with a number of important additions and revisions under Khusrau II (590–628, e.g. when the name of Egypt was added in the description of the Sasanian realm, which can only apply to a brief period under Khusrau) and Yazdgird III (633–651). This new book would become known under the title *xwadāynāmag* "Book of the Lords". A *written* redaction of such a record can only be imagined at a time when literacy was more widespread. Writing was far from generalized, but clearly the upper social classes had mastered reading. It is writing that allows people to think over their own remote past and to get interested in it. By and by, different kinds of collective memory (popular, sacerdotal, heroic) merged with royal tradition. By the first centuries after the arrival of Islam, written history with a different way of thinking had replaced the art of the minstrels. Plato had already recognized it: writing is only a remedy (φάρμακον), not of memory (μνήμης), but of reminiscence (ὑπομνήσεως).

*****

As I mentioned in the first part of my paper when speaking of the creation of the Avestan alphabet, one of the main features of an oral society on its way to (generalised) literacy is a clear tendency to preserve of what remains of the old tradition. A second particularity is its homeostatic character,[56] which means that such a society is constantly trying to find an equilibrium by eliminating the recollection of past events unless they still have a direct bearing on the present. The curiosity of the past for curiosity alone, without a direct link to the present, is considered to be vain in oral societies. This is what explains the "structural amnesia" Ehsan Yarshater spoke about a quarter of a century ago. Since the process of adapting the past to the present (and therefore to people's expectations) is a continuous development, anthropologists speak of "dynamic homeostasis".[57] This phenomenon may, for example, help to explain why in certain cultures divinities disappear from the pantheon once they have accomplished their function. It also explains the changes royal genealogies undergo in the course of time: remote generations are described with a wealth of details, but none of them is of historical value and everything remains in the sphere of myth or legend; intermediate generations are hardly remembered (anthropologists speak of a "floating gap"[58]); and only for the three or four most recent generations is there a real historical knowledge. The overall phenomenon is sometimes described as the "hourglass effect":[59] transposed to the level of Sasanian history, it makes one understand the above-mentioned similarities between the accounts of Agathias and Tabari. Transposed to the level of pre-Islamic Iranian history, it helps one understand why nothing more remains of the Achaemenids except some vague recollection of a few names, or why the Arsacids have disappeared altogether from the xwādaynāmag (and later from the Shahnama). Of course, the early Sasanians were able to learn of their own past thanks to the Roman historians, and later on through Jewish tradition, but I am quite sure they never used it and neither did they ever claim themselves to be heirs of the Achaemenids. The alleged Sasanian claim of former Achaemenid territories is almost certainly an *interpretatio romana* (to borrow a term used by Erich Kettenhofen[60]). As I have tried to show elsewhere,[61] the Romans had always been aware of the Achaemenid descent of the Sasanians: as late as the third century CE, the Roman emperor Gordianus, before breaking up for war against Shapur I, organised games in honour of Athena Promachos, the same goddess the Athenians had made offerings to in the early fifth century BCE after their victory over the unlucky Xerxes. And if Kayanid names and elements appear in the Sasanian royal titles of the fifth century CE, they do not show up out of nowhere because of an inexplicable sudden longing of the two Yazdgirds to break with existing traditions. There was no abrupt recollection of past Kayanid values — a development entirely incompatible with the dynamics of oral societies. It can only mean that Kayanid legends had already been present for a very long time in the south-western parts of Iran.

Notes:

1. Many of the topics only briefly touched upon in the present paper have been dealt with at far greater length in a chapter entitled "Histoire orale et écrite en Iran ancien entre mémoire et oubli" of my as yet unpublished *thèse d'habilitation* (Paris, 2003). The oral character of my presentation at the London Symposium has been maintained here, but it is my intention to publish the complete material in due time in a revised and extended monograph.
2. Derakhshani 1995; Gnoli 2000.
3. Daryaee 1995; 2001–2002.
4. Shahbazi 2001; Huyse 2002 (with a summary of earlier literature).
5. Huyse 1999 [2002].
6. Cereti, forthcoming. Cf. also Kellens 1998: 482f. and Cantera 2004: 106–163, esp. 135–162.
7. Gnoli 2000.
8. Kellens 2001; 2006.
9. Gnoli 2000: 144 and 149.
10. Cf. Vansina 1985: 3.
11. Cf. Finnegan 1970.
12. *Ibid.* 27.
13. Cf. Thomas 1989: 15–34.
14. Finley 1985: 16.
15. *Ibid.* 16f.
16. As is clearly shown in the passage from the *Herbedestān* 16.1f. (14): "(A man) who has ears that cannot hear (*asruṯ.gaošō*) or who cannot speak (*afrauuaocō*) (and therefore) has never studied (*aiβiiā(i)š*) a single phrase (of a holy text), (such a man) then does not make himself guilty by not studying".
17. Boyce 1977: 61.
18. Cf. Bailey 1943: 169.
19. Henning 1958: 72 n. 1.
20. Sundermann 1985: 112f.
21. Cf. Kellens 1998: 482.
22. Kellens 1998.
23. Cantera 2004: 106–163 (chap. III: "Die Überlieferung des Avesta und dessen schriftliche Fixierung").
24. Hoffmann and Narten 1989.
25. De Menasce 1967: 60.
26. De Blois 1990.
27. Kellens 1998: 483.
28. This view was recently repeated in Kellens 2006: 24f.
29. Cantera 2004: 135–162.
30. Cantera 2004: 163.
31. Cf. Geiger 1956: 154* with table LXX 2, 4.
32. Cf. Huyse 1998: 114–116 for the details.
33. Cf. Huyse 1999 [2002]; 9, 27, 34, 49, 58, 63.
34. Seal and a fortiori datable coin legends also corroborate the idea that cursive script was used as early as the fifth century, but it is not before the sixth century that we find a more systematic practice when it had completely replaced the lapidary script; this argument is elaborated with much detail in Cereti, forthcoming.
35. This was pointed out by K. Barr in Andreas and Barr 1933: 94.

36. Andreas 1910: 870.
37. Huyse 2003a.
38. This was discovered by Belardi 1986: 18.
39. Cf. Huyse 2003b: 62–65.
40. Andreas 1910: 870f. had dated the first translation to the time between the Synod of Seleucia in 410 and the death of Yazdgird I in 421, since this was a short, but very propitious period for the Christians in the Sasanian Empire.
41. Cf. Hartmann 2002.
42. One might also add here that when Tabari writes three centuries later about the period of Bahrām Jūr, i.e. Wahrām Gōr (421–439), he lets the king ask for "erudite educators, well trained in the methods of teaching, who can instruct me in the art of writing, archery and the knowledge of the law" (transl. Bosworth 1999: 83). Needless to say, however, this remark is more instructive of Tabari's lifetime than of Wahr"m G.r's.
43. Boyce 1957 (and 2002).
44. Boyce 1957: 11 and 2002: 167b.
45. Briant 2003a: 775 and 2003b: 579.
46. Cameron 1969–70: 112–119 (esp. 115).
47. Transl. Bosworth 1999: 23.
48. *Ibid.* 23–39.
49. The reign of Bahram I is dealt with in three lines only (in the translation of Bosworth 1999: 43), that of Bahram II covers a third of a page (*ibid.* 46), and both that of Bahram III (*ibid.* 47) and Narsē/Narseh (*ibid.* 48) a quarter of a page.
50. *Ibid.* 60.
51. *Ibid.* 50–66.
52. *Ibid.* 70–74.
53. *Ibid.* 128–139.
54. *Ibid.* 146–162; 252–267; 285–294.
55. *Ibid.* 295–411.
56. Ong 1982: 46–49.
57. Vansina 1985: 120.
58. Vansina 1985: 23f.
59. Vansina 1985: 169; Thomas 1989: 158.
60. Kettenhofen 1984.
61. Huyse 2002.

Abbreviations

A.M.	Ammianus Marcellinus
AASH	*Acta Antiqua Academiae Scientiarum Hungaricae*
Afo	*Archiv für Orientforschung*
AIr	*Acta Iranica*
AirWb	Bartholomae 1904.
AJA	*American Journal of Archaeology*
AMI (T)	*Archäologische Mitteilungen aus dem Iran (und Turan)*
AMI ns	*Archäologische Mitteilungen aus dem Iran, new series*
AOAT	*Alter Orient und Altes Testament*
ArO	*Archiv Orientálni*
AS	*Anatolian Studies*
BAI	*Bulletin of the Asia Institute*
BiOr	*Bibliotheca Orientalis*
BPahl.	Book Pahlavi
BSOAS	*Bulletin of the School of Oriental and African Studies*
CAH	*Cambridge Ancient History*
CHIr	*Cambridge History of Iran*
CPD	MacKenzie 1971.
CUP	*Cambridge University Press*
DAFI	*Délégation archéologique française en Iran*
Dd	*Dādestān ī dēnīg*, cf. Jaafari-Dehaghi 1998.
Dk, Denkard	Adurbad i Emedan, *Denkard.*

The following editions have been used: Dhanjishah Meherjibhai Madan, (ed.) *The complete text of the Pahlavi Dinkard*, (2 volumes), Bombay 1911; Dresden, M.J. (ed.), *Denkart — a Pahlavi text.* Facsimile edition of manuscript B of the K.R. Cama Oriental Institute Bombay, Wiesbaden: 1966; Sanjana, P.B. and Sanjana (Sunjana), D.P. (eds.), *The Dinkard*, (19 volumes), Bombay 1874–1928. For *Dk* Book 3, the division of chapters as indicated in the edition of P.B. and D.P. Sanjana has been used, with a further internal division introduced by Shaul Shaked.

EncIr	*Encyclopaedia Iranica*
Elam.	Elamite
Herb.	Kotwal and Kreyenbroek 1992.
IrAnt	*Iranica Antiqua*
JA	*Journal Asiatique*
JNES	*Journal of Near Eastern Studies*
JRAS	*Journal of the Royal Asiatic Studies*
JSAI	*Jerusalem Studies in Arabic and Islam*

(man./inscr.) MP	(Manichaean/inscriptional) Middle Persian
MHD	*Mādayān ī hazār dādestān*; cf. Perikhanian 1997; Macuch 1993.
OIP	*Oriental Institute Publications*
OP	Old Persian
(O./Y.) Av.	(Old/Young) Avestan
PersRiv	*Dārāb Hormazyār's Rivāyat*, by Ervad Manockji Rustamji Unvālā, with an introduction by Shams-ul-Ulma Jivanji Jamshedji Modi, (2 volumes), Bombay 1922; (English translation, see Dhabhar 1932).
Purs	JamaspAsa and Humbach 1971.
RE	*Pauly's Real-Encyclopädie der klassischen Altertumswissenschaften*
SEL	*Studi Epigrafici e Linguistici sul Vicino Oriente*
ŠKZ	The inscription of Shapur at Ka'ba-i Zardusht; for an edition and translation see Back 1978.
SNS I	see Alram and Gyselen 2003.
SNS II	see Alram and Gyselen (forthcoming).
SNS III	see Schindel 2004.
StIr	*Studia Iranica*
WZ	*Wizīdagīhā ī Zādsparam*, cf. Gignoux and Tafazzoli 1993.
ZDMG	*Zeitschrift der deutschen morgenländischen Gesellschaft*

The Idea of Iran

Bibliography:

'Abbas, I. (1967). *'Ahd-i ardashīr*, Beirut.

Adams, R.McC. (1965). *Land Behind Baghdad: A History of Settlement on the Diyala Plains*, Chicago.

— (1981). *Heartland of Cities: Surveys of Ancient Settlement and Land Use on the Central Floodplain of the Euphrates*, Chicago.

— (forthcoming). "Central strategies of irrigation and resettlement in the late Sasanian province of Kaskar: new evidence from satellite imagery", in Kennet, D. and Luft, P. (eds), *Current Research in Sasanian Archaeology, Art and History*. Proceedings of a Conference held at Durham University, November 3rd and 4th, 2001, Durham.

Adams, R.McC. and Hansen, D.P. (1968). "Archaeological reconnaissance and soundings in Jundi Shapur", *Ars Orientalis* 7: 53–73.

Ahn, G. (1992). *Religiöse Herrscherlegitimation im achämenidischen Iran*, *AI* 31, Leiden.

Al-Faraid (1955). *Al-Faraid Arabe-Français*, Beirut.

Alram, M. (1999). "The beginning of sasanian coinage", *BAI* 13: 67–76.

— (2007). "Ardashir's eastern campaign and the numismatic evidence", *Proceedings of the British Academy* 133: 227–242.

Alram, M. and Gyselen, R. (2003). *Sylloge Nummorum Sasanidarum – Paris – Berlin – Wien, Bd. I: Ardashir I. – Shapur I*, Verlag der Österreichischen Akademie der Wissenschaften, Vienna.

— (forthcoming). *Sylloge Nummorum Sasanidarum, Paris – Berlin – Wien, vol. II: Ohrmazd I – Ohrmazd II*, Vienna.

Alram, M. and Klimburg-Salter, D.E. (eds.) (1999). *Coins, Art and Chronology. Essays on the Pre-Islamic History of the Indo-Iranian Borderlands*, (Denkschriften der Österreichischen Akademie der Wissenschaften, Philosophisch-historische Klasse 280), Vienna.

Alram, M., Blet-Lemarquand, M. and Skjærvø, P.O. (2007). "Shapur, king of kings of Iranians and non-Iranians", *Res Orientales* XVII: 11–40.

Altheim, F. and Stiehl, R. (1954). *Ein asiatischer Staat: Feudalismus unter den Sasaniden und ihren Nachbarn*, Wiesbaden.

Aman ur Rahman, Grenet, F. and Sims-Williams, N. (2006). "A Hunnish Kushan-shah", *Journal of Inner Asian Art and Archaeology* 1: 125–131.

Andreas, F.C. (1910). "Bruchstücke einer Pehlewi-Übersetzung der Psalmen aus der Sassanidenzeit", *Sitzungsberichte der Preußischen Akademie der Wissenschaften, philosophisch-historische Klasse 1910*: 869–872.

— (1933). "Bruchstücke einer Pehlewi-Übersetzung der Psalmen", *Sitzungsberichte der Preußischen Akademie der Wissenschaften, philosophisch-historische Klasse 1933*: 91–152.

Azarnoush, M. (1981). "Excavations at Kangavar", *AMI* ns 14: 69–94.

— (1994). *The Sasanian Manor House at Hajiabad, Iran*, Monografie di Mesopotamia III, Florence.

Back, M. (1978). *Die sassanidischen Staatsinschriften. Studien zur Orthographie und Phonologie des Mittelpersischen der Inschriften zusammen mit einem etymologischen Index des mittelpersischen Wortgutes und einem Textcorpus der behandelten Inschriften*, AIr 18, Leiden.

Bahār, M. (1369). *Bundahiš*, Tehran.

Bailey, H.W. (1943). *Zoroastrian Problems in the Ninth-Century Books*, Ratanbai Katrak Lectures, Oxford [reprinted 1971].

— (1989): "Baga ii. In Old and Middle Iranian", *EncIr.*

Balkhi (1912). *Description of the Province of Fars in Persia at the Beginning of the Fourteenth Cent. AD.*, translated by G. Le Strange from the MS. of Ibn al-Balkhi in the British Museum, London.

Bartholomae, C. (1904). *Altiranisches Wörterbuch*. Strasbourg [reprinted Berlin and New York, 1974].

— (1961). *Altiranisches Wörterbuch*, Berlin.

Bayliss, G.M. (1987). *Imperial War Museum. Operations in Persia* 1914–1919, London.

Belardi, W. (1986). "La scrittura di fine di parola nel pahlavico dei libri", in Schmitt, R. and Skjærvø, P.O. (eds.), *Studia grammatica iranica. Festschrift für Helmut Humbach*, München: 11–26.

Bier, L. (1983). "A sculptured building block from Istakhr", *AMI ns* 16: 307–326, pls 25–30.

Bivar, A.D.H. (1979). "The absolute chronology of the Kushano-Sasanian governors in Central Asia", in Harmatta, J. (ed.), *Prolegomena to the sources on the history of Pre-Islamic Central Asia*, Budapest: 317–332.

— (1983). "The history of Eastern Iran", in Yarshater, E. (ed.), *CHIr* III/1, Cambridge: 181–231.

Blockley, R.C. (1985). *The History of Menander the Guardsman*, Liverpool.

— (1992). *East Roman Foreign Policy: Formation and Conduct from Diocletian to Anastasius*, Leeds.

Blois, F. de (1990). "The Middle Persian inscription from Constantinople: Sasanian or Post-Sasanian?", *StIr* 19: 209–218.

— (forthcoming). "Du nouveau sur la chronologie bactrienne post-hellénistique: l'ère de 223/224 ap. J.-C.", *Comptes rendus de l'Académie des Inscriptions et Belles-Lettres*, séance du 2 juin 2006.

Börm, H. (2007). *Prokop und die Perser*, Oriens et Occidens 16, Stuttgart.

Bosworth, C.E. (1983). "Iran and the Arabs before Islam", *CHIr* 3 (1).

— (1999). *The History of al-Tabarī, V: The Sāsānids, the Byzantines, the Lakhmids, and Yemen*, Translated and annotated, Albany, N.Y.

Boyce, M. (1957). "The Parthian *gōsān* and Iranian minstrel tradition", *JRAS*: 10–45.

— (1968a). *The Letter of Tansar*, Rome.

— (1968b). "Middle Persian literature", *Handbuch der Orientalistik*, 4. Bd. 2., Abschn. 1., Lief. Iranistik-Literatur, Leiden, Cologne: 31–66.
— (1977). *A Word-List of Manichaean Middle Persian and Parthian*, Tehran and Liège.
— (1979). *Zoroastrians: their Religious Belief and Practices*, London.
— (1984). *Textual Sources for the Study of Zoroastrianism*, Manchester.
— (2002). *"Gōsān"*, *EncIr* XI/2: 167a–170b.
Briant, P. (2001) *Bulletin d'histoire achéménide II*, Persika 1, Paris.
— (2002). *From Cyrus to Alexander the Great. A History of the Persian Empire*, Winona Lake, Indiana.
— (2003a). "Perses et Iraniens après la disparition de l'empire achéménide: histoire et historiographie", *Annuaire du Collège de France 2001–2002. Résumé des cours et travaux*: 763–85.
— (2003b). *Darius dans l'ombre d'Alexandre*, Paris.
Brock, S. (1979/1980). "Syriac historical writing: a Survey of the main sources", *Journal of the Iraqi Academy (Syriac Corporation)* 5: 1–30.
— (1982). "Christians in the Sasanian empire: a case of divided loyalties", in Mews, S. (ed.), *Religion and National Identity*, Studies in Church History 18, Oxford: 1–19.
Brody, R. (1990). "Judaism in the Sasanian empire: A case study in religious coexistence", in Shaked, S. and Netzer, A. (eds.), *Irano-Judaica* II: 52–62.
Browne, E.G. (1905). *History of Tabaristān*, London.
Callieri, P. (1998). "A proposito di un'iconografia monetale dei dinasti del Fārs post-achemenide", *OCNUS: quaderni della Scuola di specializzazione in archaeologia* 6: 25–38.
— (2003). "At the roots of the Sasanian royal imagery: the Persepolis graffiti", in Compareti, M., Raffetta, P. *et al.* (eds.), *Eran and Aneran. Studies Presented to Boris Ilich Marshak on the Occasion of his 70th Birthday*: http://www.transoxiana.org/Eran/Articles/callieri.html.
Calmeyer, P. (1976). "Zur Genese altiranischer Motive", *AMI* ns. 9: 45–95, 63–68, figs 3–4.
Cameron, A. (1969–1970). "Agathias on the Sasanians", *Dumbarton Oaks Papers* 23–24: 69–183.
— (1995). *The Byzantine and Early Islamic Near East*, III *States, Resources and Armies*, Princeton.
Cantera, A. (2004). *Studien zur Pahlavi-Übersetzung des Avesta*, Iranica 7, Wiesbaden.
Carter, M.L. (1985). "A numismatic reconstruction of Kushano-Sasanian history", *American Numismatic Society Museum Notes* 30: 215–281.
Cereti, C.G. (2001). *La letteratura pahlavi. Introduzione ai testi con referimenti alla storia degli studi e alla tradizione manoscritta* (Sīmorγ. Collana di Studi Orientali), Milan.
— (forthcoming). "On the Pahlavi cursive script and the Sasanian Avesta".
Chaumont, M-L. (1960). "Recherches sur le clergé zoroastrien: le hërbad", *Revue de l'Histoire des Religions* CVIII: 55–80; 161–79.

Choksy, J.K. (1988). "Sacral kingship in Sasanian Iran", *BAI* 2: 35–52.

— (1989). "A Sasanian monarch, his queen, crown prince, and deities: the coinage of Wahram II", *American Journal of Numismatics* 1: 117–135.

Christensen, A. (1944). *L'Iran sous les sassanides*, Copenhagen.

Christensen, P. (1993). *The Decline of Iranshahr: Irrigation and Environments in the History of the Middle East 500 B.C. to A.D. 1500*, Copenhagen.

Colledge, M.A.R. (1977). *Parthian Art*, London.

Creswell, A. (1940). *Early Muslim Architecture*, II, Oxford.

Cribb, J. (1990). "Numismatic evidence for Kushano-Sasanian chronology", *SIr* 19/2: 151–193.

Crone, P. (1991). "Kavād's heresy and Mazdak's revolt", *Iran* 29: 21–42.

Curtis, V.S. (1998). "The Parthian costume and headdress", *in Wiesehöfer, J. (ed.), Das Partherreich und seine Zeugnisse*, Stuttgart: 61–73.

— (2007a). "Religious iconography on ancient Iranian coins", in Cribb, J. and Herrmann, G. (eds.), *After Alexander. Central Asia before Islam*. Proceedings of the British Academy 133: 413–434, Oxford and New York.

— (2007b). "The Iranian revival in the Parthian period", in Curtis, V.S. and Stewart, S. (eds.), *The Age of the Parthians: The Idea of Iran II*, London: 7-25.

Darmesteter, G. (1960) *Le Zend-Avesta: traduction nouvelle avec commentaire historique et philologique*, vol. II, Paris.

Daryaee, T. (1998). National history or Kayanid history? The nature of Sasanid Zoroastrian historiography", *Iranian Studies* 31/3–4: 129–141.

— (2001–2002). "memory and history: the construction of the past in late antique Persia", *Nāme-ye Irān-e Bāstān, The International Journal of Ancient Iranian Studies* 1/2: 1–14.

— (2002). "Sight, semen, and the brain: ancient Persian notions of physiology in Old and Middle Iranian texts", *Journal of Indo-European Studies* 30, 1–2: 103–128.

— (2003). "The ideal king in the sasanian world: Ardaxšīr ī Pābagān or Xusrō Anūšag-ruwān?", *Nāme-ye Irān-e Bāstān, The International Journal of Ancient Iranian Studies* 3/4: 33–46.

— (2007). "Ahamiyat-e nahād-e pādešāhi-ye sulukī dar šekl-girī-ye ideology-ye šāhanšāhī dar Iran-e bāstān (The Importance of Seleucid Institution of Kingship in the formation of Imperial Ideology of Ancient Iran)", *Bulletin of Ancient Iranian History* 2: 1–12.

De la Vaissière, E. (2002). *Histoire des marchands sogdiens*, Paris.

Derakhshani, J. (1995). *Grundzüge der Vor- und Frühgeschichte Irans. Geschichte und Kultur des Alten Ostiran. Bd. I/Heft 1. Die Zeit Zarathustras. Rekonstruktion der altiranischen Chronologie*, Tehran.

DeShazo, A.S. (1993). "The order of Narseh's coin portraits", *Pahlavi Palaver* 2: 2–3.

Dhabhar, B.N. (1932). *The Persian Rivayats of Hormazyar Framarz and Others*, Bombay.

Dodgeon, M.H and Lieu, S.N.C. (1991). *The Roman Eastern Frontier and the Persian Wars AD 226–363: A Documentary History*, London.

Drijvers, J.M. (2006). "Ammianus Marcellinus' image of Sasanian society", in Wiesehöfer and Huyse 2006: 45–69.

Duchesne-Guillemin, J. (1955). "L'homme dans la religion iranienne", in Bleeker, C.J. (ed.), *Anthropologie religieuse, l'homme et sa destinée à la lumière de l'histoire des religions*, Leiden: 93–107.

Enoki, K. (1959). "On the nationality of the Ephthalites", *Memoirs of the Research Department of the Toyo Bunko* 18: 1–58.

Ferdowsi, Abu 'l-Qāsem (1877). (transl.) Mohl, J., *Le livre des rois*, V, Paris.

— (2003). *The Shahnama: a Reprint of the Moscow Edition*, (2 volumes), Tehran.

Fiey, J.M. (1967). "Topograhy of al-Mada´in (Seleucia-Ctesiphon Area)", *Sumer* 23: 3–38.

Finley, M.I. (1985). *Ancient History. Evidence and Models*, London.

Finnegan, R. (1970). "A note on oral tradition and historical evidence", *History and Theory* 9: 195–201.

Frye, R.N. (1954). *The History of Bukhara*, Cambridge.

— (1964). "The charisma of kingship in ancient Iran", *IrAnt* 4: 36–54.

Fukai, S. *et al.* (1972). *Taq-i Bustan II*, Tokyo.

— (1984) Taq-i *Bustan IV*, Tokyo.

Gall, H. von. (1990). *Das Reiterkampfbild in der iranischen und iranisch beeinflußten Kunst parthischer und sasanidischer Zeit, Teheraner Forschungen*, VI, Berlin.

Gariboldi, A. (2004a). "Royal ideological patterns between Seleucid and Parthian Coins: The case of θεοπάτωρ", *Commerce and Monetary Systems in the Ancient World: Means of Transmission and Cultural Interaction.* Proceedings of the Fifth Annual Symposium of the Assyrian and Babylonian Intellectual Heritage Project Held in Innsbruck, Austria, October 3rd–8th 2002, ed. K. Schnegg, Melammu Symposia V: 366–384.

— (2004b). "Astral symbology on Iranian coinage", *East and West* 54: 31–53.

— (in press). "The role of gold and silver in the Sasanian economy", in Panaino, A. and Piras, A. (eds), *Societas Iranologica Europaea — Proceedings 2003*, vol. I, Milan.

Garrison, M.B. (1991). "Seals and the elite at Persepolis", *Ars Orientalis* 21: 1–30.

Gawlikowski, M. (2005). "Der Neufund eines Mosaiks in Palmyra", in Schmidt-Colinet A. (ed.), *Palmyra, Kulturbegegung im Grenzbereich*, Mainz am Rhein: 29–31.

Geiger, B. (1956). "The Middle Iranian texts", in Bellinger, A.R., Brown, F.E., Perkins, A. and Welles, C.B. (eds.), *The Excavations at Doura-Europos Conducted by Yale University and the French Academy of Inscriptions and Letters*, Final Report VIII, Part I, New Haven: 283–417.

Gershevitch, I. (1959). *The Avestan Hymn to Mithra*, Cambridge.

Gheiby, B. (1999). *Ayādgār ī Zarērān*, Pahlavi Literature Series, 4, Bielefeld.

Ghirshman, R. (1956). *Bichapour* II, *Les mosaïques sasanides*, Paris.

— (1962a). *Iran. Parthes et Sassanides*, Paris.

— (1962b). *Iran. Parthians and Sasanians*, London.

— (1971). *Bichapur* I, Paris.

Gignoux, P. (1968). "L'inscription de Kartir à Sar Mašhad", *JA* CCLVI: 387–417.

— (1983). "La chasse dans l'Iran sassanide". *Orientala Romana.* Essays and Letters 5, Iranian Studies: 101–118.

— (1984a). "Church-state relations in the Sasanian period", in Prince, H.I.H. and Mikasa, T. (eds.), *Monarchies and Socio-Religious Traditions in the Ancient Near East*, Wiesbaden: 72–80.

— (1984b). *Le livre d'Ardā Vīrāz*, Paris.

— (1986). *Iranisches Personennamenbuch II. Mittelirananische Personennamen. Faszikel 2: Noms propres sassanides en moyen-perse épigraphique* (Iranisches Personennamenbuch, II/2), Vienna.

— (1990). "Le *spāhbed* des sassanides", *Jerusalem Studies in Arabic and Islam* 13: 1–14.

— (1991). *Les quatre inscriptions du mage Kirdīr*, StIr, Cahier 9, Paris.

— (1995). "Dinar. i. In pre-Islamic Persia", *EIr* VII/4: 412–413; *EIr* VII/4: 424–426.

— (1998). "Les inscriptions en moyen-perse de Bandian", *StIr* 27: 251–258.

— (1999). "Matériaux pour une histoire du vin dans l'Iran ancien", in Gyselen, R. and Szuppe, M. (eds.), *Matériaux pour l'histoire économique du monde iranien*, *StIr*, Cahier 21: 35–50.

— (2006). "Prolégomènes pour une histoire des idées de l'Iran sassanide: convergences et divergences", in Wiesehöfer and Huyse 2006: 71–82.

Gnoli, G. (1989). *The Idea of Iran, An Essay on its Origin*, Serie Orientale Roma 62, Rome.

— (1998). "L'Iran tardoantico e la regalià sassanide", *Mediterraneo antico, economie, societa, culture* 1/1: 115–139.

— (2000). *Zoroaster in History*, Biennial Yarshater Lecture Series, University of California, Los Angeles (April 21–25, 1997), No. 2, New York.

— (2003). *Il manicheismo.* Volume 1. *Mani e il manicheismo*, Introduzione e cura di Gherardo Gnoli, Fondazione Lorenzo Valla, Rome.

Göbl, R. (1959). "Narse und nicht Bahram III", *Numismatische Zeitschrift* 78: 5–13.

— (1967). *Dokumente zur Geschichte der iranischen Hunnen in Baktrien und Indien*, (4 volumes), Wiesbaden.

— (1971). *Sasanian Numismatics*, Braunschweig.

— (1974). *Der Triumph des Sāsāniden Šāhpuhr über die Kaiser Gordianus, Philippus und Valerianus. Die ikonographische Interpretation der Felsreliefs*, Vienna.

— (1984). *System und Chronologie der Münzprägung des Kušānreiches*, Vienna.

— (1993). *Donum Burns. Die Kušānmünzen im Münzkabinett Bern und die Chronologie*, Vienna.

Gold, M. (1976). (transl.) *The Tarikh-e Sistan*, Rome.

Goldman, B. (1985). "A Dura-Europos dipinto and syrian frontality", *Oriens Antiquus* XXIV: 279–300.

— (1999). "Pictorial graffiti of Dura-Europos", *Parthica* 1: 19–106.

Gray, E.W. (1973). "The Roman Eastern *Limes* from Constantine to Justinian: Perspectives and Problems", *Proceedings of the African Classical Associations* 12: 24–40.

Greatrex, G. (1998). *Rome and Persia at War, 502–532*, Leeds.

Greatex, G. and Lieu, S.N.C. (2002). *The Roman Eastern Frontier and the Persian Wars, Part II AD 363–630: A Narrative Sourcebook*, London.

Grenet, F. (2002). "Regional interaction in Central Asia and Northwest India in the Kidarite and Hephthalite periods", in Sims-Williams, N. (ed.), *Indo-Iranian Languages and Peoples*, Proceedings of the British Academy CXVI, Oxford: 203–224.

— (2006). Review of Gyselen 2002, *StIr* 35: 144–148.

Grenet, F., Lee, J., Martinez, P. and Ory, F. (2007). "The Sasanian relief at Rag-i Bibi (northern Afghanistan)", in Cribb, J. and Herrmann, G. (eds.), *After Alexander. Central Asia before Islam*. Proceedings of the British Academy 133, Oxford and New York: 243–267.

Grignaschi, M. (1966). "Quelques spécimens de la littérature sassanide conservés dans les bibliothèques d'Istanbul", *JA* 254: 1–142.

— (1984). "La chute de l'empire hephthalite dans les sources byzantines et perses et le problème des Avar", in Harmatta, J. (ed.), *From Hecataeus to al-Ḫuwārizmī*, Budapest: 219–248.

Gutschmidt, A. von (1880). "Bemerkungen zu Tabaris's Sasanidengeschichte, übersetzt von Th. Nöldeke", *Zeitschrift der Deutschen Morgenländischen Gesellschaft* 34: 721–749.

Gyselen, R. (1989). *La géographie administrative de l'empire sasanide*, Res Orientalis I, Paris.

— (1997). "Economy V. iv. In the Sasanian period", *EIr* VIII/1: 104–107.

— (2002). *Nouveaux matériaux pour la géographie historique de l'empire sassanide. Sceaux administratifs de la collection Ahmad Saeedi*, Paris.

— (2003). "La reconquête de l'est iranien par l'empire sassanide au VIe siècle d'après les sources 'iraniennes'", *Arts asiatiques* 58: 162–167.

— (2004). "New evidence for Sasanian numismatics: the collection of Ahmad Saeedi", *Res Orientales* XVI: 49–140.

Gyselen, R. and Gasche, H. (1994). "Suse et Ivan-e Kerkha, capitale provinciale d'Eran-Xwarrah-Sapur", *StIr* 23: 19–35.

Gyselen, R. and Kalus, L. (1983). *Deux trésors monétaires des premiers temps de l'Islam*, Paris.

Hamza al-Isfahani (1848). (ed.) Gottwaldt, J.M., *Hamzae Ispahanensis annalium libri* X, Leipzig.

Harper, P.O. (1990). "An Iranian silver vessel from the tomb of Feng Hetu", *BAI* 4: 51–59.

— (2006). *In Search of a Cultural Identity. Monuments and Artifacts of the Sasanian Near East 3rd to 7th century*, New York.

Harper, P.O. and Meyers, P. (1981). *Silver Vessels of the Sasanian Period* I, New York.

Hartmann, U. (2002). "Geist im Exil. Römische Philosophen am Hof der Sasaniden", in Schuol, M., Hartmann, U. and Luther, A. (eds.), *Grenzüberschreitungen. Formen des Kontakts zwischen Orient und Okzident im Altertum*, Oriens et Occidens 3, Stuttgart: 123–168.

Henning, W.B. (1953). "A new Parthian inscription", *JRAS*: 132–136.

— (1958). "Mitteliranisch", in *Handbuch der Orientalistik* I/IV/I, Leiden and Cologne: 20–130.

Herman, G. (2005). *The Exilarchate in the Sasanian Era*. Unpublished PhD thesis, Hebrew University of Jerusalem.

Herrenschmidt, C. (1976). "Désignation de l'empire et concepts politiques de Darius I d'après ses inscriptions en vieux-perse", *StIr* 5: 33–65.

Herrmann, G. (1969). "The Darabgird relief — Ardashir or Shapur. A Discussion in the Context of Early Sasanian sculpture", *Iran* 7: 63–88.

— (1977a). *The Iranian Revival*, Oxford.

— (1977b). *Naqsh-i Rustam 5 and 8*, (Iranische Denkmaler 8, Reihe 2), Berlin.

— (1998). "Shapur I in the east. Reflections from his victory reliefs", in Curtis, V.S., Hillenbrand, R. and Rogers, J.M. (eds.), *The Art and Archaeology of Ancient Persia. New Light on the Parthian and Sasanian Empires*, London and New York: 38–51.

— (2000). "The rock reliefs of Sasanian Iran", in Curtis, J. (ed.), *Mesopotamia and Iran in the Parthian and Sasanian Periods. Rejection and Revival c. 238 BC–AD 642*. Proceedings of a Seminar in memory of Vladimir G. Lukonin, London: 35–45.

Herzfeld, E. (1920). "Der Thron des Khosro: Quellenkritische und ikonographische Studien über Grenzgebiete der Kunstgeschichte des Morgen- und Abendlandes", *Jahrbuch der Preussischen Kunstsammlungen* 41: 1–24, 103–147.

— (1921). *Archäologische Reise im Euphrat und Tigris Gebiet*, II, Berlin.

— (1926). "Reisebericht", *Zeitschrift der Deutschen Morgenländischen Gesellschaft* 80, N.S. 5: 225–284.

— (1941). *Iran in the Ancient East*, London and New York.

Hinz, W. (1969). *Altiranische Funde und Forschungen*, Berlin.

Hoffmann, K. (1975). "Zum Zeicheninventar der Awesta-Schrift", *Aufsätze zur Indoiranistik I*, I, Wiesbaden: 316–325.

Hoffmann, K. and Narten, J. (1989). *Der Sasanidische Archetypus. Untersuchungen und Lautgestalt des Awestischen*, Wiesbaden.

Howard-Johnston, J. (1995). "The two great powers in late antiquity: a comparison", in Cameron 1995: 157–226.

— (1999). "Heraclius' Persian campaigns and the revival of the eastern Roman empire, 622–630", *War in History* 6: 1–44.

Huff, D. (1969/1970). "Zur Rekonstruktion des Turmes von Firuzabad", *Istanbuler Mitteilungen* 19/20: 319–338.

— (1971). "Qal'a-ye Dukhtar bei Firuzabad. Ein Beitrag zur sasanidischen Palastarchitektur", *AMI* ns. 4: 127–171.

— (1972). "Der Takht-i Nishin in Firuzabad", *Archäologischer Anzeiger* 1972: 517–540.

— (1974). "An Archaeological Survey in the Area of Firuzabad, Fars, in 1972", in Bagherzadeh, F. (ed.), *Proceedings of the 2ⁿᵈ Annual Symposium on Archaeological Research in Iran. 29th October–1st November 1973*, Tehran: 155–179.

— (1976). "Ausgrabungen auf Qal'a-ye Dukhtar 1975", *AMI* ns 9: 157–173.

— (1978). "Ausgrabungen auf Qal'a-ye Dukhtar bei Firuzabad 1976", *AMI* ns11: 117–147.

— (1989). "Das Qasr Nuweijis bei Amman", *Istanbuler Mitteilungen* 39: 223–236.

— (1991). "Baidha", in Kiani, M.Y. (ed.), *Iranian Cities* 4, Tehran: 46–69.

— (1993). "Sassanidische Architektuur", in Koniglijke Musea voor Kunst en Geschiedenis (ed.), *Hofkunst van de Sassanieden (Splendeur des Sassanides)*, Brussels: 45–61.

— (1995). "Darabgerd", in Kiani, M.Y. (ed.), *Iranian Capitals*, Tehran: 407–446.

— (in press). "The 'Parthian' Bronze Bust in the Berlin Museum for Islamic Art, and Parthian-Sasanian aristocratic head-gear", in Hagedorn, A. and Shalem, A. (eds.), *Facts and Artefacts. Art in the Islamic World*, Leiden: 205–229.

Huyse, P. (1998). "Kerdīr and the first Sasanians", in Sims-Williams, N. (ed.), *Proceedings of the Third European Conference of Iranian Studies held in Cambridge, 11th to 15th September 1995*, Pt. 1. *Old and Middle Iranian Studies*, Beiträge zur Iranistik 17, Wiesbaden: 109–120.

— (1999). *Die dreisprachige Inschrift Šābuhrs I. an der Ka'ba-i Zardušt (ŠKZ)*, vol. 1, Part III. Pahlavi Inscriptions, Corpus Inscriptionum Iranicarum, London.

— (1999 [2002]). "Some further thoughts on the Bisitun monument and the genesis of the Old Persian cuneiform script", *BAI* 13: 45–66

— (2002). "La revendication de territoires achéménides par les sassanides: une réalité historique?", in Huyse, P. (ed.), *Iran: questions et connaissances. Actes du IVe congrès européen des études iraniennes organisé par la Societas Iranologica Europaea. Paris, 6–10 Septembre 1999. Vol. I. La période ancienne*, StIr, cahier 25, Paris: 297–311.

— (2003a). *Le y final dans les inscriptions moyen-perses et la "loi rythmique" proto-moyen-perse*, StIr, cahier 29, Paris.

— (2003b). "Ein erneuter Datierungsversuch für den Übergang vom Schluß-y der mittelpersischen Inschriften zum Endstrich im Buchpahlavi (6.–7. Jh.)", in Weber, D. (ed.), *D.N. MacKenzie Memorial Volume. Languages of Iran: Past and Present*, Iranica 8, Wiesbaden: 51–68.

— (2005). *La Perse antique*, Guide Belles Lettres des Civilisations, Paris.

— (2006). "Die sasanidische Königstitulatur: eine Gegenüberstellung der Quellen", in Wiesehöfer, J. and Huyse, P. (eds.), *Ērān ud Anērān, Studien zu den Beziehungen zwischen dem Sasanidenreich und der Mittelmeerwelt, Beiträge des Internationalen Colloquiums in Eutin, 9.–9. Juni 2000*, Stuttgart: 182–201.

Insler, S. (1975). *The Gāthās of Zarathustra*, AIr 8, Leiden.

Invernizzi, A. (1976). "Ten years' research in the Al-Madaʿin area. Seleucia and Ctesiphon", *Sumer* 32: 167–175.

— (1998). "Parthian Nisa. New Lines of Research", in Wiesehöfer, J. (ed.), *Das Partherreich und seine Zeugnisse*, Stuttgart: 45–59.

— (2001). "Arsacid Dynastic Art", *Parthica* 3: 133–157.

Jaafari-Dehaghi, M. (1998). *Dādēstān i dēnīg*, Part I. Transcription, translation and commentary, StIr, Cahier 20, Paris.

Jamasp, D.H. (1907). *Vendidâd,* Avesta Text with Pahlavi Translation, vol. I, Bombay.

JamaspAsa, K.M. and Humbach, H. (1971). *Pursišnīhā. A Zoroastrian catechism*, (2 volumes), Wiesbaden.

Jeffreys, E., Jeffreys, M. and Scott, R. (1986). *The Chronicle of John Malalas: A Translation*, Melbourne.

Jong, A. de. (2005). "The first sin: Zoroastrian ideas on culture and religion before Zarathustra", in Shaked, S. (ed.), *Genesis and regeneration*, Jerusalem: 192–209.

Karnamak (1879). (transl.) Nöldeke, T., *Geschichte des Artachsir i Papakan, aus dem Pehlevi übersetzt*, Göttingen.

Kawami, T.S. (1987). *Monumental Art of the Parthian Period in Iran*, Leiden.

Kellens, J. (1998). "Considérations sur l'histoire de l'Avesta", *Journal Asiatique* 286/2: 451–519.

— (2001). "Zoroastre dans l'histoire ou dans le mythe? À propos du dernier livre de Gherardo Gnoli", *Journal Asiatique* 289/2: 171–184.

— (2006). *La quatrième naissance de Zarathushtra*, Paris.

Kennedy, H. (2007). *The Great Arab Conquests: How the Spread of Islam Changed the World we Live in*, London.

Kent, R.G. (1953). *Old Persian Grammar, Texts, Lexicon*, (second edition), American Oriental Society, New Haven, Connecticut.

Kettenhofen, E. (1984). "Die Einforderung des Achämenidenreiches durch Ardašir: eine interpretatio romana", *Orientalia Lovaniensia Periodica* 15: 177–190.

Kister, M.J. (1968). "Al-Hīrā. Some notes on its relations with Arabia", *Arabica* 15: 143–169. (Reprinted in idem, *Studies in Jāhiliyya and early Islam*, London).

Klíma, O. (1957). *Mazdak: Geschichte einer sozialen Bewegung im sassanidischen Persien*, Prague.

Kotwal, F.M. and Kreyenbroek, P.G. (1992). *The Hērbedestan and Nērangestān*. Vol. 1, *Hērbedestān*, Paris.

— (2003). *The Hērbedestān and Nērangestān III: Nērangestān, Fragard 2*, Paris.

Kreyenbroek, [P.]G. (1987a). "The Zoroastrian priesthood after the fall of the Sasanian empire", in Gignoux, P. (ed.), *Transition Periods in Iranian History*, Louvain: 151–166.

— (1987b). "The Dādestān ī Dēnīg on priests", *Indo-Iranian Journal* 30: 185–208.

— (forthcoming). "Zoroastrianism under the Achaemenians: a non-essentialist approach", in Curtis, J. and Simpson, S. (eds), *Proceedings of the Achaemenid Conference, London 30 September-1 October 2005*.

Lassner, J. (1970). *The Topography of Baghdad in the Early Middle Ages*, Detroit.

Lazard, G. (1990). *Dictionnaire persan-français*, Leiden.

Le Patourel, J. (1976). *The Norman Empire*, Oxford.

Lieu, S.N.C. (1985). *Manichaeism in the Late Roman Empire and Medieval China: a historical survey*, Manchester.

— (1994). *Manichaeism in Mesopotamia and the Roman East*, Leiden.

Lincoln, B. (1992). "čehr", *EIr*, ed. E. Yarshater, V: 118–119.

Loginov, D. and Nikitin, A.B. (1993). "Sasanian coins of the third century from Merv", *Mesopotamia* 27: 225–241.

Lombard, M. (1971). *L'Islam dans sa première grandeur (VIIIe-XIe siècle)*, Paris.

Lukonin, V.G. (1961). *Iran v epokhu pervikh sasanidov*, Leningrad.

— (1968). "Monnaie d'Ardachir I et l'art officiel sassanide", *Iran* 8: 106–117.

— (1969). *Kultura sasanidskogo irana*, Moscow.

McKenzie, D.N. (1971). *A Concise Pahlavi Dictionary*, London (reprinted 1986, with corrections).

— (1987). "Avroman documents", *EIr* III/1: 111.

— (1989). "Kerdir's inscription", in Herrmann, G., MacKenzie, D.N. and Caldecott, R.H., *The Sasanian rock reliefs at Naqsh-i Rustam* (Naqsh-i Rustam, 6; Iranische Denkmäler, Lief. 13, Reihe II), Berlin: 35–72.

— (1998). "Ērān, Ērānšahr", *EIr* VIII: 534–535.

Mackintosh, M.C. (1973). "Roman influences on the victory reliefs of Shapur I of Persia", *California Studies in Classical Antiquity* 6: 63–88.

Macuch, M. (1976). *Das sasanidische Rechtsbuch "Mātakdān i Hazār Dātistān"*, Teil II, Berlin.

— (1990). "Die 'Tagesration' in den Pahlavi-Schriften", in Gyselen, R. (ed.), *Prix, salaires, poids et mesures*, Res Orientales II, Bures-sur-Yvette: 139–142.

— (1993). *Rechtskasuistik und Gerichtspraxis zu Beginn des siebenten Jahrhunderts in Iran. Die Rechtssammlung des Farrohmard I Wahraman*, Iranica, I, Wiesbaden.

Malandra, W. (1983). *An Introduction to Ancient Iranian Religion: Readings from the Avesta and Achaemenid Inscriptions*, Minneapolis.

Malek, H.M. (1993). "A seventh-century hoard of Sasanian drachms", *Iran* 31: 77–93.

Markwart, J. (1931). (ed.) Messina, G., *A Catalogue of the Provincial Capitals of Eranshahr*. Pahlavi Text, Version and Commentary, Rome.

Masson, V.M. (1982). *Das Land der tausend Städte*, Munich.

Matheson, S. (1972). Persia: *An Archaeological Guide*, London and Boston.

Mathiesen, H.E. (1992). *Sculpture in the Parthian Empire I, II*, Aarhus.

Mayrhofer, M. (1976). *Kurzgefaßtes etymologisches Wörterbuch des Altindischen*, Carl Winter Universitätsverlag, Lieferung 26, Heidelberg.

Melzer, G. (2006). "A copper scroll inscription from the time of the Alchon Huns", in Braarvig, J. (ed), *Manuscripts in the Schøyen collection*, I: *Buddhist manuscripts*, III, Oslo: 251–278.

Menasce, J.P. de (1967). "L'inscription funéraire pehlevie d'Istanbul", *IrAnt* 7: 59–71.

— (1975). "Zoroastrian literature after the Muslim conquest", in Frye, R.N. (ed.), *CHIr* Vol. 4. *The period from the Arab invasion to the Saljuqs*: 543–565.

Meyer, M. (1990). "Die Felsbilder Shapurs I", *Jahrbuch des deutschen Archäologischen Instituts* 105: 237–302.

Millar, F. (1993). *The Roman Near East 31 BC–AD 337*, Cambridge and London.

Miroschedji, P. de (1980). "Un chahar taq dans la plaine de Darab", *Iran* 18: 157–160.

Mirza, H.P. (1954). "The Frahang-i Pahlavik, XXX", *Prof. Jackson Memorial Volume*, The K.R. Cama Oriental Institute, Bombay: 7–12.

Mitchiner, M. (1978). *Oriental Coins and Their Values: The Ancient and Classical World, 600 B.C.–A.D. 600*, London.

Modi, J.J. (1922). *The Religious Ceremonies and Customs of the Parsees*, Bombay.

Morony, M.G. (1984). *Iraq after the Muslim Conquest*, Princeton.

— (2003). "Magic and society in late Sasanian Iraq", in Noegel, S., Walker, J. and Wheeler, B. (eds.), *Prayer, magic and the stars in the ancient and late antique world*, University Park, PA: 83–107.

Nasrullahzadeh, C. (1383/2004–2005) "Shapur Pabagan, King of Pars. Genealogy and rulership". *Quarterly Journal of Historical Studies*. Journal of the Faculty of Letters and Humanities, Ferdowsi University, Mashhad, 5-6, Fall/Winter: 183-192.

Neusner, J. (1963). "Parthian political ideology", *IrAnt* 3, 1963: 40–59.

Nikitin, A.B. (1999). "Notes on the chronology of the Kushano-Sasanian kingdom", in Alram, M. and Klimburg-Salter, D. (eds.), *Coins, Art and Chronology, Essays on the pre-Islamic History of the Indo-Iranian Borderlands*, Vienna: 259–263.

Nöldeke, T. (1879). *Geschichte der Perser und Araber zur Zeit der Sasaniden. Aus der arabischen Chronik des Tabari übersetzt und mit ausführlichen Erläuterungen und Ergänzungen versehn*, Leiden.

Nokandeh, J., Sauer, E., Rekavandi, H.O. *et al.* (2006). "Linear barriers of northern Iran: The great wall of Gorgan and the wall of Tammishe", *Iran* 44: 121–173.

Northedge, A. (forthcoming). "The Sasanians and the Nahrawan canal", in D.Kennet and P. Luft (eds), *Current Research in Sasanian Archaeology, Art and History*. Proceedings of a Conference held at Durham University November 3rd and 4th, 2001, Durham.

Nyberg, H.S. (1938). (transl.) Schaeder, H.H., *Die Religionen des alten Irans*, Leipzig.

Nyberg, S.H. (1974). *A Manual of Pahlavi*, Part II: *Glossary*, Wiesbaden.

Ong, W.J. (1982). *Orality and literacy. The technologizing of the world*, London.

Ouseley, W. (1821). *Travels in Various Countries of the East. More Particularly Persia*, II, London.

Panaino, A. (1992). *Tištrya, The Avestan Hymn to Sirius, vol. ii,* Istituto Italiano per il medio e estremo oriente, Rome.

— (2003). "The baγān of the Fratarakas: gods or 'divine' kings?", in Cereti, C., Maggi, M. and Provasi, E. (eds.), *Religious Themes and Texts of Pre-Islamic Iran and Central Asia: Studies in Honour of Professor Gherardo Gnoli on the Occasion of His 65th Birthday on 6th December 2002*, Beiträge zur Iranistik, Wiesbaden: 265–288.

— (2004). "Astral characters of kingship in the Sasanian and Byzantine worlds", *La Persia e Bisanzio*, Accademia nazionale dei lincei, Rome: 555–594.

Pellat, C. (1954). *Le livre de la couronne attribué à Jahiz*, Paris.

Perikhanian, A.G. (1974). "Le contumace dans la procédure iranienne et les termes pehlevis *hacašmānd* et *srād*", in Gignoux, P. and Tafazzoli, A. (eds.), *Mémorial Jean de Menasce*, Paris: 305–318.

— (1979). "L'ordalie et le serment dans la procédure judiciaire de l'Iran pré-islamique", *Peredneaziatiskij Sbornik* III, Moscow: 182–192.

— (1997). Farraxwmart ī Vahrāmān. *The book of a thousand judgements (A Sasanian law-book)*, Introduction, transcription and translation of the Pahlavi text. Translated from the Russian by N. Garsoïan (St. Petersburg Branch of the Institute of Oriental Studies, Russian Academy of Sciences; Center for Iranian Studies, Columbia University, New York; Persian Heritage Series, No. 39), Costa Mesa, CA and New York.

Piras, A. (2002). "Preliminary remarks on MELAMMU database: the continuity of Mesopotamian culture showed by Iranological evidences", in Panaino, A. and Pettinato, G. (eds.), *Second Melammu Symposia III*, Milan: 205–214.

— (2004). "Mesopotamian sacred marriage and pre-Islamic Iran", in Panaino, A. and Piras, A. (eds.), *Melammu Symposia IV*, Milan: 249–259.

Pisani, V. (1933). "Note miscellanée", *Rivista degli Studi Orientali*, vol. xiv, fasc. I, Rome: 83–86.

Potts, D.T. (2007). "Foundation houses, fire altars and the frataraka: interpreting the iconography of some post-Achaemenid Persian coins", *IrAnt* 42: 271–300.

Puech, H-C. (1949). *Le manichéisme. Son fondateur, sa doctrine*, (Musée Guimet, Bibliothèque de Diffusion, 56), Paris.

Rahbar, M. (1998). "Découverte d'un monument d'époque sassanide à Bandian, Dargaz (Nord Korassan). Fouilles 1994 et 1995", *StIr* 27: 213–250.

— (forthcoming). "Excavations at Bandiyan at Darr Gaz in N.E. Iran", in Kennet, D. and Luft, P. (eds), *Current Research in Sasanian Archaeology, Art and History*. Proceedings of a Conference held at Durhqm University November 3rd & 4th, 2001, Durham.

Razmjou, S. (2005). "Ernst Herzfeld and the Study of Graffiti at Persepolis", in Gunter, A.C. and Hauser, S.P., (eds.), *Ernst Herzfeld and the Development of Near Eastern Studies 1900–1950*, Leiden and Boston.

Reuther, O. (1930). *Die Ausgrabungen der Deutschen Ktesiphon-Expedition im Winter 1928/29*, Berlin.

— (1938). "Sasanian architecture", in Pope, A.U. (ed.), *A Survey of Persian Art*, I, London and New York: 493–578.

Ritter, H.W. (1965). *Diadem und Königsherrschaft*, Vesitigia VII, Munich.

Rubin, Z. (1986). "The Mediterranean and the dilemma of the Roman empire in late Antiquity", *Mediterranean Historical Review* 1: 13–62.

— (1995). "The reforms of Khusrau Anūshirwān", in Cameron 1995: 227–297.

— (2004). "Nobility, monarchy and legitimation under the Later Sasanians", in Haldon, J. and Conrad, L.I. (eds.), *The Byzantine and Early Islamic Near East VI, Elites Old and New in the Byzantine and Early Islamic Near East*, Princeton: 235–273.

Safa-Isfehani, N. (1980). *Rivāyat-i Hēmīt-i Ašawahistān*, Harvard Iranian Series 2, Harvard, Mass.

Sami, A. (1958/1959, 1338 H). *Gozareshhaye bastanshenasi*, Shiraz.

Schindel, N. (2004). *Sylloge Nummorum Sasanidarum, Paris – Berlin – Wien, vol. III/1 and III/2: Shapur II – Kavad I/2. Regierung*, Vienna.

— (2005). "Adhuc sub iudice lis est? Zur Datierung der Kushanosasanidischen Münzen", in Emmerig, H. (ed.), *Vindobona docet: 40 Jahre Institut für Numismatik und Geldgeschichte der Universität Wien 1965–2005*, (Numismatische Zeitschrift 113–114), Vienna: 217–242.

— (2006). "Sasanian gold coinage: an overview", *Dal denarius al dinar. L'oriente e la moneta romana. Atti dell'incontro di studio, Roma 16–18 settembre*, Rome: 105–129.

Schippmann, K. (1990). *Grundzüge der Geschichte des sasanidischen Reiches*, Darmstadt.

Schmidt, E.F. (1970). *Persepolis III. The Royal Tombs and Other Monuments*, Chicago.

Schmidt-Colinet A. (ed.) (2005). *Palmyra, Kulturbegegung im Grenzbereich*, Mainz am Rhein.

Schmitt, R. (1977). "Königtum in Alten Iran", *Saeculum* 28: 384–395.

— (1997). "Onomastica Iranica Symmicta", in Ambrosini, R., Bologna, M.P., Motta, F. and Orlandi, C. (eds.), *Scríbthair a ainm nogaim. Scritti in memoria di E. Campanile,* Pisa: 921–927.

Schwarz, P. (1896–1934). *Iran im Mittelalter nach den arabischen Geographen*, Hildesheim and New York (reprinted 1969).

Seipel, W. (ed.) (1996). *Weihrauch und Seide – Alte Kulturen an der Seidenstrasse*, Vienna.

Shahbazi, A.S. (2001). "Early Sasanians' claim to Achaemenid heritage", *Nāme-ye Irān-e Bāstān, The International Journal of Ancient Iranian Studies* 1/1: 61–74.

Shaked, S. (1967). "Some notes on Ahreman, the Evil Spirit, and his creation", *Studies in mysticism and religion presented to G.G. Scholem*, Jerusalem: 227–254 (Reprinted in Shaked 1995, III).

— (1969). *Esoteric trends in Zoroastrianism*, Proceedings of the Israel Academy of Sciences and Humanities, vol. 3, No. 7, Jerusalem. (Reprinted as *Proceedings of the Israel Academy of Sciences and Humanities* 3 (1970): 175–221; also in Shaked 1995, I).

— (1984). "From Iran to Islam: notes on some themes in transmission", *Jerusalem Studies in Arabic and Islam* 4: 31–67 (Reprinted in Shaked 1995, VI).

— (1987). "Paymān: an Iranian idea in contact with Greek thought and Islam", *Transition Periods in Iranian History. Actes du Symposium de Fribourg-en-Brisgau (22–24 mai 1985)* (StIr, Cahier 5), Paris: 217–240. (Reprinted in Shaked 1995, VIII).

— (1990). "Zoroastrian polemics against Jews in the Sasanian and early Islamic period", in Shaked, S. and Netzer, A. (eds.), *Irano-Judaica* II, Jerusalem: 85–104.

— (1992). "The myth of Zurvan: cosmogony and eschatology", in Gruenwald, I., Shaked, S. and Stroumsa, G.G. (eds.), *Messiah and Christos. Studies in the Jewish origins of Christianity presented to David Flusser* (Texte und Studien zum antiken Judentum, 32), Tübingen: 219–240 (Reprinted in Shaked 1995, V).

— (1995). *From Zoroastrian Iran to Islam. Studies in Religious History and Intercultural Contacts* (Collected Studies Series, CS505), Aldershot.

— (1997). "Popular religion in Sasanian Babylonia", *Jerusalem Studies in Arabic and Islam* 21: 103–117.

— (forthcoming). "La vision humaine selon les livres pehlevis", (Bucarest conference of the Romanian Association for the History of Religions, 2006).

Shapira, D. (1998). *Studies in Zoroastrian Exegesis: Zand*. Unpublished PhD thesis, Hebrew University of Jerusalem.

— (2005/2006). "On the scriptural sources of Mazdak's teachings", *Nāme-ye Irān-e Bāstān* 5: 63–82.

Shayegan, R.M. (1998). "The evolution of the concept of xwadāy 'god'", *Acta Orientalia Academiae Scientiarum Hungaricae* 51/1–2: 31–54.

Sims-Williams, N. (1989). "Baga iii. The use of Baga in Names", *EIr* III: 405–406.

— (1997). *New light on ancient Afghanistan: the decipherment of Bactrian*, London.

— (1999). "From the Kushan-shahs to the Arabs. New Bactrian documents dated in the era of the Tochi inscriptions", in Alram and Klimburg-Salter 1999: 245–258.

— (2000). *Bactrian Documents from Northern Afghanistan I: Legal and Economic Documents*, CII Part II, vol. VI, London.

— (2001). *Bactrian Documents from Northern Afghanistan*, I: *Legal and Economic Documents*, Oxford, 2000 [2001].

— (2005a). "Bactrian legal documents from 7th and 8th century Guzgan", *BAI* 15, 2001 [2005]: 9–29.

— (2005b). "Some Bactrian seal inscriptions", in Bopearachchi, O. and Boussac, M-F. (eds.), *Afghanistan, ancien carrefour entre l'est et l'ouest*, Turnhout: 335–346.

— (2007). *Bactrian Documents from Northern Afghanistan*, II: *Letters and Buddhist Texts*, London (= BD2).

Sims-Williams, N. and Blois, F. de (1998). "The Bactrian calendar", BAI 10: 149–165.

— (2006). "The Bactrian calendar: new material and new suggestions", in Weber, D. (ed.), *Languages of Iran: Past and Present. Iranian Studies in Memoriam David Neil MacKenzie*, Wiesbaden: 185–196.

Skjærvø, P.O. (1983). "Kirdir's vision: translation and analysis", *AMI* ns16: 296–306.

— (1997). "The joy of the cup: a pre-Sasanian Middle Persian inscription on a silver bowl", *BAI* 11: 93–104.

— (2003). "Paleography", in Alram, M. and Gyselen, R. (eds.), *Sylloge Nummorum Sasanidarum Paris – Berlin – Wien, Bd I, Ardashir I – Shapur I*, Verlag der Österreichischen Akademie der Wissenschaften, Vienna.

Soudavar, A. (2003). *The Aura of Kings, Legitimacy and Divine Sanction in Iranian Kingship*, (Bibliotheca Iranica, Intellectual Tradition Series, No. 10), Costa Mesa.

— (2006). "The significance of čiθra, čiça, čihr and čehr for the Iranian cosmogony of light", *IrAnt* 41: 1–26.

Stein, A. (1936). "An archaeological tour in ancient Persis", *Iraq* 3: 111–230.

Stöllner, T. and Mir Eskanderi, M. (2003). "Die Höhle der Anāhitā?", *Antike Welt* 5: 505–516.

Sundermann, W. (1985). "Schriftsysteme und Alphabete im alten Iran", *Altorientalische Forschungen* 12: 101–113.

Tabari (1869). (transl.) Zotenberg, H., *Chronique de Tabari, sur la version Persane d'Abou-Ali Mohammed Bel'Ami,* II, Paris.

— (1879). (transl.) Nöldeke, T., *Geschichte der Perser und Araber zur Zeit der Sasaniden,* Graz. (reprinted 1973).

— (1999). (transl.) Bosworth, C.E., *The History of al-Ṭabari, The Sāsānids, the Byzantines, the Lakmids, and Yemen,* New York.

Tanabe, K. (1998). "A newly located Kushano-Sasanian silver plate" in Curtis, V.S., Hillenbrand, R. and Rogers, J.M., *The Art and Archaeology of Ancient Persia,* London and New York: 93–102.

— (2001). "A Kushano-Sasanian plate and Central Asian tigers", *Silk Route Art and Archaeology* 7: 167–186.

Tha'alibi (1900). (transl.) Zotenberg, H., *Histoire des rois des Perses,* Paris.

Thiesen, F. (2005). "Eleven etymologies", in Weber, D. (ed.), *Languages of Iran: Past and Present. Iranian Studies in Memoriam David Neil MacKenzie,* Wiesbaden: 213–216.

Thomas, R. (1989). *Oral Tradition and Written Record in Classical Athens,* Cambridge Studies in Oral and Literate Culture, Cambridge.

Thomson, R.W. (1991). *The History of Łazar P'arpec'i,* Atlanta.

Thomson, R.W. and Howard-Johnston, J. (1999). *The Armenian History Attributed to Sebeos,* Translated Texts for Historians 31, Liverpool.

Tremblay, X. (2003). "La résurrection du bactrien: à propos des bactrian documents", *Indo-Iranian Journal* 46: 119–133.

Trombley, F.R. and Watt, J.W. (2000). *The Chronicle of Pseudo-Joshua the Stylite,* Translated Texts for Historians 32, Liverpool.

Unvala, J.M. (1921). *The Pahlavi Text King Husrav and his Boy,* Paris.

— (1921–1923). "Draxt i Asurik", *BSOAS* 2: 637–678.

Utas, B. (1988). *Frahang ī Pahlavīk,* ed. from the posthumous papers of Henrik Samuel Nyberg, Wiesbaden.

Vanden Berghe, L. and Smekens, E. (1984). *Reliefs rupestres de l'Iran ancien,* Brussels.

Vansina, J. (1985). *Oral tradition as History,* London and Nairobi.

Venco Ricciardi, R. (1968/1969). "The excavations at Choche: seasons 1966, 1967 and 1968", *Mesopotamia* 3–4: 57–68.

— (1996). "Wall paintings from Building A at Hatra", *IrAnt* 31: 147–165.

— (1998). "Pictorial graffiti in the city of Hatra", *Electrum* 2, Krakow: 187–205.

— (2004). "Imagini graffite dall'edificio A di Hatra", *Parthica* 6: 203–226.

Watelin, L.C. (1967). "Sasanian architecture C. The Sasanian buildings near Kish" in Pope, A.U. (ed.), *A Survey of Persian Art*, Tokyo: 584–592.

Watt, J.C.Y. (2004). *China Dawn of a Golden Age*, New York.

Whitby, M. (1988). *The Emperor Maurice and His Historian*, Oxford.

Whitby, M. and Whitby, M. (1986). *The History of Theophylact Simocatta*, Oxford.

Widengren, G. (1959). "The sacral kingship in Iran", *La Regalità sacra*, Leiden: 242–257.

— (1969). *Der Feudalismus im alten Iran: Männerbund, Gefolgswesen, Feudalismus in der iranischen Gesellschaft im Hinblick auf die indogermanischen Verhältnisse*, Cologne.

— (1971). "The establishment of the Sasanian dynasty in the light of new evidence", in *La Persia nel Medioevo*. (Atti del Convegno Internazionale, Rome 31.3.–5.4. 1970). Rome: 711–784.

Wiesehöfer, J. (1994). *Die "dunklen Jahrhunderte" der Persis: Untersuchungen zu Geschichte und Kultur von Fārs in frühhellenistischer Zeit (330–140 v. Chr.)*, Zetemata 90, Munich.

— (1996). "'King of kings' and Philhellên: Kingship in Arsacid Iran", in Bilde, P., Engberg-Pedersen, T., Hanestad, L. and Zahle, J. (eds.), *Aspects of Hellenistic Kingship*, Aarhus: 55–66.

— (2001). *Ancient Persia: from 550 BC to 650 AD*, London and New York

— (2005). *Iraniens, grecs et romains*, StIr Cahier 32, Paris.

— (2007). "Fars under Seleucid and Parthian rule", in Curtis, V.S. & Stewart, S. (eds.), *The Age of the Parthians. The Idea of Iran*, London and New York, vol. II: 37–49.

Wiesehöfer, J. and Huyse, P. (2006). *Ērān ud Anērān: Studien zu den Beziehungen zwischen dem Sasanidenreich und der Mittelmeerwelt*, Oriens et Occidens 13, Munich.

Wolska-Conus, W. (1968–1973). *Cosmas Indicopleustès, topographie chrétienne*, Sources chrétiennes 141, 159, 197, Paris.

Wolski, J. (1990). "Le titre de 'roi des rois' dans l'idéologie monarchique des arsacides", in *From Alexander the Great to Kül Tegin: Studies in Bactrian, Pahlavi, Sanskrit, Arabic, Aramaic, Armenian, Chinese, Türk, Greek, and Latin sources for the history of pre-Islamic Central Asia*, Budapest: 11–18.

Yaqut (1861). (transl.) Barbier de Meynard, C., *Dictionnaire géographique, historique et littéraire de la Perse*, Paris.

Yoshida, Y. (2003). Review of Sims-Williams, N. (2001). *Bactrian Documents from Northern Afghanistan*, I, *BAI* 14, 2000 [2003]: 154–159.